Ātreyaśīkṣā

Ātreyaśīkṣā

A Śikṣā of the Taittirīya School

Critically edited & translated by

Deepro Chakraborty

With a Foreword by

Girish Nath Jha

PRINTWORLD

Publishers of Indian Traditions

Cataloging in Publication Data — DK
[Courtesy: D.K. Agencies (P) Ltd. <docinfo@dkagencies.com>]

Ātreyaśīkṣā.
Ātreyaśīkṣā : a śikṣā of the Taittirīya school : with a foreword by Girish Nath Jha / critically edited & translated by Deepro Chakraborty.
pages cm
In Sanskrit (Devanagari and roman); translation and introductory matter in English.
Includes bibliographical references (pages).
ISBN 13: 9788124608234

1. Sanskrit language – Phonology. 2. Sanskrit language – Phonetics. I. Chakraborty, Deepro, 1988-, translator. II. Ātreyaśīkṣā. English. III. Title.

DDC 491.215 23

ISBN 13: 978-81-246-0823-4
First published in India in 2015

Printed and published by:
D.K. Printworld (P) Ltd.
Regd. Office: 'Vedasri', F-395, Sudarshan Park
(Metro Station: Ramesh Nagar), New Delhi - 110 015-11
Phones: (011) 2545 3975; 2546 6019; Fax: (011) 2546 5926
e-mail: indology@dkprintworld.com
Website: www.dkprintworld.com

Dedicated to
my Grandmother,

Late Anjali Basu,

Who was the guiding spirit
behind all my endeavour
and is still so

Foreword

One of the most sophisticated intellectual traditions of ancient India has been its systematic study of sounds. Śikṣā or the school of phonetics-phonology was a critical necessity of India's oral tradition than a pretentious intellectual exercise. No wonder that four out of the six disciplines of study (Vedāṅgas) in the Vedic tradition dealt with linguistic analysis – Nirukta (etymology), Chandas (metrics), Śikṣā (phonetics-phonology), Vyākaraṇa (grammar) – with Śikṣā being the foremost among them. *Ātreyaśīkṣā* is a mature text of the Taittirīya school of the *Kṛṣṇa-Yajurveda* and presents a set of instructions primarily dealing with precise pronunciation and recitation methods of the Vedic hymns. Unlike some other texts of the *Śikṣā-Prātiśākhya* genre, *Ātreyaśīkṣā* deals with a wide range of topics including the core areas like enumeration, general description and properties of sounds, their place and manner of articulation, *pāṭha* techniques and sound combination rules. The text also discusses some general ancillary concepts and of course the merits of correct pronunciation/recitation and demerits if not done the prescribed way.

The manuscripts of the text were not easy to find. With painstaking effort, Deepro Chakraborty – the editor of this volume – was able to locate one of them in the Staats- und Universitätsbibliothek, Hamburg, Germany and the other in Oriental Research Institute and Manuscripts Library, Sri Venkateswara University, Tirupati. While some earlier efforts to edit *Ātreyaśīkṣā* could not succeed completely, Deepro was able to reach his efforts to a meaningful conclusion. The book will be extremely useful for any authentic study of the Vedic texts in general and of the Taittirīya school in particular. The students of linguistics and Vyākaraṇa alike will benefit from this critical edition and translation. An empirical study of some nuances of pronunciation typical to this school of Vedic tradition may be the next step for research students of Sanskrit phonetics and phonology.

I congratulate Deepro Chakraborty for undertaking this serious academic exercise with sincerity and commitment for his M.Phil. research and making sure that the work reaches conclusion in the short span of two years. I offer my deep appreciation to the publisher for agreeing to publish this important text of India's long, continuous and unbroken intellectual tradition. Finally I thank Special Centre for Sanskrit Studies, Jawaharlal Nehru University (JNU) for facilitating this research and to the library of JNU for supporting the acquisition of the manuscript from the Hamburg Library, Germany.

February 2015

Girish Nath Jha
Special Centre for Sanskrit Studies,
JNU, New Delhi

Preface

आम्नायानामृषिभ्यो धिषणरुचिदृशा दर्शनाच्छान्तरेभ्यः
शाखाप्रावर्तकेभ्यो यजुष ऋतधिया पार्षदस्य प्रणेत्रे ।
शीक्षाणां ख्यापकेभ्यः श्रुतिनिपठकृतेऽहं तथा भाष्यकृद्भ्यः
सश्रद्धः सौस्मितेयः सततकृतनुतिः सम्प्रदायं च वन्दे ॥

THE field of Sanskrit phonetics is always my favourite interest. However, when I searched for the primary works in this area I discovered that a huge number of Sanskrit phonetic texts, which mainly consists of the Śikṣā and the commentaries of Śikṣā and Prātiśākhya texts, are still unexplored, i.e. they have not undergone any proper edition or translation. These texts are important not only because they depict the proper method of pronouncing the Vedas but also because they are actually the documents of early Indian contemplations on phonetics and phonology. Therefore, these texts, which comprise a number of significant phonetic thoughts, are very important from the perspective of history of linguistics. A deep analytical study of these texts can throw light on the chronological development of linguistics in early India, a hitherto comparatively unexplored area of knowledge. The fact is that we know very little about the historical development of Sanskrit literature on phonetics whereas we know much more about grammar and its gradual growth. Scarcity of printed texts is the chief obstacle for linguistic and historical research in this field. The printed editions, too, require translation and explanation in order to be accessible to those researchers who are not skilled in handling Sanskrit texts. There is a need for critical editions, translations and explications of Śikṣā literature for facilitating further research.

As for *Ātreyaśīkṣā* it is a handbook for the Taittirīya Vedic reciters who recite the phonic sequences along with *saṁhitā, pada, krama* and *jaṭā*. However, this text does not include methods of other artificial readings such as *ghana, śikhā*, *dhvaja*, etc. As a Śikṣā text, *Ātreyaśīkṣā* contextually describes many phonetic laws, most of which can be traced to *Taittirīya Prātiśākhya*. Also, the way in which the subject matter of *Ātreyaśīkṣā* is arranged appears to be very similar to *Pāriśikṣā*. Therefore, *Taittirīya Prātiśākhya* and its commentaries, especially *Vaidikābharaṇa* and *Tribhāṣyaratna*, and *Pāriśikṣā* and its commentary *Yājuṣabhūṣaṇa* facilitated the interpretation of *Ātreyaśīkṣā* verses. I sometimes consulted *Vyāsaśikṣā* and *Sarvasammataśikṣā* along with their commentaries, *Vedataijasa* and *Sarvasammataśikṣā-Vivaraṇa* respectively.

Also, *Ātreyaśīkṣā* contains a versified content list called *Ātreyaśīkṣā-Kārikā,* which is rare not only in the Śikṣā literature but also in the whole corpus of the Sanskrit texts, adds another unique feature to the text in focus. Additionally, some new topics which are not usually discussed in other texts of the same category are found in *Ātreyaśīkṣā.* The sections dealing with the dos and don'ts during Vedic recitation, the classification of *śabda,* the inner functions of the human body, the activities of the five vital airs and the detailed account of differing fruits of Vedic studies are unique themes which are rarely found in other texts of the same genre. I drew upon the expertise of and the scrutiny and proper explication by scholars who are well-versed in the yogic knowledge for interpretation of the section that deal with the inner activities of the human body and the five vital airs.

I took the project of critically editing and translating the text *Ātreyaśīkṣā* as part of my M.Phil. dissertation that was submitted to the Special Centre for Sanskrit Studies, Jawaharlal Nehru University (JNU) in August 2013 under the supervision of Dr Girish Nath Jha. My first and foremost thanks go to him for his sincere and meticulous guidance. His observations and corrections enriched my text and clarified my ideas. It is he who actually suggested me to work on this particular text and encouraged me to publish this work. His is a great contribution behind the publication of this work.

I thank Prof. Shashiprabha Kumar who sincerely helped me in every respect as a chairperson of Special Centre for Sanskrit Studies, JNU. My indebtedness to her is beyond expresssions.

I express my gratitude to Dr Srinivasa Varakhedi, Dean, Shastra Faculty, Karnataka Samskrit University, Bangalore; Dr Dipak Bhattacharya, Retired Professor, Department of Sanskrit, Pali and Prakrit, Visva Bharati, Shantiniketan; Dr Nabanarayan Bandyopadhyay, Professor and Director, School of Vedic Studies, Rabindra Bharati University, Kolkata; Dr Dilip Kumar Rana, Director, Chinmaya International Foundation Shodha Sansthan, Adisankaranilayam, Ernakulam; Dr Nirmala R. Kulkarni, Professor, Centre of Advanced Study in Sanskrit, University of Pune, Pune; and Dr Siddharth Y. Wakankar, Professor, Centre for Ancient History & Culture, Jain University, Bangalore, who helped me at the initial stage of my project.

I sincerely thank the following libraries for providing me resources for my research – Staats- und Universitätsbibliothek, Hamburg, Germany; Punjab University Library, Lahore, Punjab; Oriental Research Institute and Manuscripts Library, Sri Venkateswara University, Tirupati, Andhra Pradesh; Oriental Research Institute and Manuscripts Library, University of Kerala, Kariavattom, Kerala; D.A.V. College, Chandigarh; Vishveshvaranand Vedic Research Institute, Hoshiarpur, Punjab; Government Oriental Manuscript Library, Chennai, Tamil Nadu and Kalanidhi, Indira Gandhi National Centre for Arts, New Delhi. I also thank University Grants Commission, New Delhi for granting me fellowship.

My indebtedness goes to Mr Hans-Walter Stork, Manuscript Librarian, Western and Non-European Manuscripts, Staats- und Universitätsbibliothek; Mr Hamid Ali, Senior Librarian (Manuscripts), Punjab University Library; Mr Narasimha, Library staff, ORI & ML, Sri Venkateswara University; Mr Shaji Lal, Library staff, ORI & ML, University of Kerala; Mrs Deepti Madaan, Librarian, D.A.V. College; Mr Peter Freund, Tape Librarian, Maharishi University of Management, Fairfield, Iowa, USA; Ranjana Ray, Librarian, Kalanidhi, IGNCA; Ramesh Chandra Gaur, Librarian, Central Library, JNU; Dr Shim Jaekwan, Research Professor, Sangji University, Wonju, South Korea; Dominik Wujastyk, Department of South Asian, Tibetan and Buddhist Studies, University of Vienna, Vienna, Austria and N.V. Ramachandran, Director, ACIP Sanskrit Project, Kerala Centre, Palghat, Kerala who helped me by providing manuscripts and other information essential to my project.

Besides, I gratefully acknowledge Peter Scharf, S. Jagannatha, Shriramana Sharma, Viroopaksha Jaddipal, P. Ramanujan, Anjalika Mukhopadhyay and Mridula Saha for their sincere response to my queries occurring at different times of my editing the text. Special mention must be made of Dr Chandrashekhar Ramaswamy who helped me in deciphering a Telugu manuscript and provided a number of references.

A host of friends connected with my project must be remembered with gratitude. I am greatly indebted to Varsha Patel for her enormous help. Shilpi Sarkar, Sujoy Sarkar too helped me in various ways. I am also grateful to Meera Vishvanathan and Aniruddha Kar for their help. I had fruitful discussions on my topic with Diwakar Mishra, Jay Saha, Rishiraj Pathak and Shweta Deshpande. Seniors and friends who also helped in different ways are Manji Bhadra, Biplob Sardar, Parthasarathi Sil, Archana Tiwari, Devalina Saikia, Jnanesh Marathe, Arjun Kashyap, A. Eswaran and Pallavi Pal.

Lastly, I express my indebtedness to my family, especially my mother Susmita Basu, sister Sutanoya Chakraborty, father Dipankar Chakraborty, my closest friend Anirban Das and another well-wisher Arup Lodh for their assistance and for being constant sources of inspiration. Without the help of all the above-mentioned people I could not have done this work as I have done it.

Finally I have to offer my thanks to Mr Susheel Kumar Mittal of the D.K. Printworld for venturing into publishing the work of a green-horn like me.

17 February 2015 (Śivarātri) **Deepro Chakraborty**

Transliteration Keys

a	अ	gh	घ्	ṣ	ष्
ā	आ	ṅ	ङ्	s	स्
ā$_3$	आ३	c	च्	h	ह्
i	इ	ch	छ्	ḷ	ळ्
ī	ई	j	ज्	ṁ	ं (anusvāra)
ī$_3$	ई३	jh	झ्	ḥ	ः (visarga)
u	उ	ñ	ञ्	ẖ	× (velar fricative)
ü	उ (hiatal u)	ṭ	ट्	ḫ	× (labial fricative)
ū	ऊ	ṭh	ठ्	~	ँ (nasalized)
ū$_3$	ऊ३	ḍ	ड्	´	(acute)
r̥	ऋ	ḍh	ढ्	`	(independent circumflex)
r̥̄	ॠ	ṇ	ण्		
r̥̄$_3$	ॠ३	t	त्		
l̥	ऌ	th	थ्		
l̥̄	ॡ	d	द्		
l̥̄$_3$	ॡ३	dh	ध्		
e	ए	n	न्		
e$_3$	ए३	p	प्		
ai	ऐ	ph	फ्		
ai$_3$	ऐ३	b	ब्		
o	ओ	bh	भ्		
o$_3$	ओ३	m	म्		
au	औ	y	य्		
au$_3$	औ३	r	र्		
k	क्	l	ल्		
kh	ख्	v	व्		
g	ग्	ś	श्		

Abbreviations

AK	*Ātreyaśīkṣākārikā*
AS	*Ātreyaśīkṣāmūla*
AS2	The second variety of *Ātreyaśīkṣā*
C	Siglum for the Chandigarh MS of *Ātreyaśīkṣā*
H	Siglum for the Hamburg MS of *Ātreyaśīkṣā*
K	Siglum for the Kariavattom MS of *Ātreyaśīkṣā*
L	Siglum for the Lahore MS of *Ātreyaśīkṣā*
M	Siglum for the Madras MS of *Ātreyaśīkṣā*
T	Siglum for the Tirupati MS of *Ātreyaśīkṣā*
TA	*Taittirīya Āraṇyaka*
TB	*Taittirīya Brāhmaṇa*
TP	*Taittirīya Prātiśākhya*
TS	*Taittirīya Saṁhitā*

Contents

Foreword vii
Preface ix
Transliteration Key xiv
Abbreviations xv

Chapter I: Introduction 1

1.1. Śikṣā 2
1.1.1. Śikṣā as a Vedāṅga 2
1.1.2. Subject Matter of Śikṣā 5
1.1.3. Śikṣā vs Prātiśākhya 7
1.1.4. Available Literature in the Field of Śikṣā 9
1.2. The Ātreyaśīkṣā 11
1.2.1. Śikṣā vs Śīkṣā 11
1.2.2. Three Different Ātreyaśikṣās 12
1.2.3. The "Original" Ātreyaśikṣā 15
1.2.4. Structure of the Text 19
1.2.5. Subject Matters 20
1.2.6. Affiliation to the Kr̥ṣṇa-Yajurveda of the Taittirīya School 25
1.2.7. South Indian Origin 26
1.2.8. Authorship 27
1.2.9. Date 38
1.3. Description of the Manuscripts 42
1.3.1. MS H 42

1.3.2. MS T 48
1.3.3. Stemmatics 54
1.4. Methodology 55
1.4.1. Critical Apparatus 55
1.4.1.1. Emendations 55
1.4.1.2. Treatment of Variant Readings 56
1.4.1.3. Treatment of the Headings 59
1.4.1.4. Orthography 65
1.4.2. Roman Transcription 67
1.4.3. Translation 68
Chapter II: **Critically Edited Text: आत्रेयशीक्षा** 71
आत्रेयशीक्षाकारिका 71
आत्रेयशीक्षामूलम् 73
परिभाषा 73
संहिताविषयम् 74
वेदपारायणफलम् 74
पारायणक्रमः 74
अनध्ययनप्रकरणम् 75
वाग्वृत्तिः 75
पदलक्षणम् 75
क्रमलक्षणम् 76
जटालक्षणम् 77
केवलवर्णक्रमलक्षणम् 77
द्वित्वप्रकरणम् 78
आगमः 78
अभिनिधानम् 79
केवलागमः 79
यमाः 79

यमनिषेधः	79
नादः	79
द्वित्वागमनिषेधः	80
स्वरभक्तिविषयम्	80
स्वरभक्तीनां सोदाहरणसंज्ञाः	81
विवृत्तिलक्षणं तस्याः संज्ञाश्च	81
विवृत्त्युदाहरणम्	82
व्यक्तिमध्यस्थनासिक्यः	83
रङ्गप्लुताः	83
रङ्गदीर्घाः	83
स्वरितोदात्तकम्पविषयम्	84
वैकृतप्राकृते	84
नासिक्यत्वोरस्यत्वे	84
व्यक्तिमध्यस्थविसर्गः	84
जिह्वामूलीयोपध्मानीयविधिः	85
स्थितिसन्धिः	85
स्वरहीनस्य वर्णस्य वाचकं नाम	85
केवलानुस्वारः	85
प्रणवलक्षणम्	85
सन्धिनिषेधः	85
स्वरवर्णक्रमलक्षणम्	86
उदात्तादीनां संज्ञा	86
सप्तस्वरितलक्षणानि सोदाहरणानि	86
स्वरितानां प्रयत्नभेदाः	88
मात्रावर्णक्रमलक्षणम्	88
मात्राकाललक्षणम्	88
मात्राकालोक्तिविवेकः	89
अङ्गवर्णक्रमलक्षणम्	89

अङ्गलक्षणम्	89
पराङ्गपूर्वाङ्गलक्षणम्	90
अङ्गवर्णक्रमोक्तिलक्षणम्	90
वर्णसारभूतवर्णक्रम इत्यस्य नाम्नो निर्वचनम्	91
वर्णधर्मक्रमः	91
अनुस्वारभक्तिकम्पविषये रङ्गप्लुतविषये च	92
शब्दोत्पत्तिप्रकरणम्	93
तत्प्रकारः	93
ध्वनिनिरूपणप्रकरणे शरीरान्तर्गतजाठराग्निस्थितिः	93
प्राणादीनां पञ्चानां वायूनां स्थानस्थित्यादिकम्	94
तेषां स्थूलसूक्ष्मरूपचेष्टाविशेषः	94
ध्वनिभेदाः	95
तज्जातवर्णाः	95
वर्णानां स्थानकरणविवेकः	96
वर्णानां प्रयत्नभेदाः	98
देवतालक्षणम्	98
जातिलक्षणम्	98
वर्णसंज्ञा	98
उदात्तादीनां देवतानियमः	99
जातिः	99
गुणलक्षणम्	99
हस्तस्वरविन्यासलक्षणम्	99
स्वरविन्यासफलम्	100
अङ्गाद्यवस्था	100
षड्जादिस्वरनिरूपणम्	100
उदात्तादिस्वरोत्पत्तिस्थानम्	101
वेदाध्ययनफलम्	101
वेदमहिमा	101

अध्ययनरहितदोषः 102
साङ्गवेदाध्ययनफलम् 102
Chapter III: Transliteration and Translation 103
ĀTREYAŚĪKṢĀKĀRIKĀ 103
ĀTREYAŚĪKṢĀMŪLA 106
Explanatory Rules and Terms 106
The Topic Related to Saṁhitā 108
Fruit of Vedic Recitation 109
System of Vedic Recitation 110
Discussion on Intermission in Vedic Recitation 110
Mode of Speech 111
Definition of Word-Reading 111
Definition of Sequential Reading 112
Definition of Tangled Reading 114
Definition of the Phonic Sequence 115
Discussion on Duplication 117
Increment 118
Adjacent Imposition 119
Insertion 119
Twin Phones 119
Prevention of Twin Phones 120
Final Nasal Stop 120
Prevention of Duplication and Increment 121
The Topic Related to Anaptyxis 122
Appellations of the Anaptyxes along with Examples 123
Definition of Hiatus and Its Appellations 124
Examples of Hiatus 126
Intermediate Nasal within a Hiatus 127

Nasally Modified Protracted a-Vowel 128

Nasally Modified Long a-Vowel 129

Topic Related to Circumflex and Acute Tremulous 129

Modification and Originality 131

Nasalization and Pulmonic-ness 131

Intermediate ḥ within a Hiatus 131

Rule for ẖ and ḫ 132

Stability in Juncture 132

Proper Names of the Phones [Designated] without Vowel 132

Pure ṁ 133

Definition of Om 133

Prevention of Euphonic Change 133

Definition of Accentual Phonic Sequence 134

Appellations of (the Accents that) Begin with Acute 134

Definitions of the Seven Circumflex Accents with Examples 135

Varieties of the Manners of Articulation of the Circumflexes 138

Definition of Moraic Phonic Sequence 139

Definitions of Moraic Time Durations 139

Discussion on the Recitation of Moraic (Phonic Sequence) 140

Definition of Adjunctive Phonic Sequence 142

Definition of Adjunct 142

Definition of Adjuncts of Subsequent and Antecedent (Vowel) 143

Accurate Description of the Recitation of Adjunctive Phonic Sequence 144

Etymology of the Term Varṇasārabhūtavarṇakrama 145

Order of Attributes of the Phones 146

(Order of Attributes) in the Contexts of ṁ, Anaptyxis, Tremulous and Nasally Modified Protracted a-Vowel 148

Section on the Origin of Sound 150

Its Types 150

Situation of Stomach Fire inside the Body in the Section on Determination of Speech Sound 151

(Aspects such as) Location, Situation of the Vital Airs Starting with Respirational Air 152

Speciality of Their Gross and Subtle Activities 153

Types of Speech Sound 156

Phones Originated from Them 156

Discussion on the Places of Articulation and Articulators of the Phones 157

Various Manners of Articulation of the Phones 162

Definition of Deities 163

Definition of Class 163

Designations of the Phones 164

Precept Regarding the Deities of (the Accents) Beginning with the Acute 164

Class 164

Qualities 165

Feature of Manual Demonstration of Accents 165

Fruit of Accentual Demonstration 167

Conditions of Organs, etc. 167

Determination of the Notes Beginning from Ṣaḍja 168

Place of Origin of the Accents Beginning with the Acute 169

Fruit of Vedic Studies 169

Magnificence of the Veda 170

Harm Done for not Studying (the Veda) 170

Fruit of the Comprehensive Study of the Veda		171
Appendix I:	***Index of Half-Verses***	173
Appendix II:	***Index I: References Used in This Book***	183
	Index II: Important Terms Occurring in Ātreyaśīkṣāmūla	187
Appendix III:	***English Equivalents of Some Important Sanskrit Terms Used in Ātreyaśīkṣāmūla***	199
Appendix IV:	***The Text in Grantha Script with the Spellings Found in the Manuscripts***	206
Appendix V:	***The Ātreyaśīkṣāmūla and Taittirīya Prātiśākhya: Comparative References***	240
Bibliography		248

1

Introduction

THIS work is concerned with producing an edition of *Ātreyaśīkṣā*, a Śikṣā work associated with the Taittirīya School of the *Kṛṣṇa-Yajurveda*. *Ātreyaśīkṣā* is an excellent work, for such a comprehensive, well-structured, clear and complete text is very rare in the whole body of the Śikṣā literature. It is, however, not widely acknowledged by the commentators on the Śikṣā and Prātiśākhya literature and no commentary of this text has yet been found. It is also true that the text which clearly describes the topics in a very simple and lucid language would hardly require a commentary.

This book is divided into three chapters followed by five appendices. The first chapter is the introduction which provides an elementary notion about the Śikṣā literature, a survey of all the available literature in this field, an account of the various aspects of the *Ātreyaśīkṣā*, a detailed description of the two MSS which are used for this edition and the methodology adopted for this research. The second chapter presents the critically edited text along with its variant readings. The third chapter provides a Roman transcription using IAST and the English translation of the text.

Verse index, the glossary of important terms used in the main text and English renderings of some important Sanskrit terms are provided in the appendices. In order to acquaint the reader with the orthography of the original MSS the text of *Ātreyaśīkṣā* in Grantha script with the spellings as found in the MSS is appended with this book. As *Ātreyaśīkṣā* closely resembles the *Taittirīya Prātiśākhya* in terms of most of its subject matters, an appendix of the comparative references to *AS* and *Taittirīya Prātiśākhya* is also provided in order to facilitate further research.

Śikṣā

ŚIKṢĀ AS A VEDĀṄGA

Śikṣā constitutes one of the six auxiliary sciences of the Vedas (Vedāṅga)[1] and flourished as a major discipline in early India. Although etymologically the word Śikṣā means "teaching", "training" or "learning", technically, it refers to the specific branch of knowledge that deals with proper articulation and pronunciation. While some of these disciplines, although originating as a Vedāṅga, have received independent status (allowing them to incorporate even those topics which are not directly related to the Vedas), in the case of the Śikṣās (as we find them today), it appears that such development did not take place. In other words, general topics of phonetics and phonology irrespective of the Vedas could not become the subject matter of the discipline Śikṣā. Almost all Śikṣā texts are associated with one or the other Vedic schools. The following list contains the extant Śikṣā texts which belong to different Vedic schools:

- The Śikṣās of *R̥gveda*:
  - *Svaravyañjanaśikṣā*
  - *Svarāṅkuśaśikṣā*
  - *Śamānaśikṣā*
  - *Pāṇinīyaśikṣā*

---

[1] The *Pāṇinīyaśikṣā* uses the metaphor "nose" for the discipline Śikṣā as an organ of the Vedas:

chandaḥ pādau tu vedasya hastau kalpo 'tha paṭhyate ।
jyotiṣām ayanañ cakṣur niruktaṁ śrotram ucyate ॥

śikṣā ghrāṇan tu vedasya mukhaṁ vyākaraṇaṁ smr̥tam ।
tasmāt sāṅgam adhītyaiva brahmaloke mahīyate ॥ 41-41

— Ghosh 1938: 75

— *Śaunakaśikṣā*
— *Śaiśirīyaśikṣā* (belongs to the Śaiśirīya School)

• The Śikṣās of *Kṛṣṇa-Yajurveda*
— *Cārāyaṇīyaśikṣā* (belongs to the Cārāyaṇīya School)
— *Vyāsaśīkṣā* (belongs to the Taittirīya School)
— *Lakṣmīkāntaśikṣā* (belongs to the Taittirīya School)
— *Ātreyaśīkṣā* (belongs to the Taittirīya School)
— *Bhāradvājaśikṣā* (belongs to the Taittirīya School)
— *Śambhuśikṣā* (belongs to the Taittirīya School)
— *Kauṇḍinyaśikṣā* (belongs to the Taittirīya School)
— *Pāṇinīyaśikṣā* (belongs to the Taittirīya School)
— *Kauhalīyaśikṣā* (belongs to the Taittirīya School)
— *Vasiṣṭhaśikṣā* (belongs to the Taittirīya School)
— *Vararuciśikṣā* (belongs to the Taittirīya School)
— *Sarvasammataśikṣā* (belongs to the Taittirīya School)
— *Āraṇyaśikṣā* (belongs to the Taittirīya School)
— *Pāriśikṣā* (belongs to the Taittirīya School)
— *Siddhāntaśikṣā* (belongs to the Taittirīya School)
— *Āpiśaliśikṣā* (belongs to the Taittirīya School)
— *Kālanirṇayaśikṣā* (belongs to the Taittirīya School)

• The Śikṣās of *Śukla-Yajurveda*
— *Yājñavalkyaśikṣā* (belongs to the Mādhyandina School)
— *Mādhyandinī Śikṣā* (belongs to the Mādhyandina School)
— *Laghumādhyandinī Śikṣā* (belongs to the Mādhyandina School)
— *Kramakārikāśikṣā* (belongs to the Mādhyandina School)
— *Kramasandhānaśikṣā* (belongs to the Mādhyandina School)
— *Pārāśarī Śikṣā* (belongs to the Mādhyandina School)

— *Varṇaratnadīpikā Śikṣā* (belongs to the Mādhyandina School)
— *Prātiśākhyapradīpaśikṣā* (belongs to the Mādhyandina School)
— *Vāsiṣṭhī Śikṣā* (belongs to the Mādhyandina School)
— *Keśavī Śikṣā* (belongs to the Mādhyandina School)
— *Amoghanandinī Śikṣā* (belongs to the Mādhyandina School)
— *Māṇḍavī Śikṣā* (belongs to the Mādhyandina School)
— *Manassvāraśikṣā* (belongs to the Mādhyandina School)
— *Galadṛkśikṣā* (belongs to the Mādhyandina School)
— *Yajurvidhānaśikṣā* (belongs to the Mādhyandina School)
— *Kauśikī Śikṣā*
— *Katyāyanī Śikṣā*
— *Traisvaryaśikṣā*
— *Padakārikāratnamālā Śikṣā* (belongs to the Kāṇva School)

- The Śikṣās of *Sāmaveda*
  — *Nāradaśikṣā*
  — *Lomaśī Śikṣā*
  — *Gautamī Śikṣā*
- The Śikṣā of *Atharvaveda*
  — *Māṇḍukī Śikṣā*

Sometimes *Pāṇinīyaśikṣā* is, however, considered to be the "general Śikṣā", i.e. common to all Vedas.[2] A close examination of these Śikṣā texts clearly indicates their Vedāṅgic nature. Moreover, these texts are often categorized under the title "Vedalakṣaṇa". While this term is prevalent in south India, it is also commonly used as one of the subject titles of Vedic literature in many library

---

2 Cf. *Prasthānabheda — tatra sarvavedasādhāraṇī śikṣā 'atha śikṣām pravakṣyāmi' ityādipañcakhaṇḍātmikā pāṇininā prakāśitā* ।
— Sarasvatī 1912: 7

catalogues. Vedalakṣaṇa texts which include Śikṣās, Prātiśākhyas, Anukramaṇīs, Baiṭhs, Saptalakṣaṇas, works on accents and different forms of recitation, etc. assist the Vedic reciters in determining, understanding and preserving the pure and definite form of the Vedas. Hence, they are called Lakṣaṇagrantha.[3] Certain Śikṣās such as *Śamānaśikṣā, Bhāradvājaśikṣā, Ātreyaśīkṣā* (the first variety mentioned by Aithal (1991: 128))[4] are comprised of mere lists of some Vedic words which mostly come under the Saptalakṣaṇa[5] category. Since no concerted attempt was made by the Śikṣākāras to expand its scope beyond the Vedas, Śikṣā remained a Vedāṅga in the true sense, in contrast with some of the other Vedāṅgas such as Vyākaraṇa, Chandas and Jyotiṣa.

SUBJECT MATTER OF ŚIKṢĀ

In essence, Śikṣās are the guidelines for the proper articulation

---

3 The *Tribhāṣyaratna* designates itself as a commentarial *lakṣaṇa* of the Prātiśākhya — *bhaktiyuktaḥ praṇamyāhaṅ gaṇeśacaraṇadvayam* । *gurūn api girān devīm idal̃ lakṣaṇav̄ vakṣyāmi. Tribhāṣyaratna* on the *Taittirīya Prātiśākhya* 1.1 (Sastri and Rangacarya 1906: 1). The *Vaidikābharaṇa* calls the Prātiśākhya as *lakṣaṇa: "prātiśākhyan nāma lakṣaṇam praṇīyate". Vaidikābharaṇa* on the *Taittirīya Prātiśākhya* 1.1 (Sastri and Rangacarya 1906: 3).

4 Cf. *Vedic Studies* (Kulkarni 2006c.: 269).

5 The *saptalakṣaṇa*s are: *śamāna* (the Vedic words whose final *visarga*s are dropped due to euphonic change), *vilaṅghya* (the Vedic words with a final *e, ai, o* or *au* which have undergone euphonic change because of a subsequent vowel), *avarṇi* (the Vedic words with an initial *a* merging with the antecedent vowel), *āvarṇi* (the Vedic words with an initial *ā* merging with the antecedent vowel), *tapara* (the Vedic words with a final *t* that is assimilated with a subsequent *n*), *napara* (the Vedic words with a final *n* that is assimilated with one of these subsequent sounds *c, ch, j, t, d, dh, n, m* and *l*), *aniṅgya* (the Vedic words which are not separated in the word reading). Cf. *Vedalakṣaṇānukramaṇikā — śamānañ ca vilaṅghyañ ca naparan taparan tathā* । *avarṇyāvarṇyaniṅgyāntaṁ saptalakṣaṇam ucyate* ॥ (Suryakanta 1940: 1).

and pronunciation of the Vedas.[6] At the phonological level, Vedic Sanskrit and Classical Sanskrit share almost the same sound pattern if the accentuation and some other particularities of the Vedas are kept aside. Pronunciation varies in different Vedic schools on account of dialectal variations. Classical Sanskrit, which is the standard, commonly accepted and consequently artificial form of the so-called old Indo-Aryan language, can be said to have originated from these different dialects of Vedic Sanskrit.

In the ancient Indian tradition, Śikṣā is considered the science of articulatory phonetics and phonology. The second *anuvāka* of the first chapter (Śīkṣā Vallī) of the *Taittirīya Upaniṣad* that is the seventh chapter (*prapāṭhaka*) of the *Taittirīya Āraṇyaka*, which is one of the earliest references to Śikṣā, mentions six subject matters of Śikṣā — 1. *varṇa* (phones), 2. *svara* (accent or intonation), 3. *mātrā* (mora or moraic time duration), 4. *bala* (manner of articulation), 5. *sāman* (balanced way of pronunciation), and 6. *santāna* (euphonic combination).[7] The Śikṣā texts remarkably contain very minute details of the sound inventory of the language, detailed description and classification of the phones with regard to their places of articulation, manners of articulation and active articulators, euphonic combinations, accentuation, moraic quality, duplication, increment, adjunction, nasalization, syllabication, aspiration, voicing and so on. Such an advanced and accurate state of the discipline was without contemporary parallels and constitutes, by all accounts, a unique achievement of the Indian intellectual tradition.

The establishment of the Asiatic Society in CE 1784 by William

6 Madhusūdana Sarasvatī says in his monograph *Prasthānabheda* — *tatra śikṣāyā udāttānudāttasvaritahrasvadīrghaplutādiviśiṣ-ṭasvara vyañjanātmakavarṇoccāraṇaviśeṣajñānam prayojanam, tadabhāve mantrāṇām anarthakatvāt* || (1912: 7) Sāyaṇa comments — *śikṣā vidyopādāne iti dhātuḥ* | *śikṣyante vedanīyatvenopadiśyante svaravarṇādayo yatrāsau* Śikṣā . . . on *TA* 7.2 (Phaḍake 1898: 493).

7 *śīkṣāṁ vyākhyāsyāmaḥ* | *varṇas svaraḥ* | *mātrā balam* | *sāma santānaḥ* | *ity uktaś śīkṣādhyāyaḥ* |

Jones and others led to the introduction of Sanskrit knowledge to the Western world. As a consequence, Western knowledge of phonetics was heavily influenced and developed by the advanced Indian knowledge of phonetics. In this connection, Allen (1953: 3) says:

> Moreover the link between the ancient Indian and the modern Western schools of linguistics is considerably closer in phonetics than in grammar. For whilst Pāṇinean techniques are only just beginning to banish the incubus of Latin grammar, our phonetic categories and terminology owe more than is perhaps generally realized to the influence of the Sanskrit phoneticians . . . In a paper on 'The English School of Phonetics'[8] Professor J.R. Firth has said of this great orientalist,[9] 'Without the Indian grammarians and phoneticians whom he introduced and recommended to us, it is difficult to imagine our nineteenth century school of phonetics.

ŚIKṢĀ *vs* PRĀTIŚĀKHYA

Despite structural differences, there is a close affinity between the Śikṣās and the Prātiśākhyas in terms of subject matter. While the Śikṣā texts are composed metrically and the Prātiśākhya texts are composed aphoristically, in most of the cases their subject matter is almost the same. The term Prātiśākhya suggests that these texts are related to particular branches of the Vedic schools.[10] Compared to the Śikṣās, the Prātiśākhyas are also fewer in number.

The extant Prātiśākhyas are as follows — *R̥gveda Prātiśākhya* of the Śākala branch of *R̥gveda,* ascribed to Śaunaka; *Taittirīya Prātiśākhya* of the Taittirīya branch of the *Kr̥ṣṇa-Yajurveda*; *Maitrāyaṇīya Prātiśākhya*[11] of the Maitrāyaṇī branch of *Kr̥ṣṇa-*

[8] Firth 1946: 92-132.

[9] Sir William Jones has been referred to here.

[10] Cf. Anantabhaṭṭa, the commentator of the *Vājasaneyi-prātiśākhya* interprets the term Prātiśākhya as — *śākhāyāṁ śākhāyāṁ prati pratiśākham, pratiśākham bhavam prātiśākhyam* (Sharma 1934: 2)

[11] This Prātiśākhya is not yet published. No public manuscript library has a MS of this text. It is, however, known from the references to this Prātiśākhya by Mīmāṁsaka (1984: 401-02) that it is still →

Yajurveda; Vājasaneyi-prātiśākhya of the Mādhyandina branch of *Śukla-Yajurveda,* ascribed to Kātyāyana; *Puṣpasūtra* (alternatively *Phullasūtra*) of the Kauthuma and Rāṇāyanīya branch of the *Sāmaveda,* ascribed to Vararuci or Puṣpa, *R̥ktantra* and *Sāmatantra* of the Kauthuma branch of *Sāmavedā*[12] ascribed to Śākaṭāyana[13] and Audavraji[14] respectively; *Śaunakīyā Caturadhyāyikā* of the Śaunaka branch of *Atharvaveda,* ascribed to Kautsa, and *Atharvaveda Prātiśākhya* of the Śaunaka branch of *Atharvaveda.* The Prātiśākhyas also foreground the pronunciational aspects of their respective Vedic branches.

Uvaṭa, in his commentary on *R̥gveda Prātiśākhya*, tries to point out the distinctive features of the Prātiśākhya. According to him, the Śikṣā, Chandas and Vyākaraṇa define their subject matter from a general perspective, whereas the Prātiśākhyas describe the special aspects of their respective Vedic branches and sometimes also discuss new topics which are not found in the former traditions.[15] In keeping with this, Śikṣā can be considered as "general phonetics" and the Prātiśākhyas as "applied phonetics".[16] The Prātiśākhyas sometimes refer to Śikṣā[17] or quote from Śikṣā.[18] The commentators of the Prātiśākhyas often quote various verses from the Śikṣās in support of their views. Even a core Vedic portion (*TA* 7.1) comprises a section on Śikṣā which certainly proves the

← preserved in MS forms in some private collections in Maharashtra. The references to those persons who possess the MSS of the *Maitrāyaṇīya Prātiśākhya* are given as follows: "श्री रा० रा० भाऊ साहेब त्यात्या साहेब मुटे पञ्चवटी, नासिक अथवा श्री रा० रा० शंकर हरि जोशी अभोणकर जि० नासिक, ता० कुलवण, पो० मु० अभोणे ।"

12 Suryakanta 1933: 3.

13 Suryakanta 1940: 5.

14 Aithal 1991: 658.

15 Uvaṭa's commentary on *R̥gveda Prātiśākhya* 1.1 (Shastri 1931: 21-23).

16 Cf. Varma 1929: 5.

17 Cf. *atha śikṣāvihitāḥ* । — *Vājasaneyi-prātiśākhya* 1.29

18 Cf. *TP* 17.8, 24.6, etc.

importance and antiquity of this discipline. Śikṣā also enjoys the status of the Vedāṅga which Prātiśākhya does not possess. It is, therefore, conjectured that Śikṣā offered to Prātiśākhya the general principles of phonetics and consequently it has a higher rank than that of Prātiśākhya.

However, the Śikṣā texts, as we find them today, can hardly be considered to be the prototypes of the Prātiśākhyas; rather, they seem to be the followers of the Prātiśākhyas. Many implicit concepts of the Prātiśākhyas are clearly explained in the Śikṣā texts. Some Śikṣā texts refer to some of the prātiśākhyakāras.[19] This certainly proves the posteriority of the Śikṣā texts. None of the extant Śikṣā texts predate any of the Prātiśākhyas. The *Sarvasammataśikṣā* explicitly declares the subservience of the Śikṣā texts with regard to the Prātiśākhyas in terms of their authority.[20] It is, therefore, no longer possible to prove the hypothesis that views the Śikṣā as the archetype of the Prātiśākhyas. However, some scholars opine that a Śikṣā used to exist before the Prātiśākhyas and it provided the phonetic principles to the Prātiśākhyas. The available Śikṣā texts are developed from that "original" Śikṣā. Several extant Śikṣā texts share some similar expressions even when they belong to different branches of the Vedic schools. The nature of the so-called "original" Śikṣā can be traced in these verses.[21]

AVAILABLE LITERATURE IN THE FIELD OF ŚIKṢĀ

Numerous MSS of the Vedalakṣaṇa texts in different manuscript repositories worldwide are still awaiting disclosure. There have not been many editions of the Śikṣā texts even though they contain salient phonetic theories par excellence. Amongst the publications of

19 *Yājñavalkyaśikṣā* 81 (Jha 2005: 44) refers to Śaunaka.

20 *śikṣā ca prātiśākhyañ ca virudhyete parasparam | śikṣaiva durbalety āhus siṁhasyaiva mṛgī yathā ||* *Sarvasammataśikṣā* 42 (Franke 1886: 43). The *Sarvalakṣaṇamañjarī* also quotes a similar verse: *śikṣā ca prātiśākhyañ ca virudhyete yadā tadā | prātiśākhyam balīyas syād avakāśo na cet sadā ||* (Sastri 1976: 124)

21 Cf. Bhagavaddatta 1921: 10-12.

the Śikṣā texts related to the Taittirīya School, the German editions of *Sarvasammataśikṣā* and *Vyāsaśikṣā* by Franke (1886) and Lüders (1894), respectively, are noteworthy. *Vyāsaśikṣā* has undergone some more editions among which Pattabhirama Sastri's edition (1976) is popular. Amongst the few editions of *Bhāradvājaśikṣā*, the Poona edition (1938) is significant. However, *Pāṇinīyaśikṣā* has the maximum number of editions. *Āpiśaliśikṣā* has also undergone a number of editions. *Kauhaliśikṣā* and *Kauṇḍinyaśikṣā* are edited by Sadhu Ram (1981) and Sriramachandra (1980), respectively.

The other Śikṣās of the Taittirīya School do not have any exclusive edition. Raghu Vira transcribed some Śikṣā texts from the MSS which are preserved in the Adyar Library. These transcriptions are published by his son Lokesh Chandra (1981) under the title *Sanskrit Texts on Phonetics* that comprises some of the major Śikṣā texts of the Taittirīya School, such as *Āraṇyaśikṣā, Vāsiṣṭhaśikṣā, Kālanirṇayaśikṣā, Lakṣmīkāntaśikṣā, Śambhuśikṣā, Pāriśikṣā,* etc. This publication, however, cannot be called a proper edition of those texts as it is a handwritten transcription of the MSS and is not error free. A comparatively recent edition of *Pāriśikṣā* and *Sarvasammataśikṣā* by Ralf Stautzebach (1994) is a significant contribution in this area. He edited and translated *Pāriśikṣā* along with its commentary *Yājuṣabhūṣaṇa* and the two different versions of *Sarvasammataśikṣā* with their commentaries. The Śikṣā texts of other Vedic schools which have undergone some important editions, are *Yājñavalkyaśikṣā, Māṇḍukī Śikṣā, Gautamī Śikṣā* and *Nāradaśīkṣā. Śikṣāsaṅgraha,* another important publication within this field, comprises thirty-three Śikṣā texts, most of which are associated with the schools of *Śukla-Yajurveda.* Kauṇḍinyāyana appended eight Śikṣā texts, viz. *Śaunakaśikṣā, Śaiśirīyaśikṣā, Vyāḍiśikṣā, Cārāyaṇīyaśikṣā, Kauhalīyaśikṣā, Sarvasammataśikṣā, Pāriśikṣā* and *Āpiśalīyaśikṣā* to his work, *Kauṇḍinyāyanaśikṣā* using an unconventional (but supported by the principles of traditional Sanskrit phonetics) orthography. Aithal (1991) has provided an easy ground for researchers in this field by creating an exhaustive bibliography of the Vedalakṣaṇa texts both published and unpublished.

Since there is a paucity of the printed original texts in the field of Śikṣā literature, analytical studies of Śikṣā texts are consequently scarce. Though some discussions are scattered in different journals and in the introductions of some of the printed texts, full-fledged analytical studies are not copiously available. Varma (1929) and Allen (1953) should be remembered in this context. Varma's treatise is specially recognized since it provides a systematic discussion on the chronology of the Śikṣā and Prātiśākhya texts. Kauṇḍinnyāyana (1992) gives a detailed account on the Śikṣā and Prātiśākhya literature in the introduction of his work. However, the publications of Mishra (1972) and Chaturvedi (2003) appear to be merely descriptive. Pataskar (2010) has also written a book on this topic which unfortunately, I was unable to access. Keilhorn's (1876) short article on Śikṣā is also worth mentioning. The editors of some Śikṣā and Prātiśākhya texts discuss many allied issues in their introductions to the various texts as well. Whitney (1862), Franke (1886), Lüders (1894), Sastri and Rangacarya (1906), Bhagavaddatta (1921), Suryakanta (1940), Ghosh (1938), Shastri (1956), Deshpande (1998), Kulkarni (2004), etc. have additionally contemplated upon related issues.

The Ātreyaśīkṣā

ŚIKṢĀ *vs* ŚĪKṢĀ

The seventh chapter (*prapāṭhaka*) of the *Taittirīya Āraṇyaka*, which is the first chapter (*vallī*) of the *Taittirīya Upaniṣad* (alternatively *Sāṁhitī Upaniṣad*) in turn, is called Śīkṣā Vallī. Its second *anuvāka* enumerates the topics of Śikṣā. Śikṣā is spelled as *śīkṣā* herein. According to the commentators,[22] Śīkṣā is the irregular Vedic form of the word Śikṣā. Many Śikṣā texts of the Taittirīya School adopt

[22] ... *śikṣā saiva śīkṣā* ... Sāyaṇa on *TA* 7.2 (Phaḍake 1927: 493). *chāndaso dīrghaḥ* । Kūra Nārāyaṇa Muni on *Taittirīyopaniṣad* 1.2 (Chariar 1905: 4).

this spelling, making it unique to this Vedic school. Consequently, *AS*, which is a Śikṣā text of the Taittirīya School, uses the spelling *śīkṣā*.

THREE DIFFERENT ĀTREYAŚIKṢĀS

Aithal's (1991: 128-30) catalogue states that three texts are available in the MS form with the appellation *Ātreyaśikṣā*. Although the titles of these texts are the same, they are entirely different from one another. Applying the terminology provided by Suryakanta (1940: 1) we can put the first form of *Ātreyaśīkṣā* in the group of nomenclatory *lakṣaṇa*s while the others in the group of prescriptive *lakṣaṇa*s because the first variety just enumerates some of the separable words (*iṅgya*) that occur in the word-reading of *Taittirīya Saṁhitā* and the other two varieties are in prescriptive as well as in descriptive style as a Śikṣā text is expected to be. The first variety of *Ātreyaśikṣā* has already been edited by Kulkarni.[23] This book brings forward the third variety of *Ātreyaśikṣā*.

The MSS of these texts are deposited in different repositories including private archives. Aithal mentions five MSS of the first variety of *Ātreyaśīkṣā,* one (M) of which is deposited in Government Oriental Manuscripts Library, Chennai, another one is supposed to be in National Library, Kolkata, while the other three are in some private collections as mentioned by Oppert.[24] Out of these MSS of the first variety, I could acquire only the copy of M that is inscribed in the Telugu script. As Oppert's catalogue is not a descriptive one, the other three MSS of *Ātreyaśikṣā* which are deposited in the private archives cannot be surely assigned as copies of the first variety. It is, however, erroneously mentioned by Kulkarni (2006c: 265) that this text deals with non-separables, i.e. *aniṅgya*s

23 Kulkarni 2006c: 265-75.

24 Oppert 1880: 525(1) Belonged to Pola Lakshmanavadhani of Vijayanagaram, vol. I: #7126.

Oppert 1880: 527(2) Belonged to Ivattur Nandikesvara Sastri of Vijayanagaram, vol. 1: #7168.

Oppert 1885: 419(3) Belonged to Venkatarama Sastri of Pillur, Mayavaram Taluk, vol. 2: #7344.

in the word-reading. In fact, it is just the opposite — this is clearly stated in the initial verse[25] of the text that it enumerates some of the separable words of the word-reading of *Taittirīya Saṁhitā*. This variety of *Ātreyaśikṣā* consisting of 27 *anuṣṭubh* verses is allegedly based on *Atrisūtra* or *Ātreyasūtra*.[26] According to Oppert, there is one text called *Atrisūtra* that belongs to Narasiṁhācāryār of Chingleput in Tamil Nadu.[27] Unless this MS is obtained, the ascription of *Ātreyaśikṣā* to *Atrisūtra* cannot be verified.

Though Aithal accurately adverts to the three varieties of *Ātreyaśikṣā* he made a small mistake in grouping the MSS based on the three varieties. He kept the Tirupati MS (T) in the list of the *AS2* while it should have been kept in the group of the third variety along with the Hamburg MS (H) of the same. I collected both H and T whereupon this edition is based. Both these MSS are in Grantha script.

Apart from T, Aithal also mentions three MSS of the second variety of the *Ātreyaśikṣā* (*AS2*). Out of these, two MSS (C and K) which are preserved in D.A.V. College, Chandigarh, and in Oriental Research Institute and Manuscripts Library, University of Kerala, Kariavattom, Thiruvananthapuram, are fragmented and incomplete. C is written in Grantha script and has three leaves. On the first leaf *Pāriśikṣā* ends and *Ātreyaśikṣā* begins. It contains five initial verses of *Ātreyaśikṣā*. The second leaf is an isolated leaf and does not seem to be the part of *Ātreyaśikṣā*. Perhaps, it is mistakenly placed along with the other two leaves of *Ātreyaśikṣā*. The third leaf contains eight full verses and a half verse of the final part of *Ātreyaśikṣā*, after which the *Siddhāntaśikṣā* begins. Possibly this MS of *Ātreyaśikṣā* was a part of a larger compilation of some Taittirīya Vedalakṣaṇa texts. K is written in Telugu script. It also has three leaves and its abrupt conclusion suggests that the MS is incomplete.

---

25 *ātreyokteṣu sūtreṣu sthitānīṅgyapadāny aham* ।
ślokarūpeṇa vakṣyāmi saukaryāya supāṭhinām ॥ —*Ātreyaśikṣā* 1

26 Ibid.

27 MS no. 15 (Oppert 1880: 4).

Furthermore, the lower and the upper areas of the left parts of the second and the third leaves respectively of K are torn. Therefore, some verses could not be deciphered therein. Another MS (L) of the same text is preserved in Punjab University Library, Lahore. It is a complete paper MS written in Grantha script. It contains sixty *anuṣṭubh* verses. Although appearing to be a complete MS of *Ātreyaśikṣā*, it in fact lacks a number of verses which are even found in K. Moreover, the final verses of *Ātreyaśikṣā* which are found in C are not there in L. Consequently, it is almost impossible to represent the full text of *AS2* unless some other complete MS of this text is discovered.

The author of the *AS* and the *AS2* are two different persons. Even though their texts belong to the same genre of the literature of the same Vedic school, there are no identical verses to be found in these two texts. Even the same rule is written differently therein. For example, the *AS* reads:

pāthaeṣo 'tidhāmātibhūteparamapūrvikāḥ ।
tathopasargapūrvāś cāgamañ chakhibhujā iyuḥ ।।59।।

The *AS2* reads the same rule as:

chakhibhujā iyuḫ pūrvan dhāmāpāty upasargataḥ ।
bhūte ca pāthaeṣo 'tiparamād ūrdhvatas sthitaḥ ।।[28]

In another instance, the *AS* reads:

tadhottare ṅato 'nantyād āgamau staḫ kagau kramāt ।

The same thing is stated in the *AS2* as follows:

ṅānunāsikapūrvas tu kakāro madhya āgamaḥ ।।
gakāraś ca takāre ca dhakāre ca yathākramam ।[29]

The styles of their compositions also seem to be very different.

---

28 L folio no. 12, 17-19th lines.

29 L folio no. 13, 4-6th lines. Commenting on *TP* 14: 23, *Tribhāṣyaratna* as well as *Vaidikābharaṇa* quote (Sastri and Rangacarya 1906: 393) a very similar verse.

The language in the *AS2* appears to be older than that of the *AS*.

THE "ORIGINAL" ĀTREYAŚIKṢĀ

An important concern for research would be the identification of the "original" *Ātreyaśikṣā* amidst these texts. Such an identification would not mean that *Ātreyaśikṣā*s other than the original are fake, but they would definitely become inferior to or of lesser importance than the original one. Here, the term "original" requires some clarification: I have used it to indicate the text which is usually found referred to in other works with the appellation *Ātreyaśikṣā*. References to and recognition of the said *AS* in other Sanskrit texts are usually the primary parameter to identify the "original". In order to locate such references to *Ātreyaśikṣā*, one needs to survey related literature that primarily includes *Taittirīya Prātiśākhya* and its commentaries, Śikṣās belonging to the Taittirīya School and their available commentaries and other Lakṣaṇa texts of the same Vedic school.

The paucity of printed Sanskrit texts related to this field makes it difficult to find references to *Ātreyaśikṣā*. In such a situation, checking all the MSS of the related texts is not a handy solution. Therefore, my arguments are based on whatever little material was available to me. Further publications of related texts can certainly modify my considerations.

Another problem is the tendency of the commentators to quote verses from the Śikṣā texts without indicating the source. Thus, the commentators of *Taittirīya Prātiśākhya* frequently quote verses from the related Śikṣā texts in order to strengthen their opinions but hardly ever mention the source of those Śikṣā verses. It is also the case that the Śikṣā texts share a lot of identical verses. For instance, from the last line of the second verse up to the first line of the fifth verse of *AS* and also from the last line of the 160th verse up to the first line of the 161st verse of *AS* are identical with

Āpiśaliśikṣā 7-9[30] and 14[31] respectively, *Śaiśirīyaśikṣā* 6-7[32] are identical with *Pāṇinīyaśikṣā* 3-4,[33] *Māṇḍukī Śikṣā* 1.4[34] is identical with *Yājñavalkyaśikṣā* 55.[35] Since several such instances occur, it is hard to identify the sources of the verses which are anonymously quoted by the commentators of the *Taittirīya Prātiśākhya*. Even though a verse that is quoted by a commentator is found in a Śikṣā text we cannot assert that the commentator took the verse from that very Śikṣā. Thus identifying the Śikṣā verses is not an easy task.

With regard to the available printed texts related to this field, references to *Ātreyaśikṣā* are very scarce. I could find two commentarial texts which directly attribute a verse quoted therein to *Ātreyaśikṣā*. They are *Lakṣaṇacandrikā,* a very recent (nineteenth century CE) commentary on the *Taittirīya Prātiśākhya* by Mahādeva Rāmacandra Gadre and the *Vedataijasa,* a commentary on *Vyāsaśikṣā* by Sūryanārāyaṇa Surāvadhānin.

Lakṣaṇacandrikā quotes several verses from *Ātreyaśikṣā* most of which are found in *AS2*. No such verse, which is said to be taken from *Atreyaśikṣā,* however, is traced in *AS*. The following verses of *AS2* are cited in *Lakṣaṇacandrikā*:

padadvayanimittaỹ yad ekābhāve 'pi tatra tu ।
saṁhitāvat kramo jñeyas tadvaj jñeyā jaṭā budhaiḥ ॥[36]

svaravarṇād abhedasya yat padadvitayasya ca ।
jaṭāvicakṣaṇair uktaṁ kramoccāraṇam atra tu ॥[37]

---

30 Vira 1981: 347.

31 Ibid.: 348.

32 Chowdhury 1981: 405.

33 Ghosh 1938: 49-50.

34 Bhagavaddatta 1921: 17.

35 Tripāṭhī 1989: 7.

36 L folio no. 8, 4-6th lines. Under *TP* 8.12, *Lakṣaṇacandrikā* quotes this line (Kulkarni 2004: 101).

37 L folio no. 8, 6-8th lines. Under *TP* 8.12, *Lakṣaṇacandrikā* quotes this line (Kulkarni 2004: 101).

sthāstanbhor eva lopas sa nimittena yathā bhavet ।[38]

cādīnām eva vo lopaḥ…[39]

… mo lopaẖ kvipparasya tu ।[40]

adhyāye taittirīyāṇām anusvāro yadā bhavet ।
tasyādyardho gakāras syāt tac cheṣam anunāsikam ।।[41]

eṣa sa sya halūrdhve ca visargo lupyate tathā ।[42]

mithunī na bhaved atra hy anārṣe tu svare pare ।[43]

hrasvapūrvāv anusvārayogādīñ cāntagau naṅau ।[44]

chakhibhujā iyuẖ pūrvan dhāmāpāty upasargataḥ ।
bhūte ca pātha-eṣo 'ti-paramād ūrdhvatas sthitaḥ ।।[45]

ṅānunāsikapūrvas tu kakāro madhya āgamaḥ ।
gakāraś ca takāre ca dhakāre ca yathākramam ।।[46]

rephāt pūrvo nakāro yaẖ padānto yatra dr̥śyate ।

---

38 L folio no. 8, 13th line. Under *TP* 5.14, *Lakṣaṇacandrikā* quotes this line (Kulkarni 2004: 84).

39 L folio no. 8, 13-14th lines. Under *TP* 5.13, *Lakṣaṇacandrikā* quotes this line (Ibid.: 84).

40 L folio no. 8, 14th line. Under *TP* 13.4, *Lakṣaṇacandrikā* quotes this line (Ibid.: 128).

41 L folio no. 9, 3-5th lines. Under *TP* 15.3, *Lakṣaṇacandrikā* quotes this line (Ibid.: 142).

42 L folio no. 10, 9-11th lines. Under *TP* 5.15, *Lakṣaṇacandrikā* quotes this line (Ibid.: 84).

43 L folio no. 11, 13-14th lines. Under *TP* 10.18, *Lakṣaṇacandrikā* quotes this line (Ibid.: 116).

44 L folio no. 12, 15-16th lines. Under *TP* 14.1, *Lakṣaṇacandrikā* quotes this line (Ibid.: 133).

45 L folio no. 12, 17-19th lines. Under *TP* 14.8, *Lakṣaṇacandrikā* quotes this line (Ibid.: 135).

46 L folio no. 13, 4-6th lines. Under *TP* 14.23, *Lakṣaṇacandrikā* quotes this line (Ibid.: 137).

viśeṣan tatra jānīyād dvitvam ity abhidhīyate ||[47]

lakārasya vakārasya saỹyoge svarito yadi |
viśeṣas tatra jānīyād dvitvam ity abhidhīyate ||[48]

nakārāntam padam pūrvaỹ yavaheṣu pareṣu ca |
nakārayavahā madhye tatra varṇam asaỹyutam ||[49]

nakārāntam padapūrvaṽ vakārād r̥pare yadi |
saỹyuktan tatra jānīyād dvitvam ity abhidhīyate ||[50]

avagraho nakāro yaḫ padānto yatra dr̥śyate |
viśeṣan tatra jānīyād dvitvam ity abhidhīyate ||[51]

saỹyuktau navakārau ca yakāraḫ parato yadi |
viśeṣan tatra jānīyād dvitvam ity abhidhīyate ||[52]

ūṣmottarasya rephasya svarabhaktir budhais smr̥tāḥ |
lakārasya tadūrdhve ca svarabhaktitvam ucyate ||[53]

The verse of *Ātreyaśikṣā* that is quoted in *Vedataijasa*[54] is not found in the MSS of *AS2*. The verse is as follows:

adukāramakāraś ca jñeyās santi sadā 'tra tu |
tasmāt sarvaś caturmātra om iti praṇavas smr̥taḥ ||

---

[47] L folio no. 13, 14-16th lines. Under *TP* 14.28, *Lakṣaṇacandrikā* quotes this line (Kulkarni 2004: 139).

[48] L folio no. 13, 16-18th lines. Under *TP* 14.28, *Lakṣaṇacandrikā* quotes this line (Ibid.: 139).

[49] L folio no. 13, 19-20th lines. Under *TP* 14.28, *Lakṣaṇacandrikā* quotes this line (Ibid.: 139).

[50] L folio no. 14, 1-3rd lines. Under *TP* 14.28, *Lakṣaṇacandrikā* quotes this line (Ibid.: 140).

[51] L folio no. 14, 3-5th lines. Under *TP* 14.28, *Lakṣaṇacandrikā* quotes this line (Ibid.: 140).

[52] L folio no. 14, 5-7th lines. Under *TP* 14.28, *Lakṣaṇacandrikā* quotes this line (Ibid.: 140).

[53] L folio no. 14, 20th line; folio no. 15, 1-2nd lines. Under *TP* 21.16, *Lakṣaṇacandrikā* quotes this line (Ibid.: 165).

[54] Sastri 1976: 175.

Since this verse is not there in *AS* it is possibly a verse from *AS2* itself. If a complete MS of *AS2* is discovered this verse can be traced therein.

It is clear from the previous discussion that *Ātreyaśikṣā* which was chiefly known by the then Vedic scholars of the Taittirīya School is not *AS* but *AS2*. A close comparative study of these two *Ātreyaśikṣā*s would reveal that *AS* appears to be of a later date. This will be discussed in detail in the sub-section "DATE" later. Here we can conclude with the decision that the so-called originality should be attributed to *AS2*.

STRUCTURE OF THE TEXT

Ātreyaśīkṣā is divided into two parts, viz. *Ātreyaśīkṣākārikā* (*AK*) and *Ātreyaśīkṣāmūla* (*AS*). The *AK* consisting of seventeen *anuṣṭubh* verses and a half-verse is a comprehensive table of contents of *AS* while *AS* is the main body of the text. Such an exhaustive content list is very rare in the Sanskrit literature and I have never seen any other Śikṣā text with such a versified table of contents. The contents mentioned in *AK* exactly correspond to the subject matters of *AS* sequentially.

The body of *AS* is well-structured comprising 294 verses out of which 293 verses are composed in the *anuṣṭubh* (*vaktra*) metre followed by the concluding verse in *rathoddhatā* metre. However, the rule for a *vaktra* metre says that the fifth and the sixth syllable of each hemistich should be *laghu* and *guru* respectively and the seventh syllable of the second and fourth should be *laghu,*[55] is not always followed. The text starts with a proper benediction to the Ultimate light, i.e. the *Brahman* and ends with a *phalaśruti* verse that states the fruit of Vedic recitation.

---

[55] *pañcamaĪ laghu sarvatra saptaman dvicaturthayoḥ* ।
guru ṣaṣṭhañ ca jānīyāt śeṣeṣv aniyamo mataḥ ॥

prayoge prāyikam prāhuḫ ke 'py etad vaktralakṣaṇam ।
loke 'nuṣṭub iti khyātan tasyāṣṭākṣaratā matā ॥

— *Chandomañjarī* 5.4-5

The body of *AS* is duly divided into sections, the headings of which are found on the margins of the respective manuscripts. The headings of the sections tally with the contents mentioned in *AK* if not word-by-word.

SUBJECT MATTERS

In general, most of the extant Śikṣā texts are ill-structured and composed in an unplanned manner. Some Śikṣā texts of the Taittirīya School, however, are the exceptions. Fortunately, *AS* is one of them. It is very well-structured in terms of arranging its topics of discussion. When compared to the other Śikṣās of the Taittirīya School, *AS* in keeping its focus on the discussion on the different methods of Vedic recitation namely, word-reading (*padapāṭha*), sequential reading (*kramapāṭha*), tangled reading (*jaṭāpāṭha*) and the five varieties of the reading of the phonic sequences (*varṇakrama*s), holds a unique position in the corpus of Śikṣā literature. Though, to some extent, *Pāriśikṣā* also consists of similar kind of topics, the structure and topics of *AS* seem to be more comprehensive than that of *Pāriśikṣā*. *Pāriśikṣā* mostly deals with the phonic sequences (*varṇakrama*s) whereas *AS* describes not only the phonic sequences but also the tangled reading and the three natural recitations, viz. continuous reading (*saṁhitā*), word-reading (*pada*) and sequential reading (*krama*). A close reading of the text shows that the main aim of the text is to explain the practical aspects of the different ways of Vedic recitation, in whose connection it describes the theoretical elements of Śikṣā too. It, therefore, serves as a practical guidebook to Vedic recitors who recite the above-mentioned readings of *Kṛṣṇa-Yajurveda* along with the continuous reading. While describing the methods of recitation *AS*, however, does not neglect theoretical nuances as the recitor cannot grasp the rules prescribed in the text properly if his theoretical base is not profound. Therefore, the theories, most of which are expressed in *Taittirīya Prātiśākhya*, are also illustrated in this text.

As mentioned before, the 294 verses of *AS* are divided into various sections on different subject matters with no sub-sections. But an overall perspective investigating the text may group the sections in the following hierarchical manner:

- Explanatory Terms and Rules (*paribhāṣā*)
- *Saṁhitā* and Its Different Natural and Artificial Readings (*saṁhitāviṣaya*)
    - The Fruits of the Vedic Recitation (*vedapārāyaṇaphala*)
    - The System of Vedic Recitation (*pārāyaṇakrama*)
    - Intermission in Vedic Recitation (*anadhyayana*)
    - Modes of Speech (*vāgvṛtti*)
    - Word-reading (*padapāṭha*)
    - Sequential Reading (*kramapāṭha*)
    - Tangled Reading (*jaṭāpāṭha*)
    - Simple Phonic Sequence (*kevalavarṇakrama*)
        - Duplication (*dvitva*)
            - Final Nasal Stop (*nāda*)
        - Increment (*āgama*)
            - Adjacent Imposition (*abhinidhāna*)
            - Insertion (*kevalāgama*)
            - Twin Phones (*yama*)
            - Prevention of the Twin Phones (*yamaniṣedha*)
        - Prevention of Duplication and Increment (*dvitvāgama-niṣedha*)
        - Anaptyxis (*svarabhakti*)
            - Definition (*lakṣaṇa*)
            - Appellations (*saṁjñā*) and Examples (*udāharaṇa*)
        - Hiatus (*vivṛtti*)
            - Definitions and Appellations (*lakṣaṇa* and *udāharaṇa*)

        - Examples (*udāharaṇa*)
        - Intermediate Nasal within a Hiatus (*vyaktimadhya-sthanāsikya*)
    - Nasally Modified *a*-Vowel (*raṅga*)
        - Nasally Modified Protracted *a*-Vowel (*raṅgapluta*)
        - Nasally Modified Long *a*-Vowel (*raṅgadīrgha*)
    - Circumflex Tremulous (*svaritakampa*) and Acute Tremulous (*udāttakampa*)
    - Modification (*vaikr̥ta*) and Originality (*prākr̥ta*) of the Sibilants
    - Nasalization (*nāsikyatva*) and Pulmonicness (*urasyatva*) of the Aspirate
    - Intermediate *ḥ* within a Hiatus (*vyaktimadhyasthavisarga*)
    - *ẖ* (*jihvāmūlīya*) and *ḫ* (*upadhmānīya*)
        - Stability in Juncture (*sthitisandhi*)
    - Proper Names (*vācaka nāman*) of the Phones Designated without Vowel (*svarahīna varṇa*)
    - Pure *ṁ* (*kevalānusvāra*)
    - Om (*praṇava*)
    - Prevention of Euphonic Change (*sandhiniṣedha*)
- Accentual Phonic Sequence (*svaravarṇakrama*)
    - Definition (*lakṣaṇa*)
    - Appellations of the Accents (*svara*)
    - Seven Circumflexes (*sapta svarita*)
        - Definitions and Examples (*lakṣaṇa* and *udāharaṇa*)
        - Different Manners of Articulation (*prayatnabheda*)
- Moraic Phonic Sequence (*mātrāvarṇakrama*)
    - Definition (*lakṣaṇa*)

   - Measurement of Moraic Time Duration (*mātrākālanirūpaṇa*)
   - Discussion on the Recitation of Moraic Phonic Sequence (*mātrākāloktiviveka*)
- Adjunctive Phonic Sequence (*aṅgavarṇakrama*)
   - Definition (*lakṣaṇa*)
   - Definition of Adjunct (*aṅgalakṣaṇa*)
   - Adjuncts of Subsequent and Antecedent (*parāṅga* and *pūrvāṅga*) Vowel
   - Description of the Recitation of Adjunctive Phonic Sequence (*aṅgavarṇakramoktilakṣaṇa*)
- Phonic Sequence of the Phonic Attributes (*varṇasārabhūtavarṇakrama*)
   - Etymology of the Term (*varṇasārabhūtavarṇakrama*)
   - Number of Attributes of a Phone (*varṇadharmasaṅkhyā*)
   - Order of the Attributes of the Phones (*varṇadharmakrama*)
   - Speciality in the Context of *ṁ*, Anaptyxis, Tremulous (*anusvārabhaktikampaviṣaya*) and Nasally Modified Protracted *a*-Vowel (*raṅgaplutaviṣaya*)
      - ♦ Speech Sound (*dhvani*)
         - ◊ Sound (*śabda*)
            - ❀ Origin of Sound (*śabdotpatti*)
            - ❀ Classification (*prakāra*) of Sound
            - ❀ Determination (*nirūpaṇa*) of Speech Sound
               - — Inner Activities of the Body (*śarīrāntargatavyāpāra*)
                  - * Situation of the Stomach Fire (*jāṭharāgnisthiti*)
                  - * Five Vital Airs (*pañca vāyu*)
                     - ∘ Location (*sthāna*)

- ○ Gross and Subtle Activities (*sthūla-sūkṣmarūpaceṣṭā*)
- ◇ Types of Speech Sound (*dhvanibheda*)
  - ❀ Phones Originated from Them (*tajjātavarṇa*)
- ◆ Places of Articulation (*sthāna*) and Articulators (*karaṇa*) of the Phones
- ◆ Manners of Articulation (*prayatna*) of the Phones
- ◆ Deities (*devatā*) of the Phones
- ◆ Class (*jāti*) of the Phones
- ◆ Designations of the Phones (*varṇasaṁjñā*)
- ◆ Deities of the Accents
- ◆ Class of the Accents
- ◆ Qualities (*guṇa*) of the Accents
- ◆ Manual Demonstration of the Accents (*hastasvaravinyāsa*)
  - ◇ The Fruit of the Accentual Demonstration (*svaravinyāsaphala*)
- ◆ Conditions of the Organs (*aṅgāvasthā*)
- ◆ Determination of the Notes (*svaranirūpaṇa*)
- ◆ Places of Origin (*utpattisthāna*) of the Accents

– Importance of the Vedic Studies (*vedādhyayana*)

- The Fruits of the Vedic Studies (*vedādhyayanaphala*)
- Harm Done for not Studying the Veda (*anadhyayanarahitadoṣa*)
- Magnificence of the Veda (*vedamahimā*)
- The Fruit of the Comprehensive Study of the Veda (*sāṅgavedādhyayanaphala*)

In keeping with this order and by following a meticulously structured manner *AS* is composed. The sections on the stomach fire and the five vital airs make this text peerless. I did not find any other Śikṣā text where the inner activities of the astral human body which are involved in producing speech sounds are depicted so elaborately. It also dedicates a number of verses for describing the importance of Vedic studies — this, too, is not very common in other Śikṣā texts.

In other places, *AS* maintains a close affinity to the other Śikṣā texts of the Taittirīya School. In many places *AS* and *Pāriśikṣā* share the same contents in same order with similar verbal expressions. However, they do not share many identical verses. The metrical representations of their verses are also different. Except the final verse *AS* is entirely composed in *anuṣṭubh* verses whereas *Pāriśikṣā* is mostly in *upajāti* metre and *anuṣṭubh* verses are used in some of the initial verses.

AFFILIATION TO THE KṚṢṆA-YAJURVEDA OF THE TAITTIRĪYA SCHOOL

It is certain that *AS* is affiliated to *Kṛṣṇa-Yajurveda*. There are ample reasons which affirm its association with *Kṛṣṇa-Yajurveda*. Importantly:

- Prima facie it appears that *AS* predominantly adheres to the *Taittirīya Prātiśākhya*. There are ample references to the expressions of *AS*, which have their counterparts in the *Taittirīya Prātiśākhya*.[56]
- The unusual spelling *śīkṣā* which is adopted in *AS* is the speciality of the Taittirīya School. This spelling is used in the Śīkṣā Vallī of the *Taittirīya Upaniṣad*.[57] Most of the Grantha manuscripts of the Śikṣā texts which belong to the Taittirīya School keep the spelling *śīkṣā*.
- The examples which are quoted in *AS* in the contexts of anaptyxes, hiatus, *raṅgapluta* and *raṅgadīrgha* are all found in *Kṛṣṇa-Yajurveda*.

---

56 Vide Appendix V.

57 *TA* 7.

- The text of *AS* itself refers to the Taittirīya School once.[58] Moreover, it mentions Kāṭhaka[59] twice. Out of these two it mentions one is in the context of the modification of *n* preceded by *ś*[60] and the other one is in the context of *raṅgadīrgha*. Obviously Kāṭhaka does not directly refer to the Kāṭhaka school of *Kṛṣṇa-Yajurveda* which was prevalent in Punjab and Kashmir region. Rather, it indicates the Kāṭhaka part whose recitation is still practised by the followers of the Taittirīya School along with *Kṛṣṇa-Yajurveda*. The second occurrence of the word *kāṭhaka*, however, refers to the eight *Kāṭhaka Āraṇyaka*s which are the first two chapters of the *Taittirīya Āraṇyaka*. There are several references to the association of *AS* with *Yajurveda*.[61]
- *AS* maintains a close affinity to the other Śikṣā texts such as *Pāriśikṣā*, *Sarvasammataśikṣā*, *Vyāsaśikṣā* which are affiliated to the Taittirīya School.

SOUTH INDIAN ORIGIN

It is certain that *AS* was composed somewhere in south India. It is affiliated to the Taittirīya School of *Kṛṣṇa-Yajurveda* which is prevalent in south India. The Śikṣā texts belonging to the Taittirīya School were probably all composed in south India since their MSS are found in this region.[62] Both of the MSS of *AS* are in Grantha script which was a predominant script for writing Sanskrit texts in Tamil Nadu and the adjacent region. The MSS of the other *Ātreyaśikṣā*s are also either in Grantha or in Telugu script, both of

---

58 *AS* 61.

59 *AS* 61, 106.

60 Cf. *Vyāsaśikṣā* (Sastri 1976: 133).

61 *AS* 5, 11, 12, 55, 198.

62 "The Śikṣās of the Taittirīya School are by far the most important contribution to Indian phonetics. As their MSS are available only in south India, they were presumably composed in that part of the country." — Varma 1929: 37.

which are south Indian scripts. The text mentions *mahāpradoṣa,*[63] a day for certain religious vow, which is mostly prevalent in south India. All these arguments corroborate the south Indian origin of the text.

AUTHORSHIP

The very name of the text suggests its association with Ātreya. The name Ātreya appears to be a generic one, connected with the *gotra* of Atri. The Vedic and Purāṇic traditions provide a long list of different Ātreyas who are associated with the family of Atri (*atri* + *ḍhak* [nominal affix] = Ātreya). The fifth *maṇḍala* of the *Ṛgveda Saṁhitā* consists of a number of hymns whose seers are different Ātreyas. *Jaiminisūtras* (5.2.18[64] and 6.1.26[65]) refer to one Ātreya. Ātreya is a renowned figure in the Āyurvedic tradition too.[66] The Purāṇas also mention different Ātreyas. No connection, however, can be established between these Ātreyas and *AS*. In the Taittirīya tradition, Ātreya is celebrated as the redactor of the word-reading of *Taittirīya Saṁhitā.*[67] It is already shown that *AS* belongs to the Taittirīya School of *Kṛṣṇa-Yajurveda.* Therefore, it would not be irrelevant to judge whether the authorship of *AS* goes to this Ātreya.

The fourth chapter of *Taittirīya Kāṇḍānukrama*[68] states that Ātreya is one of the initiators of the Taittirīya School which was first founded by Vaiśampāyana. As the tradition of the Taittirīya School came to be fully developed after Ātreya, this Vedic branch

---

63 Associated with the worship of the Hindu god Śiva — a three-hour period in the thirteenth day of every fortnight which occurs on Monday and Saturday.

64 *mukhyānantaryam ātreyaḥ, tena tulyaśrutitvād aśabdatvāt prākṛtānāṽ vyavāyaḥ* ||

65 *nirdeśād vā trayāṇāṁ syād agnyādheye hy asambandhaḫ kratuṣu brāhmaṇaśrutir ity ātreyaḥ* ||

66 Chitrao 1964: 57-58.

67 Kulkarni (1995: 11-17) elaborately discusses the references to Ātreya as the *padapāṭhakāra* of *Kṛṣṇa-Yajurveda.*

68 *Taittirīya Kāṇḍānukrama*, Chapter 4 (Weber 1855: 396).

is also known as Ātreyī *Śākhā*. He redacted the word-reading of *Taittirīya Saṁhitā* 25-27 too:

vaiśampāyano yāskāya etam prāha paiṅgaye ।
yāskas tittiraye prāha ukhāya prāha tittiriḥ ॥

ukhaś śākhām imām prāha ***ātreyāya*** *yaśasvine* ।
tena śākhā praṇīteyam ***ātreyī*** *ca socyate* ॥

yasyām padakṛd ***ātreyo*** *vṛttikāras tu kuṇḍinaḥ* ।
tāṽ vidvāṁso mahāśākhām bhadram aśnute mahat ॥[69]

The Gṛhyasūtras of Bodhāyana[70] and Hiraṇyakeśin[71] also refer to the same fact. Skandamaheśvara and Devarājayajvan in their commentaries on *Nirukta* indicate Ātreya to be the redactor of the word-reading of *Taittirīya Saṁhitā*.[72] *Taittirīya Prātiśākhya* and *Maitrāyaṇīya Prātiśākhya* mention Ātreya twice[73] and thrice[74] respectively. *Kauhalīyaśikṣā* also refers to Ātreya twice.[75] At one place it says that Ātreya is the redactor of the word-reading and elsewhere it cites the opinion of Ātreya in a particular context.

---

69 This verse is identical with the *Kauhalīyaśikṣā* 45 (Ram 1981: 397).

70 *atha dakṣiṇataḥ prācīnāvītino vaiśampāyanāya phaliṅgave tittiraye ukhāyokhyāya* ***ātreyāya padakārāya*** *kauṇḍinyāya vṛttikārāya kaṇvāya bodhāyanāya pravacanakārāyāpastambāya sūtrakārāya satyāṣāḍhāya hiraṇyakeśāya vājasaneyāya yājñavalkyāya bharadvājāyāgniveśāyācāryebhya ūrdhvaretobhyo vānaprasthebhyaḥ vaṁśasthebhya ekapatnībhyaḫ kalpayāmīti* ॥ — *Baudhāyana-Gṛhyasūtra* 3.9.6 (Sastri 1920: 98)

71 *vaiśampāyanāya paliṅgaye tittirāyokhāy***ātreyāya padakārāya** *kauṇḍinyāya vṛttikārāya sūtrakārebhyaḥ satyāṣāḍhāya pravacanakartṛbhya ācāryebhya ṛṣibhyo vānaprasthebhya ūrdhvaretobhya ekapatnībhya iti* ॥ — *Hiraṇyakeśi-Gṛhyasūtra* 2.20.1 (Kirste 1889: 90)

72 Vide Kulkarni 1995: 15-16.

73 *TP* 5.31 and 17.8.

74 *Maitrāyaṇīya Prātiśākhya* 2.5, 5.33, 6.8. Vide Mīmāṁsaka 1984: 403.

75 Ram 1981: 397.

It seems that the Ātreya who is the redactor of the word-reading of *Taittirīya Saṁhitā* and the Ātreya who is mentioned in the Prātiśākhyas are same. Moreover, the references to Ātreya in the Prātiśākhyas and *Kauhalīyaśikṣā* indicate that Ātreya not only redacted the word-reading of the *Taittirīya Saṁhitā* but also authored some text which was possibly a Śikṣā. The 8th aphorism of the 17th chapter of the *Taittirīya Prātiśākhya* is a cited verse which is said to be the statement of Ātreya:

nātivyaktan na cāvyaktam evaṽ varṇān udīrayet ।
payaḥpūrṇam ivāmatraṁ haran dhīro yathāmati ॥ *ity* ***ātreyaḥ***

According to *Vaidikābharaṇa* this verse is quoted from a Śikṣā text.[76] If this verse is really a statement of Ātreya and is quoted in *Taittirīya Prātiśākhya* from a Śikṣā text Ātreya is certainly the author of a Śikṣā, i.e. *Ātreyaśikṣā.*

It is, however, certain that *AS* is not this *Ātreyaśikṣā.* Neither the above-mentioned verse nor the opinion of Ātreya mentioned in the *Taittirīya Prātiśākhya* 5.31 regarding the nasalization of the vowel preceding *l* that substitutes a nasal[77] found in *AS.* Ātreya has a very old date which *AS* does not comply with. If we rely upon the traditional information which *Taittirīya Kāṇḍānukrama* provides Ātreya falls in the discipular line of the Taittirīya School. The discipular line is thus — Vyāsa → Vaiśampāyana → Paiṅgi Yāska / Paliṅgi / Phaliṅgu → Tittiri → Ūkha → Ātreya. Therefore, Ātreya should not be more than 200 years posterior to Vaiśampāyana. According to *Mahābhārata,* Vaiśampāyana was present after the great Bhārata war and he was the priest of Janamejaya, the great-grandson of Arjuna. The date of the great Bhārata war, however, is a highly discordant issue (6000 BCE to 500 BCE). Generally, the widely accepted date of the war is tenth century BCE. After the war, Yudhiṣṭhira ruled the kingdom for thirty-six years and after

76 *śikṣoktaṁ svamatam āha* । — *Vaidikābharaṇa* on *TP* 17.8 (Sastri and Rangacarya 1906: 448).

77 *uttamalabhāvāt pūrvo 'nunāsika ity* ***ātreyaḥ*** — *TP* 5.31.

him Parīkṣit, the grandson of Arjuna ruled for sixty years.[78] Then, Janamejaya became the king of the Kurus. Vaiśampāyana and Janamejaya were contemporary. If we accept tenth century BCE to be the date of the great Bhārata war, Vaiśampāyana should be from ninth century BCE. Then Ātreya should be of eighth-seventh century BCE. This date, however, is a mere conjecture since the date of the great Bhārata war is not certain and the other information is based on the mythological literature.

Baudhāyana Gṛhyasūtra also refers to Ātreya. According to Kane (1930: 30), the date of *Baudhāyana Dharmasūtra* is between 500–200 BCE. So, the date of *Gṛhyasūtra* of Bodhāyana would possibly be close to this date as *Gṛhyasūtra* and *Dharmasūtra* are the constituents of *Kalpasūtra*s of Bodhāyana. It affirms that Ātreya was already accepted as an authoritative figure in the Taittirīya School during that period. Therefore, he must have existed long before the time when *Gṛhyasūtra* of Bodhāyana was composed. In this text Ātreya is mentioned along with the other teachers of the Taittirīya School. If the order,[79] in which the teachers of the Taittirīya School are mentioned in *Gṛhasūtra* of Bodhāyana is chronological, then Ātreya was before the *vṛttikāra* Kauṇḍinya, the *pravacanakāra* Kaṇva Bodhāyana and the *sūtrakāra* Āpastamba. Ātreya is mentioned in *Taittirīya Prātiśākhya* which, as regards the view of Varma (1929: 20-28), was the oldest Prātiśākhya after *Ṛgveda Prātiśākhya.* According to him, the kernel of this Prātiśākhya must have been composed between 800–500 BCE whereas the later phase was between 500–150 BCE. The way Ātreya was mentioned in *Gṛhyasūtra* of Bodhāyana along with the other celebrated teachers of the Taittirīya School it appears that Ātreya precedes the *Gṛhyasūtra* for by at least one century. If the lower limit of this *Gṛhyasūtra* is 200 BCE the lower limit of the date of Ātreya must be 300 BCE. Kulkarni (1995: 17) suggests 500 BCE to be the lower limit of the date of Ātreya. Nevertheless, we can hardly assign the

78 Parameshwaranand 2001: 1002.

79 Vide fn. 70.

date of Ātreya to be after 300 BCE.

AS can never be as old as Ātreya, for *AS* is very much posterior to *Taittirīya Prātiśākhya* that *prima facie* succeeds Ātreya. The reasons that compel us to determine the date of *AS* after that of *Taittirīya Prātiśākhya* are discussed as follows:

- We have already seen how copiously *AS* follows *Taittirīya Prātiśākhya*. Many issues which are not there in *Taittirīya Prātiśākhya* or indicated implicitly are clearly described in *AS*. It is definitely so because of the further development of the subject.
- The use of some Pāṇinian terms in *AS* certainly proves the posteriority of *AS* to *Taittirīya Prātiśākhya*. Burnell (1875) shows that the Prātiśākhyas and the Pāṇinian grammar belong to two different grammatical traditions in which the former, as he identifies, to be of the Aindra School of grammar that was prior to Pāṇini.[80] The terms such as *ac, hal, at, it, ut, et, ot, ait, aut,* which exclusively belong to the Pāṇinian phraseology, are never found in *Taittirīya Prātiśākhya*. The way of representing the grammatical topics in *Taittirīya Prātiśākhya* is not similar to that of the Pāṇinian system too. In *AS*, the depiction of the subject matters solely follows the method of the Prātiśākhya. It uses certain Pāṇinian terms, but not in that technical sense in which those are used in the Pāṇinian system. For example, in *AS*, the term *hal*, which is used as an abbreviation (*pratyāhāra*) for certain consonants in the Pāṇinian system, refers to all consonants[81] including *ṁ, ḥ, ẖ, ḫ* which are not even reckoned in *Pratyāhārasūtras* of the Pāṇinian School of grammar. It would not be unwise to consider that though *AS* belongs to a different school of linguistic tradition it adopts some of the terms from the Pāṇinian school which

80 Burnell 1875: 2-8.

81 Vide *AS* 2-5.

surpassed the other grammatical schools through its popularity in that time. *AS*, the text of such a discipline that is very close to Vyākaraṇa in terms of the subject matters, could not remain uninfluenced by the prevailing Pāṇinian School of grammar. The same phenomenon did not take place in the case of the Prātiśākhya because the Pāṇinian School of grammar was not deeply rooted at that time in the Indian linguistic tradition.

- *Sarvasammataśikṣā* consists of a verse[82] where the Prātiśākhya is considered to be more authoritative than the Śikṣā. This may be taken in keeping with the Indian convention to consider the older work to be more authentic than a newer one. Therefore, *Taittirīya Prātiśākhya* must predate *Sarvasammataśikṣā. Sarvasammataśikṣā* reckons five varieties of the anaptyxes[83] whereas *AS* describes seven varieties of the same.[84] It is likely because of the later development of the subject. So *Sarvasammataśikṣā* probably precedes *AS*. The *Taittirīya Prātiśākhya* definitely predates *AS*.

It is, therefore, confirmed that Ātreya who was the redactor of the word-reading of *Taittirīya Saṁhitā* was not the author of *AS*.

In the Taittirīya linguistic tradition, there is, however, another Ātreya who wrote a commentary on *Taittirīya Prātiśākhya*. Somayārya, the author of *Tribhāṣyaratna* and Vīrarāghavakavi, the author of the commentary called *Śabdabrahmavilāsa* on *Taittirīya Prātiśākhya* mention[85] Ātreya as one of the previous commentators

---

[82] Vide fn. 20.

[83] *kareṇuḫ karviṇī caiva hariṇī hāriteti ca* ।
haṁsapadeti vijñeyāḫ pañcaitās svarabhaktayaḥ ॥
— *Sarvasammataśikṣā* 22 (Franke 1886: 22)

[84] *AS* 83.

[85] *vyākhyānam prātiśākhyasya vīkṣya vārarucādikam* । *kr̥tan tribhāṣyaratnaṽ yad bhāsate bhūsurapriyam* ॥ … *vārarucādikam bhāṣyajātaṽ vīkṣya nyūnātirekaparihāreṇa kr̥taṽ viracitam* । →

on *Taittirīya Prātiśākhya.* Somayārya informs that before writing the commentary on *Taittirīya Prātiśākhya* he consulted three other commentaries on the same, out of which one is authored by Ātreya. He quotes from *Ātreyabhāṣya* too.[86] That is why the name of Somayārya's commentary is named *Tribhāṣyaratna* (the jewel from the three commentaries). The other two commentators are Vararuci and Māhiṣeya. Only a single MS of Māhiṣeya's commentary was found and it is published. The commentaries of Vararuci and Ātreya are not even available in manuscript forms. As *Tribhāṣyaratna* was written using the essential portions of all these three commentaries, it alone came to be regarded as a substitute for these three. The three commentaries lost their importance and consequently their scribal transmission through manuscript forms became so insufficient that they did not survive to the present day. Fortunately, one MS of the commentary of Māhiṣeya has been found, although incomplete and full of lacunae.

Yudhisthira Mimamsaka (1984: 377-78) indicates the presence of another Ātreya who is referred to in a MS of *Pārṣadavṛtti* of Viṣṇumitra, preserved in the Deccan College Library:

> *tasya vṛttiḫ kṛtā yena tam* ***ātreyam*** *praṇamya ca* ।
> *teṣām prasādenāsyāhaṁ svaśaktyā vṛttim ārabhe* ॥ 2 ॥

In the printed edition of Shastri (1931: 1), the verse, however, is different:

> *tathā vṛttikṛtas sarvāṁs tān sūtrayaśasas tathā* ।
> *teṣām prasādād eteṣāṁ svaśaktyā vṛttim ārabhe* ॥ 2 ॥

← *ādiśabdena* ***ātreya****māhiṣeye gṛhyete* । — *Tribhāṣyaratna* on *TP* 1.1 (Sastri and Rangacarya 1906: 1).

ātreyo *māhiṣeyo vararucir api ca prātiśākhyasya cakrur vyākhyām bhāṣyāṇy amīṣām anuvidadhad atha trīṇi kaścid vipaścit* । ... — *Śabdabrahmavilāsa.* Vide Aithal 1991: 592.

86 *ekasamutthaḫ prāṇa ekaprāṇaḥ, tasya bhāvas tadbhāvaḥ, tasminn ity* ***ātreya****matam* । — *Tribhāṣyaratna* on *TP* 5.1 (Sastri and Rangacarya 1906: 163).

According to Mimamsaka, this Ātreya and the Ātreya who commented on *Taittirīya Prātiśākhya* are possibly one and the same. Based upon such little information, however, we cannot reach a reasonably reliable conclusion about this. The date of Ātreya, the commentator of *Taittirīya Prātiśākhya* is more obscure than that of the celebrated *padakāra* Ātreya. But evidently they are two different persons hailing from two different ages.

Taittirīya Prātiśākhya is far later than the *padakāra* Ātreya; but *Taittirīya Prātiśākhya* must predate its commentator Ātreya. Therefore, they cannot be one and the same. Since the date of Somayārya who exclusively mentions Ātreya as one of the commentators of *Taittirīya Prātiśākhya* is not known to us it is not possible to determine the date of Ātreya. The upper limit of the date of Somayārya cannot be after CE 1634 as there is one MS[87] of *Tribhāṣyaratna* which is dated as 1690 Vikrama Saṁvat, i.e. CE 1634. Whitney (1868: 435) observes that *Tribhāṣyaratna* mentions to be quoting passages from *Mahābhāṣya* under *Taittirīya Prātiśākhya* 2.7 and 5.2 but these are actually from the Kaiyyaṭa's gloss, *Pradīpa*. The approximate date of Kaiyyaṭa is eleventh century CE.[88] Therefore, Somayārya should not be placed before eleventh century CE. Commenting on *Taittirīya Prātiśākhya* 18.1, Somayārya quotes from *Kālanirṇayaśikṣā* too.[89] According to Burnell (1875: 49), *Kālanirṇaya* was probably written by Sāyaṇa who lived in fourteenth century CE. He, however, mistook it with

---

87 Preserved in Prajñā Pāṭhaśālā Maṇḍala, Wai. MS No. 572 (Aithal 1991: 373).

88 Coward and Raja 1990: 19, Bandyopadhyay 2000: 485.

89 *kālanirṇaye 'py evaṽ varṇitam — svādhyāyārambhaśeṣasya praṇavasya svarasya ca | adhyāyasyānuvākasyānte syād ardhatṛtīyatā || tuśabdasya prayojanam ucyate — sandhyakṣarāṇāṽ vedañ ca praṇavañ cāntarā tathā | iti kālanirṇaye |* — *Tribhāṣyaratna* on *TP* 18.1 (Sastri and Rangacarya 1906: 450). These are found in the *Kālanirṇayaśikṣā* (Chandra 1981: 273-74).

a Dharmaśāstra work[90] that is also called *Kālanirṇaya* and is ascribed to Mādhava, the brother of Sāyaṇa. Even referring to the consideration of Burnell regarding *Kālanirṇayaśikṣā,* Varma (1929: 45) did not recognize the error made by Burnell. He, however, is not consentient with the opinion to place *Kālanirṇayaśikṣā* in fourteenth century CE. He places it before thirteenth century CE arguing that *Vyāsaśikṣā,* whose date is thirteenth century CE, has borrowed a part from *Kālanirṇayaśikṣā. Vaidikābharaṇa,* another commentary on *Taittirīya Prātiśākhya* by Gārgya Gopāla Yajvan is definitely posterior to *Tribhāṣyaratna* as it refutes the view of *Tribhāṣyaratna* at many places referring to it indirectly.[91] Varma (1929: 48) suggests the probable date of the *Vaidikābharaṇa* to be fourteenth-fifteenth century CE. Therefore, Somayārya could not have been living after fourteenth century CE and we can at least place him between twelfth-fourteenth century CE. Consequently, Ātreya could not be living after thirteenth century. If Somayārya mentions the three commentators in chronological order Ātreya precedes Māhiṣeya and succeeds Vararuci. It is obscure whether Vararuci, the commentator of the *Taittirīya Prātiśākhya,* is same with the Prākṛta grammarian Vararuci or the vārttikakāra Vararuci or Kātyāyana. Even the date of Māhiṣeya, the author of the commentary called *Padakramasadana* on *Taittirīya Prātiśākhya,* is not known. Unless some other information is known it is not possible to determine the exact date of Ātreya.

Now the question is whether this Ātreya who wrote a commentary on *Taittirīya Prātiśākhya* also wrote *AS.* The answer is unknown to me. Ātreya is notably reckoned among the śikṣākāras in some texts. *Śikṣādivedāṅgasūcī,*[92] a list of authors and Vedalakṣaṇa texts enumerates Ātreya among the eighteen *śikṣākāra*s:

bhāradvāja-vyāsa-pāri-śambhu-kauhala-hāritāḥ ।
bodhāyano vasiṣṭhaś ca vālmīkiś ca mahāmuniḥ ॥

---

90 Vide Kane 1930: 375-77.

91 *Taittirīyaprātiśākhyasya Bhūmikā* (Sastri and Rangacarya 1906: 17).

92 Aithal 1991: 603.

*athāpiśala-kauṇḍinya-pāṇiny-**ātreya**-nāradāḥ* ।
pulastya-bāḍabhīkāra-plākṣi-plākṣāyaṇas tathā ॥

munayo 'ṣṭādaśa hy ete śikṣākārāḫ prakīrtitāḥ ।...

The text mentions the commentator Ātreya too:

... *syāt prātiśākhyam **ātreya**bhāṣyav̄ vararucer api* ।
syān māhiṣeyabhāṣyañ ca tathā tatsūtrakārikā ॥

tatas tribhāṣyaratnañ ca vaidikābharaṇan tathā ।...

In a MS of *Sarvasammataśikṣā* along with Mañcibhaṭṭa's commentary, a post-colophonic verse refers to nine Śikṣās of the Taittirīya School. Ātreya is enumerated in the eighth position therein:

vyāso lakṣmīr bharadvājaś śambhuḫ kāpilanirmitāḥ ।
*kauhalīyaḫ kāl**ātreyā**raṇyaśikṣā nava smṛtāḥ* ॥[93]

An almost identical verse is also found at the end of a MS[94] which is a commentary of a Vedalakṣaṇa text called *Svarasampat*. The commentator lists the Śikṣā texts in which *Ātreyaśikṣā* is mentioned as an Upaśikṣā and is kept in the third position in the enumeration of the Upaśikṣās:

prathamav̄ vyāsaśikṣā ca lakṣmīśikṣā dvitīyakā ।
bhāradvājañ ca tārtīyaṁ śikṣāraṇyā turīyakā ॥

pañcamaṁ śambhuśikṣā ca ṣaṣṭhañ cāpiśalan tathā ।
saptamam pāṇineś śikṣā aṣṭamaṅ kauhalan tathā ॥

vāsiṣṭhaśikṣā navamam ete vai nava śikṣakāḥ ।
upaśikṣā tu vaktavyā prathamaṅ gautaman tathā ॥

*agastyaśikṣā dvaitīyaṁ śikṣā "**treyan** tṛtīyakam* ।
caturthaȳ yājñavalkyañ ca viśvāmitran tu pañcamam ॥

ṣaṣṭhaṅ kāśyapaśikṣā ca plākṣāyaṇaś ca saptamam ।
kauṇḍinyaś cāṣṭamaṁ jñeyan navamaṁ hāritan tathā ।

---

93 Aithal 1991: 651.

94 Preserved in Saraswati Bhandaram Library, Mysore. MS No. 52 (Aithal 1991: 694).

ete vai śikṣākārāś ca caturvedasya lakṣaṇam ||

*pāṇiny-**atri**-bharadvāja-vasiṣṭha-vyāsa-gautamāḥ* |
śikṣākārā vararuciḥ kauhalo mahiṣo nava ||

vyāsa-lakṣmī-bharadvāja-śambhv-āpiśali-sammataḥ |
*kauhaleyaḥ kālāraṇyaś śikṣā "**treyā** nava smṛtāḥ* ||

It is noteworthy that *Ātreyaśikṣā* is not kept in the list of the main Śikṣās. According to this passage, it is a minor Śikṣā text.

There are, however, many such references where Ātreya is not considered among the śikṣākāras of the Taittirīya School. Rājā Ghanapāṭhin, the author of *Sarvalakṣaṇamañjarī,* quotes[95] similar enumerative verses which are almost identical with the first three verses of the above-mentioned passage:

prathamā vyāsaśikṣā ca lakṣmīśikṣā dvitīyikā |
bhāradvājī tṛtīyā ca śikṣā "raṇyā turīyakā ||

pañcamī śambhuśikṣā ca ṣaṣṭhī cāpiśalī tathā |
saptamī pāṇineś śikṣā aṣṭamī kauhalī tathā |
vāsiṣṭhī navamī caivan nava śikṣāḥ prakīrtitāḥ ||

Another text called *Vedalakṣaṇānukramaṇikā*[96] also enumerates nine major Śikṣās of the Taittirīya School:

bhāradvāja-vyāsa-śambhu-pāṇini-kauhalīyakam |
bodhāyano vasiṣṭhaś ca vālmīkir hāritan nava ||

It further enumerates three minor Śikṣās of the same:

sarvasammatam āraṇyan tathā siddhāntam eva ca |
upaśikṣā imāḥ proktā lakṣaṇajñānakovidaiḥ ||

Commenting on the phrase — *pūrvaśikṣāḥ parāmṛśya* — the commentator of *Siddhāntaśikṣā,* Śrīnivāsa Makhin or

95 Sastri 1976: 187. Vide *Taittirīyaprātiśākhyasya Bhūmikā* (Sastri and Rangacarya 1906: 22). Almost the same verse is found at the end of a MS work called *Saṁhitāprakārā Ekādaśa* (Aithal 1991: 629).

96 Preserved in the Government Oriental Manuscripts Library, Madras (Suryakanta 1940: 1). Also, Aithal 1991: 577-78.

Śrīnivāsādhvarīndra who is the author of *Siddhāntaśikṣā* too, refers to some śikṣākāras:[97]

> *bhāradvāja-vyāsa-pāṇini-śambhu-kauhala-vasiṣṭha-vālmīki-hārīta-bodhāyanokta-śikṣādikam parāmṛśya* . . .

Similarly, *Yājuṣabhūṣaṇa,* the commentary on *Pāriśikṣā,* also mentions some of the śikṣākāras:[98]

> . . . *bhāradvāja-vyāsa-pāri-śambhu-kauhala-hārīta-bodhāyana-vāsiṣṭha-vālmīki-prabhṛtimunigaṇavinirmitaśikṣādigranthānu-sāreṇa* . . .

Remarkably, Ātreya is not referred to in these lists. It seems that *Ātreyaśikṣā*, although known to the Vedic scholars of the Taittirīya School, was unable to acquire widespread importance as a primary text. It is also probable that the Ātreya who is reckoned in these enumerations did not compose *AS,* but was rather the author of *AS2*, for as already shown in the subsection "Original Ātreyaśikṣā", *Ātreyaśikṣā* which is quoted in some other texts is not *AS,* but *AS2.*

It is also possible that the appellation of *AS, Ātreyaśīkṣā* is not given after the name of its author, but in accordance with the name of the Vedic branch to which the Śikṣā belongs. The Taittirīya *śākhā* of *Kṛṣṇa-Yajurveda* is also known as Ātreyī Śākhā.[99] Therefore, the Śikṣā of this branch is also called *Ātreyaśikṣā.* This is, however, a mere surmise and I am unable to draw any final conclusion since the text and the related literature known to me do not provide any such evidence based on which a consensus can be reached.

DATE

Determining the date of *AS* is likewise very difficult. As the text does not provide any indication to its date, related literary evidences provide the only way to fix the date of the text. But even the dates of related texts are not properly known to us, and consequently

---

97 Aithal 1991: 673.

98 Chandra 1981: 317.

99 Vide *Taittirīya Kāṇḍānukrama*, chapter 4 (Weber 1855: 396).

there exist no strong grounds on which to settle the date of this text. References are so scarce and inadequate that no definite conclusion regarding the date of the text can be drawn. Where the verses of *Ātreyaśikṣā* are quoted, it is *AS2* not *AS;* and where actually the verses of *AS* are found quoted they are not mentioned as taken from *AS.* As the occurrences of the same or similar verses are very common in the Śikṣā literature we cannot definitely identify the source of a Śikṣā verse quoted somewhere unless the source is specified.

The comprehensiveness that marks *AS* is very rare compared to the other extant Śikṣās and it gives an impression that it must date to a later period. Such a well-structured exhaustive text cannot remain neglected by the Vedic scholars for a long time. The sections dealing with the inner activities of the astral human body are a unique part of this text, the parallel of which I have not been able to trace in any other Śikṣā text. Śikṣā texts are analogous in general and if they belong to the same Vedic School they resemble one another very closely. Had *AS* been an old Śikṣā text, the similar parts dealing with the detailed activities of the astral human body would most likely have occurred in the other homogeneous Śikṣā texts. Therefore, it seems that *AS* is of a later date than the majority of the extant Śikṣā texts of the Taittirīya School.

The last line of the second verse up to the first line of the fifth verse is found with a slight change in *Vaidikābharaṇa* (Sastri and Rangacarya 1906: 9). The *Vaidikābharaṇa* reads:

> *hrasvadīrghaplutāvarṇevarṇovarṇā r̥ r̥̄ l̥ ca* ।
> *e ai o au iti jñeyāṣ ṣoḍaśehāditas svarāḥ* ।।
>
> *kakhau gaghau ṅacachajā jhañau ṭaṭhaḍaḍhā ṇatau* ।
> *thadau dhanau paphababhamās sparśāẖ pañcaviṁśatiḥ* ।।
>
> *yarau lavau catasro 'ntassthāś ca ẖkaśaṣasaẖpahāḥ* ।
> *ṣaḍ ūṣmāṇo visargānusvārau ḷo nāsyapañcakam* ।
> *ity ekonāṣ ṣaṣṭivarṇā asmatsvādhyāyavartinaḥ* ।। *iti*

Even if we do not look at the minor differences in the first and the second verses mentioned above we cannot assign its source to be *AS* for; *AS* reads the last line as — *ity ete yājuṣā varṇā ekonā ṣaṣṭhir īritāḥ* — which is very different in this quotation by *Vaidikābharaṇa*. Moreover, the first six lines are also shared by *Āpiśaliśikṣā* (Vira 1981: 347) and *Pāriśikṣā* (Chandra 1981: 319). Therefore, the source of these verses is obscure and we cannot say that *Vaidikābharaṇa* has taken them from *AS*. Another verse which very closely resembles *AS* 108 is quoted in both *Tribhāṣyaratna* and *Vaidikābharaṇa*. But another verse, very similar to this, is found in other texts, even in *Ṛgveda Prātiśākhya* 3.34.[100] Therefore, it also cannot provide any clue.

Two verses of *AS* (152 and 283) are found in *Śambhuśikṣā*.[101] These verses are quoted in the *Tribhāṣyaratna*[102] too. The second one is quoted in *Vaidikābharaṇa* too.[103] According to Varma (1929: 39-40), *Śambhuśikṣā* seems to be a comparatively old work and possibly a contemporary of *Vyāsaśikṣā*. Lüders (1894: 107) considers the middle of the thirteen century CE to be the lower limit of the date of *Vyāsaśikṣā*. A number of verses are quoted in *Tribhāṣyaratna* and in *Vaidikābharaṇa* from *Śambhuśikṣā*. For example, commenting on *Taittirīya Prātiśākhya* 8.15,[104] 23.2[105] *Tribhāṣyaratna* quotes from *Śambhuśikṣā*;[106] commenting on *Taittirīya Prātiśākhya* 2.2 *Tribhāṣyaratna* and the *Vaidikābharaṇa* both quote[107] from *Śambhuśikṣā*.[108] It has been shown in the previous subsection that the approximate date of *Tribhāṣyaratna* is between twelfth and fourteenth century CE. Therefore, *Śambhuśikṣā* must

---

100 Shastri 1931: 125.

101 Chandra 1981: 534-35.

102 Sastri and Rangacarya 1906: 486 and 517.

103 Ibid.: 43.

104 Ibid.: 239.

105 Ibid.: 517.

106 Chandra 1981: 534-35.

107 Sastri and Rangacarya 1906: 239.

108 Chandra 1981: 534. This verse is also found in *Pāṇinīyaśikṣā*.

not be after thirteenth century CE. Twelfth-thirteenth century would be the possible date for the composition of *Śambhuśikṣā*. As *AS* possibly borrows two verses from *Śambhuśikṣā* its date should be after thirteenth century CE.

The last line of the 10th verse of *AS* is found in *Pāriśikṣā* (Chandra 1981: 325) as it is. According to Varma (1929: 47), the lower limit of the date for the composition of *Pāriśikṣā* may be assigned to the fifteenth century CE. This opinion seems to be inconsistent to me for he himself points out that *Pāriśikṣā* is quoted by *Tribhāṣyaratna*[109] and *Vaidikābharaṇa.*[110] He assigns the date of *Vaidikābharaṇa* between fourteenth to fifteenth century CE. Therefore, the lower limit of the date of *Pāriśikṣā* cannot be fifteenth century CE. If *Vaidikābharaṇa* actually quotes from *Pāriśikṣā* the date of *Pāriśikṣā* should be before fifteenth century CE. Thus, if *AS* borrows the verse from *Pāriśikṣā* the date of *AS* should be placed after *Pāriśikṣā.*

The *Vaidikābharaṇa* (Sastri and Rangacarya 1906: 39) quotes three more verses which are almost identical with the last line of the 158th verse up to the first line of the 161st verse. Another verse, found in *AS* (last line of the 231st verse and the first line of the 232nd verse), is quoted in *Vaidikābharaṇa* (Sastri and Rangacarya 1906: 81) as well as in *Yājuṣabhūṣaṇa* commentary on *Pāriśikṣā* (Chandra 1981: 333). If *Vaidikābharaṇa* really takes these verses from *AS*, the date of *AS* must be before fifteenth century CE that is the approximate upper limit of the date of *Vaidikābharaṇa*. Then *AS* can be placed between thirteenth and fifteenth century CE. Since it

---

109 On *TP* 21.1 *Tribhāṣyaratna* quotes—*yas svayaṁ rājate tan tu svaram āha patañjaliḥ* । *uparisthāyinā tena vyaṅgyav̄ vyañjanam ucyate* ॥ *Tribhāṣyaratna* mentions *śikṣāvyākaraṇa* as its source. It is the 12th verse of the *Pāriśikṣā* (Chandra 1981: 321). The last line of this verse is identical with the last line of the 164th verse of *AS*.

110 On *TP* 1.2 *Vaidikābharaṇa* quotes — *anvarthatvam mahāsaṁjñā vyañjanty arthāntarāṇi ca* । *pūrvācāryair atas tās tu sūtrakāreṇa cāśritāḥ* ॥ It is the 9th verse of the *Pāriśikṣā* (Chandra 1981: 319).

is not altogether confirmed whether *Vaidikābharaṇa* actually quotes from *AS* the probable date for its composition cannot be definitely settled. The above-mentioned information which is used to fix the dates of the texts is inadequate and consequently predictions drawn out of that are still in the level of hypothesis.

Description of the Manuscripts

This edition is based on two MSS. The details of these MSS are as follows:

MS H

A brief description of this MS is as follows:

Repository	: Staats-und Universitätsbibliothek Hamburg
Call No.	: Cod. Palmblatt 0003_8_133
Size	: 9 x 35 cm
Material	: Palm leaf
Character	: Grantha
Date	: Not given, but looks not very old[111]
Condition	: Good, well-conserved
Scribe	: Urutiṭi Cakram Ayyaṅgār
Number of leaves	: 14 (*AS* — 13 and *AK* — 1)
Number of lines	: 6 lines (5a, 14a), 7 lines (2, 3, 5, 7, 7a, 9a, 14), 8 lines (1, 1a, 2a, 3a, 4, 4a, 6, 6a, 8, 9, 10a, 11, 11a, 12, 12a, 13a), 9 lines (10, 13)

---

[111] The scribe elsewhere (the colophonic remark of the MS of the text *Sarvasammataśikṣā* contained in the same MS bundle) gives the date as — *bahudhānyanāmasaṁvatsaraṁ caitramāsaṁ kṛṣṇapakṣaṁ amāvāsyādinaṁ granthasamāpti.* S. Jagannatha, a Sanskrit scholar at the ORI, Mysore, who has enough experience working with Grantha MSS, predicts on the basis of the writing style that the MS must not be older than 300 years.

Pagination	:	The leaves are numbered on the first page.[112] The first leaf is not numbered. The leaf of *AK* is also not numbered.
The beginning (*AS*)	:	*āmnāyāyasyaniśvāsāścandrasūryaucacakṣuṣī* I *tatpraṇamyaparañjyotiśśīkṣāṁvakṣyāmi-nirmmalāṁ* I 1 I[113]. . .
The colophon (*AS*)	:	*hari om* I *ityātreyaśīkṣāmūlaṁsaṁpūrṇaṁ* I *ślokasaṁkhyā* I 294 I *śubhamastuśrīmateha-yagrīvaparabrahmaṇenamaḥ* I *ūru*[114] *tiṭicakra mayyaṅgārsvahastalikhitam* I
The beginning (*AK*)	:	*kārikāṁsaṁpravakṣyāmiprathamaṁpāribhā-ṣikaṁ* I *saṁhitāviṣayaṁvedapārāyaṇaphalantataḥ* I. . .
The colophon (*AK*)	:	*ityātreyaśīkṣākārikāsamāptā* I *hari om* I

General Comments

There are very few MSS which are so neatly written in a beautiful and legible handwriting and are highly faultless like this MS. H belongs to a larger codex that is a collection of several Vedalakṣaṇa texts.[115] It is known from the colophonic remarks of the other MSS of the same MS bundle that the scribe himself is a Vedic scholar and a practitioner of the *varṇakrama*s.[116] Therefore, his writing is almost free from scribal errors and consequently conjectural emendations were seldom required. H does not read the last hemistich of the 60th and leaves some space blank where the hemistich would have been.[117]

---

112 The south Indian MSS are always numbered on the first pages of each leaf (Katre 1941: 12).

113 The benediction is done on the left margin as: *hariḥ om* I *śubhamastu* I *avighnamastu* I

114 In the MS, *ru* is written in Tamil character.

115 Vide Aithal 1991: 574-75.

116 . . . *varṇakramapāṭhirāmasvāmiayyaṅkārsvahastalikhitam.* Vide Aithal 1991: 574.

117 MS p. 3.

Corruption

Corrupted or erroneous readings are rarely found in this MS. Only a few came to my notice. These are as follows:

Verse No.	*Accepted Reading*	*MS Pg. No. & Line*	*Erroneous Reading*
10	*tathalkāraḥ*	1, 6th line	*tathaḷkāraḥ*
14	*sarvathā*	1a, 1st line	*sarvadhā*
81	*udāhṛhaḥ*	4, 4th line	*udāhṛtam*
108	*nityābhinihita*	5, 3rd line	*nityābhinihata*[118]
131	*tatrābhinihitaś*	6, 6th line	*tatrābhinihataś*
192	*vyaṅgyān*	9a, 2nd line	*vyaṁgān*
201	*śabdoccāraṇamātrataḥ*	10, 1st line	*śabdoccāraṇamatrataḥ*
247	*karaṇa . . .*	11a, 7th line	*karaṁṇa . . .*
288	*sarvās*	13a, 2nd line	*sarve*
7 (*AK*)	*. . . dhmānīyākhya . . .*	14, 5th line	*. . . dhmanīyākhya . . .*

Erasure

The scribe adopts a very common method for the erasure, i.e. a mark that indicates a portion of the text written erroneously. He puts two dots above the miswritten characters. For instance, such marks are used in page 1, 3rd line, 6th line, etc. Somewhere he just pens through the portion without using the dots. For example, such pen through is made in page 12a, 1st line. Somewhere he neither pens through the erasable portion nor puts the dots above it. Rather, he just adds the corrected portion above or below the respective erasable portion. E.g., page 14, 4th line.

118 Though the term *abhinihita* is also used in other ancient phonetic treatises (*Ṛgveda Prātiśākhya* 3.34) it is *abhinihata* in the Taittirīya School as *TP* (20.4,10) refers to it. The scribe itself rectifies this error in the verse 278 (MS p. 13, 4th line) and he uses the correct form in the verses 137 and 144.

Addition

The scribe uses a symbol (+) to denote the addition. E.g., page 1, 7th line, page 2, 2nd line, page 14a, 5th line. Most of the cases these additions are infralineal, i.e. below the line. Somewhere the additions are supralineal, i.e. above the line. In these cases the scribe randomly inscribes the addition without putting the (+) symbol to denote the addition. E.g., page 12, 1st line; page 13a, 2nd line.

Numbering of Verses

This MS assigns numbers to some of the verses of *AS.* But it does not add numbers to the verses of *AK.* The numbering, however, is faulty at many places. The following table contains the information regarding the numbering of the verse in this MS.

AS No.	*H No.*	*AS No.*	*H No.*
1	1	99	99
5	5	100	100
8	8	105	105
9	9	107	107
12	12	113	113
24	24	114	114
29	29	115	115
30	30	123 (1st line)	122½
36	36	130 (1st line)	129½
37	37	134	134
39	39	143	142
40	40	147	146
46 (1st line)	45½	150 (1st line)	149
47	47	154	153½
48	48	161	160
52	52	168 (1st line)	167
54	54	170	169½
56	56	178 (1st line)	177

Cont.

AS No.	*H No.*	*AS No.*	*H No.*
57	57	197 (1st line)	196
58	58	197	196 1/2
59	59	228 (1st line)	227
63	63	249 (1st line)	248
67	67	252	251
68	68	255	253
69	69	259	257
71	71	260	258
75	75	261	259
76	76	262	260
78	78	274	272
83	83	276	274
88	88	282	280
95	95	283	281

Orthography

The orthography of most of the Grantha MSS is different from the conventional orthographical system that is followed in most of the Sanskrit texts printed in the Devanāgarī script. After surveying the MS, I have formulated the following general guidelines of the orthography adopted in this MS.

As most of the old MSS, H also does not use *avagraha* and *candrabindu*.

The following consonants are found duplicated when they immediately follow *r*— *n* (E.g., तयोर्न्नानुक्रमेत्); *m* (E.g., धर्म्म); *y* (E.g., कार्य्य). But सर्व, विवृत्तोर्ल्लक्षणम्, etc. In case, the consonant is either *th* or *dh*, instead of duplication, *t* and *d* are added before *th* and *dh*, respectively. E.g., अर्त्थ, अर्द्ध. Similarly, if the post-vocalic *th* and *dh* are followed by a consonant, *t* and *d* are also added before *th* and *dh*, respectively. E.g., अद्ध्याय. At many places *n* that follows *y* and *m* is duplicated. E.g., तन्न्मात्रः. Somewhere a sentence-final *n* is duplicated — सञ्चरन्न् (page 10, 6th line). However, a number of exceptions are also noticed, such as अह्न्ये सूर्यौ, कथ्यते and अन्य.

In general, *anusvāra* is used at the place of an inter-word pre-consonantal nasal and also at the place of those word-final pre-consonantal nasals which are the modifications of *m*. E.g., कंप, अंग and त्र्यंबकं. An exception: पङ्क्ति (p. 13a, 5th line). But if certain consonants follow, it gets altered to the nasal of the series (*varga*) to which the subsequent consonant belongs. These consonants are: the consonants of the *ca*-series, *ṭa*-series, *ta*-series and *m*. E.g., ग्रन्थ, द्वितीयञ्च, काण्ड, दीर्घाभ्यान्न and पदम्मुक्तवा. But before the consonant cluster *jñ* the nasal is not altered into *ñ*.[119] E.g., संज्ञा.

- Sentence-final *m* is altered to *anusvāra*.
- Pre-consonantal *t* followed by the sounds of *pa*-series except *m*, the sounds of *ka*-series and sibilants except *ś* is always written with *halanta* symbol. E.g., तत् पदम्, तत् फलम्.
- *T* and *k* followed by a non-nasal voiced stop is not modified as *d* and *g*, respectively. E.g., अल्पमहत्भवाः, पृथक्भक्ते. An exception is also found there — ओष्ठयुग्भवेत्. The pre-vocalic *t*, however, is always changed to *d*. E.g., स्यादनन्तं, etc. If a non-nasal stop precedes a pre-consonantal identical sound, it gets elided. E.g., तद्वयम्, सात्विकः.
- The *visarga* that precedes a sibilant is altered to that particular sibilant. E.g., ज्ञेयाष्षोडश, यजुश्शाखा. But if the succeeding sibilant is a member of a consonant-cluster the *visarga* is just elided. E.g., अघोषा स्युः, neither अघोषास्स्युः nor अघोषाः स्युः; अन्तस्था, neither अन्तस्स्था nor अन्तःस्था.
- *T,* followed by *ś* generally becomes *ch.* E.g., ईषच्छ्लिष्ट. Alternative form is also found: स्याच्छषसेत्यादिसंग्रहात्. Sometimes, the combination of *c* and *ch* is also written as *chś*. E.g., नियच्छ्शाति, कृच्छ्श्र.
- In the euphonic combination of *h* preceded by *k* and *c,* both peculiarly change to *gh* and *jh,* respectively. E.g., पृथग्घलि

[119] See fn. 128.

(पृथक् + हलि), अइझल् (अच् + हल्).

MS T

Repository	: Oriental Research Institute Library, Sri Venkateswara University, Tirupati
Stock No.	: 3792
Size	: Not mentioned[120]
Material	: Palm leaf
Character	: Grantha
Date	: Not given, but looks old
Condition	: Damaged, not well-conserved[121]
Scribe	: Not mentioned
Number of leaves	: 17
Number of lines	: 3 lines (17a), 6 lines (1, 1a, 5, 5a, 14, 14a, 15a, 16a), 7 lines (2, 2a, 3, 3a, 4, 4a, 6, 6a, 7, 7a, 8, 8a, 9, 9a, 10, 10a, 12, 13a, 15, 16, 17), 8 lines (11, 11a, 12a, 13)
Pagination	: The leaves are numbered on the first page.[122] The first leaf is not numbered.
The beginning	: *kārikāṁsaṁpravakṣyāmiprathamaṁpāri-bhāṣikaṁ* । *saṁhitāviṣayaṁvedapārāyaṇaphalantatathā* ।
The colophon	: *ityātreyaśīkṣāmūlaṁsaṁpūrṇam* । *hariḥom* ।

120 As the images were sent to me I could not determine the size of the MS.

121 Peter Freund provided me a photocopy of an old microfilm of this MS. From the recent images of the MS that were sent to me, I discovered that the MS has significantly deteriorated from its previous condition.

122 The left margins of most of the leaves of this MS are torn. So, the page numbers of those leaves are not visible.

śrīvedavyāsāyanamaḥ । *śrīnivāsarāghavam-ahāguravenamaḥ* ।

General Comments

This MS is not as pure as H. It does not appear to have been written carefully. Many erroneous readings are found in this MS. It, however, seems to be older than H. The margins of most of the leaves of this MS are torn therefore, a very few marginalia are legible. The leaves are worm-bitten too. This MS also does not contain the last hemistich of the 60th verse and leaves some space blank for it exactly like H.[123] Therefore, possibly both of these MSS would have a common origin.

Corruption

This MS is corrupt at many places. A detailed list of the corruption is provided below along with verse number, MS page number and line and accepted and erroneous readings.

Verse No.	*Accepted Reading*	*MS Page No. & Line*	*Erroneous Reading*
3. (*AK*)	*dvitvāgamau*	1, 2nd line	*dvitvāgama*
6. (*AK*)	. . . *kyau*	1, 5th line	. . . *kau*
11. (*AK*)	*varṇasāra* . . .	1a, 2nd line	*savarṇasāra* . . .
4.	*ẖkaṣasaẖpahāḥ*	2, 5th line	*kaśaṣasahaẖpahāḥ*
10.	*vargākhyā*	2a, 3rd line	*vargākhya*
11.	. . . *rāntarā*	2a, 4th line	. . . *rāntarau*
12.	*vikṛtīḫ*	2a, 4th line	*vikṛtiḫ*
17.	*śuddhavarṇe*	3, 2nd line	*śuddhavarṇo*
21.	*sandhyāṁ*	3, 3rd-4th lines	*saṁndhyāṁ*
22.	. . . *mānena*	3, 5th line	. . . *māsena*
32.	*pada* . . .	3a, 7th line	*padā* . . .
39.	*yadyopasargataḥ*	4, 4th line	*yadyupasargataḥ*

Cont.

123 MS p. 5a.

Verse No.	*Accepted Reading*	*MS Page No. & Line*	*Erroneous Reading*
46.	*ye atra*	4a, 3rd line	*yetra**
47.	*halām*	4a, 4th line	*halād*
54.	*hrasvapūrvau*	5, 3rd line	*dvitvapūrvau*
55.	*sarūrddhve*	5, 3rd line	*svarūrddhve*
59.	*. . . ñcha . . .*	5, 6th line	*. . . ñca . . .*
61.	*parasthitaḥ*	5a, 2nd line	*parasthitaṁ*
65.	*yamāgamaḥ*	5a, 6th line	*yadāgamaḥ*
72.	*sparśayava . . .*	6, 4th line	*sparśayavo . . .*
72.	*vr̥ṇvra*	6, 5th line	*vr̥ṇya*
74.	*syāt*	6, 6th line	*syat*
80.	*karviṇī*	6a, 4th line	*karvaṇī*
81.	*haṁsapadā*	6a, 4th line	*hasapadā*
90.	*syādeka . . .*	7, 4th line	*syāsāṇu . . .*
96.	*sedagne*	7a, 2nd line	*sadagne*
96.	*vā iyam*	7a, 2nd line	*vā idam*
99.	*saṁyattā*	7a, 4th line	*saṁyuktā*
105.	*saurāṣṭrikā*	8, 1st line	*saurāṣṭriko*
105.	*uccais tathā*	8, 2nd line	*uccaitathā*
105.	*. . . gaṁ samuccaret*	8, 2nd line	*gasamuccaret*
106.	*ava svā aha*	8, 2nd line	*aha svā aha*
110.	*uccas tvāraṇyake*	8, 5th line	*uccasvāraṇyake*
117.	*kapa . . .*	8a, 1st line	*kaṁpa . . .*
125.	*daśaitāṁs*	8a, 6th line	*deśaistāṁs*
129.	*dhr̥tapracaya-śabdaś ca*	9, 2nd line	*dhr̥tapracaya-śabdauca*
129.	*parasparam*	9, 2nd line	*parasparaḥ*
131.	*prātihataścaturtho*	9, 3rd line	*pratihataścaturtthā*
133.	*ivarṇotor*	9, 4th line	*ivarṇonor*
139.	*bhaved*	9a, 1st line	*bhāved*
143.	*āpo*	9a, 4th line	*āco*

Cont.

Verse No.	*Accepted Reading*	*MS Page No. & Line*	*Erroneous Reading*
148.	*ānupūrvyaśaḥ*	9a, 7th line	*ānupūrvaśaḥ*
155.	. . . *nādo* . . .	10, 4th line	. . . *nādā* . . .
156.	. . . *ghali*	10, 6th line	. . . *ghalī*
158.	*hrasvā* . . .	10, 7th line	*hrasvaṁ*
162.	*aṅgaṁsaṁjñā* . . .	10a, 3rd line	*aṁgasaṁjñā* . . .
169.	*parāṅgabhāk*	11, 1st line	*parāṁgatā*
170.	. . . *sthāparam*	11, 1st line	. . . *sthāḥ param*
170.	. . . *gaṁsparśako*	11, 1st line	. . . *gasparśako*
173.	*uktvā*	11, 4th line	*ukvā*
177.	*sarvantatra*	11, 6th line	*sarvatatra*
180.	*asau*	11a, 1st line	*aṁga* . . .
184.	*prokto*	11a, 4th line	*prokte*
187.	*jñeyā*	11a, 6th line	*jñeyo*
188.	*ṣaḍjādi* . . .	11a, 6th line	*ṣaḍjāti* . . .
188.	. . . *tāndaśa*	11a, 7th line	. . . *tādaśa*
192.	. . . *gātpūrva* . . .	12, 1st line	. . . *gānpūrva* . . .
195.	. . . *plute*	12, 3rd line	. . . *pluto*
197.	*sthānānnani* . . .	12, 5th line	*nasthāṁganni* . . .
202.	*ghuṭi* . . .	12a, 1st line	*ghaṭi*
204.	*vahnes*	12a, 3rd line	*vanhes*
212.	*sthūlāssūkṣmā*	12a, 8th line	*sthūlasūkṣmā*
213.	*prāṇo*	12a, 8th line	*prāṇe*
216.	. . . *deśasthe*	13, 2nd line	. . . *deśastho*
223.	*śvāsohakāra* . . .	13, 7th line	*śvāsoṁgakāra* . . .
229.	*hanū*	13a, 4th line	*hanu*
232.	*syātāmo* . . .	13a, 6th line	*syātāvo* . . .
234.	*īṣacchliṣṭo*	14, 1st line	*īṣaśliṣṭo*
235.	*oṣṭhau*	14, 2nd line	*oṣṭhā*
236.	*satryaṇukastvidut*	14, 3rd line	*syaṇukastvididut*

Cont.

Verse No.	*Accepted Reading*	*MS Page No. & Line*	*Erroneous Reading*
238.	. . . *utsu*	14, 4th line	. . . *itsu*
240.	*karaṇī*	14, 5th line	*karīṇī*
240.	*prāhurvarṇa* . . .	14, 6th line	*prāhuvarṇa*
242.	*tathā*	14a, 1st line	*tadhā*
244.	*ralayo*	14a, 3rd line	*ravayo*
245.	. . . *data*	14a, 3rd line	. . . *ntada*
245.	*ve*	14a, 3rd line	*va*
247.	*karaṇā* . . .	14a, 4th line	*kāraṇā* . . .
250.	*spr̥ṣṭa īṣat* . . .	15, 1st line	*spr̥ṣṭamīṣat* . . .
250.	*pūrvakaḥ*	15, 1st line	*pūrvakaṁ*
253.	. . . *kārāvedavarṇau*	15, 3rd line	. . . *kārauvedavarṇau*
260.	. . . *vasudhāśca*	15a, 1st line	*vasudhāca*
262.	*syātāmanudātta* . . .	15a, 2nd-3rd lines	*syātā anudātta* . . .
269.	*vinya* . . .	16, 1st line	*vinyā* . . .
271.	*kampetu*	16, 3rd line	*kaṁpetat*
272.	*vyañjanaṁ*	16, 3rd line	*vyañjane*
272.	*svatantra* . . .	16, 4th line	*svatatra* . . .
274.	*vedamimaṁ*	16, 5th line	*vedamidaṁ*
276.	*kaṇṭhakha* . . .	16, 6th line	*kaṇṭaka* . . .
277.	*dhaivataśca*	16a, 1st line	*daivataśca*
288.	*sarvāstaṁ*	17, 3rd line	*sarvātaṁ*
289.	*brāhmaṇo*	17, 4th line	*brahmaṇā*
292.	*pāpaṁ*	17, 4th line	*pāpā*

* Though *ye 'tra* is grammatically correct it causes a deficit of one mora in the metre.

Dittography

I found only one example of dittography in T. In the verse 174 the words *evavadettatra* are found in this MS as *evavadevavadettatra.*

Erasure

The scribe does not use any symbol to indicate the erasure. The portions that are intended to be erased are just penned through. For example, such kind of erasure is seen in page 4, 3rd line, page 9, 4th line, etc.

Addition

The scribe usually keeps the additions below the line. E.g., page 1, 1st line. Only once the addition is seen as supralineal — page 12, 1st line.

Overwriting

The scribe prefers overwriting than erasure and addition. Excessive use of overwriting decreases the legibility of this MS in many places. E.g., page 5a, 4th line; in page 6a, 2nd line.

Omissions

Some examples of omission are seen in this MS. They occur on page 6, 4th line, page 8, 6th line, page 8a, 2nd line and in page 17, 1st line. Haplography is done in MS page. 3a, 6th line — पद्वद्वसाने is written as पद्ावसाने.

Numbering of Verses

In this MS very few verses are numbered. Some of them are erroneously numbered. The following information regarding the numbering of the verses in this MS:

***AS* No.**	40	50	105	115	123 (1st line)	147	154	161
T No.	40	50	105	115	125	146	155	160

Orthography

The orthography adopted in this MS is almost the same as the orthography of H. However, a large number of exceptional spellings are also found in this MS. Some of these distinct features can be generalized as follows:

- In most of the cases the intervocalic *y* is duplicated if it is followed by a short *a*-vowel. E.g., तृतीय्य, जिह्वामूलीय्य.
- Unlike H this MS combines pre-consonantal *t* with the succeeding letters of *pa*-series, *ka*-series and the sibilants. E.g., हात्परे. Even a peculiar combination त्भ is found herein.
- The scribe avoids many euphonic changes. E.g., महान्श्वासः, आदौअकारः, स्थानंतदेव, अभ्यनुज्ञातः सः.
- There are many instances where a vowel follows an *anusvāra*. E.g., शब्दं उच्चैः.

The text in Grantha script is provided in Appendix III using the same orthography which is followed in the MSS.

STEMMATICS

The genealogy or the stemma of the MSS is probably as follows:

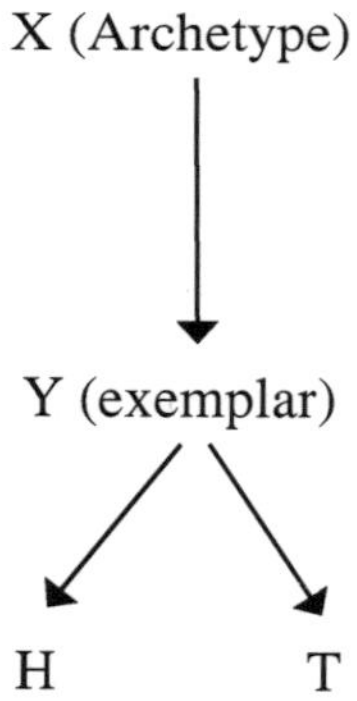

While X is the archetype H and T came from at least one common exemplar Y in the middle. The last hemistich of *AS* 60 is missing in both H and T, and both of them keep a space empty for that. The exemplar Y, from which H and T must have been directly or indirectly copied, would not have this hemistich in readable condition.

T reads the last line of *AS* 169 as *dhṛte hy ṛkāre parato rephaś ca syāt parāṅgatā.* This line is, however, grammatically incorrect. Either the word *repha* be in genitive case (*rephasya*) that can be related to the noun *parāṅgatā* or, the word *parāṅgatā* should be changed into an adjective which can go with the noun *repha.* In H, the scribe first writes it as it is in T. But then, comprehending the error, he replaces the word *parāṅgatā* with *parāṅgabhāk* making it an adjective of the word *repha.* It is, therefore, quite certain that the exemplar from which H has been copied had the same erroneous reading which T has adopted.

Although T seems to be older than H there is no reason for considering H to be copied from T. For, T has many faulty readings which are not found in H. They contain some variant readings also. *AK* is placed before *AS* in T whereas H places *AK* after *AS.*

The genealogy is, however, based on a conjectural ground and further discovery of MSS can modify this consideration.

Methodology

CRITICAL APPARATUS

Emendations

As there is a very pure MS like H the text hardly requires much conjectural emendation. I added the nasal symbol, i.e. *candrabindu* to the nasally modified vowels (*raṅga*) referred to in the verses 101 and 106 of *AS.* I changed the lateral retroflex sound (*ḷ*) that is used in the following words *viḷambitā* (*AS* 23 and 25), *kākaḷika* (*AS* 104), *sammeḷana* (*AS* 113), *nāḷī* (*AS* 200), *aṅguḷi* (*AS* 203),[124] *gaḷa* (*AS* 210, 214) and *nāḷa* (*AS* 211),[125] into its dental counterpart (*l*) as the lateral retroflex sound is not generally used in classical Sanskrit. However, the use of the lateral retroflex in Sanskrit is sometimes acceptable in the southern regions.

In the last line of *AS* 288 (*nandanti devatāḥ sarvās tav̐ vipraṁ nāviśed bhayam*) the word *sarvās* is found as *sarve* and *sarvā* in H and T, respectively. According to the noun *devatāḥ* which is in

---

[124] Not retroflexed in H.

[125] Not retroflexed in H.

feminine gender and plural in number, both the readings of the MSS are rejected and it is emended as *sarvās*. Another conjectural emendation is done in the first line of the verse 159. It is found in the MSS as follows:

dīrghāt plutāc ca tannādam ekamātram iti śrutiḥ ।

The word *nāda* is never used in neuter gender. Therefore, the sentence is ungrammatical. The same line is quoted in *Vaidikābharaṇa*[126] which reads as *dīrghāt plutāc ca tanmātram ekamātram iti śrutiḥ*. This is a plausible reading. Therefore, I emended the word *nādam* as *mātram* in accordance with the reading of *Vaidikābharaṇa*.

In the verse 229, *cauṣṭhau* is found in the MSS as *coṣṭhau*. According to the Pāṇinian grammar, the *pararūpa ekādeśa* (substitution of the former sound by the latter) is possible by the word *oṣṭha* if the euphonic change takes place in a compound word.[127] As no compound takes place in this case the form is ungrammatical. I emended it as *cauṣṭhau*.

In the MSS the last line of the verse 246 is as *kavargādiṣu yat sthānan tad eva syur yathākramam*. The subject *tat* which is in singular number does not agree with the verb *syuḥ* which is in plural number. However, I did not emend it as there is a sense of plural number that is implied by the word *yathākramam*. This should be taken as an ungrammatical form used by the author.

Treatment of Variant Readings

Apart from the erroneous readings the correct readings of the MSS H and T differ with each other at many places. Though all these readings seem to be grammatically correct this edition adopts one reading for the main body of the text keeping the other in the footnote in accordance with the principles of textual criticism.

---

126 Sastri and Rangacarya 1906: 39.

127 *otvoṣṭhayos samāse vā* । — *Vārttika, Siddhāntakaumudī* (Sharma and Sarma 1961: 96).

Readings which are entirely erroneous in terms of grammar or not at all valid in terms of the context are not kept in the footnotes. They are mentioned in the details of respective MSS. Readings which are less acceptable are also kept in the footnote if they are grammatically correct. Where both the readings of H and T are equally plausible I adopted the reading of the former for it has proved its accuracy much better than the latter. A commented list of the variant readings is provided below:

Verse No.	*Adopted Readings*	*Variant Readings*	*Comments*
1 (*AK*)	*tataḥ* (H)	*tathā* (T)	Equally plausible
2 (*AK*)	*ca* (H)	*tu* (T)	Equally plausible
9 (*AK*)	. . . *prayatnapra-deśāś* (T)	. . . *prayatnapra-bhedāś* (H)	Contextually less plausible
15 (*AK*)	. . . *saṁjñakāḥ* (H)	. . . *saṁjñikāḥ* (T)	Equally plausible
17 (*AK*)	. . . *saṁyukta* . . .(H)	. . . *saṁyukte* (T)	Equally plausible
5	*ekonāṣṣaṣṭhir* (H)	*ekonā ṣaṣṭhir* (T)	Eequally plausible
6	*krameṇa* (H & T)	*kādīnāṁ* (H*)	Equally plausible
28	*daśātroktā* . . . (H)	*daśa proktā* . . .(T)	Equally plausible
34	*pūrvaṁ pūrvaṁ padam* (H)	*pūrvapūrva-padam* (T)	Less plausible: *lectio difficilior*
35	*yadīṁgyaṁ* (H)	*yad iṁgyaṁ* (T)	Equally plausible
36	. . . *vākyāntagaṁ* (H)	*vākyāntakaṁ* (T)	Equally plausible
43	*paṭhet budhaḥ* (H)	*paṭhet punaḥ* (T)	Equally plausible
54	*yat* (H)	*tat* (T)	Equally plausible
54	*parepyaci* (H)	*parecyapi* (T)	Equally plausible
60	*Same varṇa* . . .(H)	*Same varṇe* (T)	Unpredictable†
69	. . . *dvitvalakṣaṇe* (H) *ṣaṇaṁ* (T)	. . . *dvitvalak-* *lectio difficilior*	Less plausible:
69	*pūrvāgamaścaiva* (H)	*pūrvāgamo yastu* (T)	Equally plausible
73	*yahottare* (H)	*hayottare* (T)	Equally plausible
74	. . . *vyañjanāt-makā* (H)	. . . *vyañjanāt-mikā* (T)	Equally plausible

Cont.

Verse No.	*Adopted Readings*	*Variant Readings*	*Comments*
75	*svarātmakau* (H)	*svarāsthitau* (T)	Less plausible in terms of meaning
79	*ūrdhvasvaraya* (H)	*ūrddhvaṁ parasya* (T)	Ccontextually less plausible
88	*parā* (H)	*pare* (H)	Equally plausible
100	*vyaktimadhye* (H)	*vyaktimadhyo* (T)	Equally plausible
104	*vinisrutaḥ* (H)	*vinissṛtaḥ* (T)	Equally plausible
125	*prayojya* (H)	*prayujya* (T)	Equally plausible
137	*tadā* (H)	*tathā* (T)	Contextually less plausible
140	*yā vyakti . . .* (H)	*yā vṛtti . . .*	Contextually less plausible
149	*tathā yadi* (H)	*yathāvidhi* (T)	Less plausible in terms of meaning
160	*padakāle* (H)	*pādakāle* (T)	Less plausible: unfamiliar form
177	*yathā yatra* (H)	*yatra yatra* (T)	Contextually less plausible
178	*tathā tatra* (H)	*tadā tatra* (T)	Contextually less plausible
179	*prāpitārtha* (H)	*prāpyatārtha* (T)	Less plausible in terms of meaning
182	*ka itīttham udāhṛtaḥ* (H)	*ka itīttham udāhṛtaḥ* (T)	Less possible‡
201	*mitho'pṛthaktvam (H)*	*mithaḥ pṛtha-ktvam* (T)	Ccontextually less plausible
203	*samuchśritā* (T)	*samuchśṛtā* (H)	Contextually less plausible
204	*satataṁ* (H)	*satatā* (T)	Equally plausible
205	*sañcaratā* (H)	*sañcāritā* (T)	Contextually less plausible
211	*balī prāṇo* (H)	*baliprāṇo* (T)	Less plausible: *lectio difficilior*

Cont.

Verse No.	Adopted Readings	Variant Readings	Comments
213	*bahis* (H)	*barhis* (T)	Contextually less plausible
217	*kaṇṭhoraso madhyaṁ* (H)	*kaṇṭhorasor madhyaṁ* (T)	Equally plausible
235	*cātyupasaṁhṛtau (H)*	*cāpyupasaṁhṛtau* (T)	Contextually less plausible
236	*tvokāro* . . . (H)	*tvekāro* (T)	Contextually less plausible
281	*krauñco* (H)	*kroñco* (T)	Less plausible: unfamiliar form
283	*karṇamūlīya* . . .(H)	*kaṇṭhamūlīya* . . . (T)	contextually less plausible

* Discarded reading.

† As the verse is not fully available I could not predict the correct reading.

‡ A similar verse found in *Pāriśikṣā* (Chandra 1981: 327-28) yields the sense consistent with the adopted reading:

vyañjanoccādisaẏyuktasvarasyaikasya vai punaḥ ।
ṣaḍviṁśatir īritā dharmāḫ ka ity eṣa udāhṛtaḥ ॥

Treatment of the Headings

With regard to the headings, MS T did not help much since the left margins of most of its leaves, where the marginalia are written, are damaged. There are a few headings which are not found in *AK* but are mentioned in *AS*. For example, the section *anadhyayanaprakaraṇam* is found neither in *AK* nor in H, but it is there in T and a certain portion of the text therein can be kept under this heading. Therefore, I put this heading in the edition. Again, *AK* reads *vivṛtter lakṣaṇan tasyāṁ saṁjñodāharaṇāni* (the definition of the hiatus and the appellations and examples therein). But the MSS do not have a separate heading for the appellations of the hiatus and the body of the text mentions those appellations and their definitions in such a manner that they cannot be separated in order to keep them under different headings. Therefore, the word *saṁjñā* of *AK* is ignored in this case. I could have kept it along with the heading *vivṛttilakṣaṇam* making it *vivṛtter lakṣaṇaṁ saṁjñāś ca* but as the MSS do not support this reading I did not use it in the edition. Though usually I have kept the readings of the marginalia regarding the headings as it is, sometimes I had to modify the reading where it does not fit. For example, the marginalia is *vaikṛtaprākṛtādi.* The word *ādi* in *vaikṛtaprākṛtādi* suggests that apart from the *vaikṛta* (modified) and *prākṛta* (original) there must be some more elements which are preceded by *vaikṛta* and *prākṛta*. No other topic, however, is found therein.

The next topic is *nāsikyatvorasyatve* which is also referred to in the margins of the MSS. *AK* also does not indicate any other topic there. Therefore, there is no possibility of any other topic in that section. So, in analogy with the next topic *nāsikyatvorasyatve* I have modified the name of the topic as *vaikṛtatvaprākṛtatve.* The next topic is mentioned as *nāsikyatvorasyatvādi* in the marginalia. Though the word *ādi* can signify the subsequent topic *vyaktimadhyasthavisargaḥ* which is not mentioned on the margins of the MSS I deliberately omitted the word *ādi* from the heading modifying it as *nāsikyatvorasyatve* (nasalization and pulmonic-ness) since it makes the heading vague. Compared to the other headings it looks odd too. Because of the same reason, the marginalia reading *prārambhakoṅkārādi* is not accepted in the edition. The edition retains *AK* counterpart of this heading *praṇavalakṣaṇam* which is more accurate and specific. Similarly, the marginalia heading *svarabhaktisaṁjñā* has been modified as *svarabhaktīnāṁ sodāharaṇasaṁjñāḥ* which is also supported by *AK.* The heading *svarabhaktisaṁjñā* cannot indicate the examples of the anaptyxes mentioned in that context, and which are also required to be implied through the heading. Again, there are a few headings, used in this edition, which are found neither on the margins of the MSS nor in *AK* but they can be distinctly identified as separate contexts in the body of the text. In such cases I named those sections with appropriate headings in order to separate them from the antecedent and the subsequent sections. These headings are marked with asterisks in the critical edition. The following headings are of these types — *vyaktimadhyasthavisargaḥ*, *svarahīnasya varṇasya vācakan nāma* and *kevalānusvāraḥ*:

Section Headings of the *AS*

No.	*Adopted Readings in this Edition*	*Marginalia Readings*	AK *Readings*	AK *Verse No.*
1.	*paribhāṣā*	—	*pāribhāṣikam*	1
2.	*saṁhitāviṣayam*	—	—	1
3.	*vedapārāyaṇa-phalam*	—	—	1
4.	*pārāyaṇakrama*	—	—	2
5.	*anadhyayanapra-karaṇam*	—	x	x
6.	*vāgvṛttiḥ*	—	—	2
7.	*padalakṣaṇam*	—	—	2
8.	*kramalakṣaṇam*	—	*kramasya. . . lakṣaṇam*	2-3
9.	*jaṭālakṣaṇam*	—	*jaṭāyāḥ . . . lakṣaṇam*	2-3
10.	*kevalavarṇakra-malakṣaṇam*	—	*śuddhavarṇakra-masya . . . lakṣaṇam*	2-3
11.	*dvitvaprakaraṇam*	—	*dvitva . . .*	3
12.	*āgamaḥ*	—	*āgama . . .*	3
13.	*abhinidhānam*	—	*tayor abhinidhāna-sya . . . lakṣaṇam*	3-4
14.	*kevalāgamaḥ*	—	*kevalākhyāgama-sya . . . lakṣaṇam*	3-4
15.	*yamāḥ*	—	*yamānām . . .lakṣaṇam*	4
16.	*yamaniṣedhaḥ*	—	*tanniṣedhānām . . . lakṣaṇam*	4
17.	*nādaḥ*	—	x	x

Cont.

Section Headings of the *AS* (Cont.)

No.	*Adopted Readings in this Edition*	*Marginalia Readings*	AK *Readings*	AK *Verse No.*
18.	*dvitvāgamaniṣedhaḥ*	—	*dvitvāgamaniṣedhayoḥ| lakṣaṇam*	4
19.	*svarabhaktiviṣayam*	—	*lakṣaṇaṁ svarabhaktīnām*	4
20.	*svarabhaktīnāṁ sodāharaṇasaṁjñāḥ*	*svarabhaktisaṁjñā*	*svarabhaktīnāṁ sodāharaṇasaṁjñakāḥ*	4
21.	*vivṛttilakṣaṇan tasyās saṁjñāś ca*	—	*vivṛtter lakṣaṇan tasyās saṁjñā . . .*	5
22.	*vivṛttyudāharaṇam*	—	*vivṛtteḥ ... udāharaṇāni*	5
23.	*vyaktimadhyasthanāsikyaḥ*	—	—	5
24.	*raṅgaplutāḥ*	—	*raṅgākhyapluta . . .*	5
25.	*raṅgadīrghāḥ*	—	*raṅgākhya . . . dīrgha . . .*	5
26.	*svaritodāttakampaviṣayam*	—	*lakṣaṇaṁ svaritodāttakampānām*	6
27.	*vaikṛtaprākṛte*	*vaikṛtaprākṛtādi*	*lakṣaṇam . . . vaikṛtaprākṛtayoḥ*	6
28.	*nāsikyatvorasyatve*	*nāsikyatvorasyatvādi*	*lakṣaṇam . . . nāsikyaurasyayoḥ*	6
29.	*vyaktimadhyasthavisargaḥ*	x	x	x
30.	*jihvāmūlīyopadhmānīyavidhiḥ*	*jihvāmūlīyādi*	*vidhiḥ . . . jihvāmūlīyopadhmānīyākhyayoḥ*	7
31.	*sthitisandhiḥ*	—	*sthitisandhividhiḥ*	7
32.	*svarahīnasya varṇasya vācakan nāma*	x	x	x
33.	*kevalānusvāraḥ*	x	x	x

Section Headings of the *AS* (Cont.)

No.	*Adopted Readings in this Edition*	*Marginalia Readings*	AK *Readings*	AK *Verse No.*
34.	*praṇavalakṣaṇam*	*prārambhak-oṅkārādi*	*praṇavalakṣaṇam*	7
35.	*sandhiniṣedhaḥ*	—	x	x
36.	*svaravarṇakra-malakṣaṇam*	—	*svaravarṇakramaḥ*	8
37.	*udāttādīnāṁ saṁjñā*	—	*udāttādīnān nirūpaṇam*	8
38.	*saptasvaritalakṣa-ṇāni sodāhara-ṇāni*	—	*udāharaṇasaÿyukta-saptasvaritalakṣa-ṇam*	8
39.	*svaritānām prayatnabhedāḥ*	—	*tatprayatnapra-bhedāḥ*	9
40.	*mātrāvarṇakra-malakṣaṇam*	*mātrākāla-varṇakrama-lakṣaṇam*	*mātrāvarṇakramaḥ*	9
41.	*mātrākālalakṣa-ṇam*	—	*mātrāmānanirūpam*	9
42.	*mātrākālokti-vivekaḥ*	—	*mātrākāloktividhi*	9
43.	*aṅgavarṇakra-malakṣaṇam*	—	*aṅgavarṇakramaḥ*	10
44.	*aṅgalakṣaṇam*	—	x	x
45.	*parāṅgapūrvāṅ-galakṣaṇam*	—	*parapūrvāṅga-lakṣaṇam*	10
46.	*aṅgavarṇa-kramoktilakṣaṇam*	—	*aṅgavarṇakramo-kteḥ . . . lakṣaṇam*	10
47.	*varṇasārabhūta-varṇakrama ity asya nāmno virvacanam*	—	*nirvacanaṽ varṇa-sārabhūta-varṇakramasya*	11
48.	*varṇadharma-kramaḥ*	—	*saṁkhyā varṇa-dharmāṇām . . . ānupūrvikā*	11

Cont.

Section Headings of the *AS* (Cont.)

No.	*Adopted Readings in this Edition*	*Marginalia Readings*	AK *Readings*	AK *Verse No.*
49.	*anusvārabhakti-kampaviṣaye raṅ-gaplutaviṣaye ca*	—	*bhaktyanusvāraka-mpānāṁ raṅgasya . . . uktilakṣaṇam*	12
50.	*śabdotpattipra-karaṇam*	—	*śabdotpatti . . .*	12
51.	*tatprakāraḥ*	—	*śabdotpattiprakāraḥ*	12
52.	*dhvaninirūpaṇa-prakaraṇe śarī-rāntargata-jāṭharāgnisthitiḥ*	—	*dhvaninirūpaṇam| śarīrāntargatan tatra sarvavyā-pāralakṣaṇam| jāṭharāgnisthitiḥ*	12-13
53.	*prāṇādīnām pañ-cānāṽ vāyūnāṁ sthānasthityā-dikam*	—	*pañcavāyūnāṁ sthāna . . .*	13
54.	*teṣāṁ sthūla-sūkṣmarūpa-ceṣṭāviśeṣaḥ*	—	*. . . ceṣṭikāḥ*	13
55.	*dhvanibhedāḥ*	—	—	14
56.	*tajjātavarṇāḥ*	—	*jātavarṇānāṽ viniścayaḥ*	14
57.	*varṇānāṁ sthānakaraṇa-vivekaḥ*	*varṇānāṁ sthānakaraṇa-vivekalakṣaṇam sthānakaraṇa-lakṣaṇam*	*teṣāṁ . . . sthāna-karaṇavivekas tatprakārakaḥ*	14
58.	*varṇānām prayatnabhedāḥ*	—	*prayatnabhedā varṇānām*	15
59.	*devatālakṣaṇam*	—	*varṇānān devatā . . .*	15
60.	*jātilakṣaṇam*	—	*varṇānām . . . jāti . . .*	15
61.	*varṇasaṁjñā*	—	*varṇānām . . . saṁjñakāḥ*	15
62.	*udāttādīnān devatāniyamaḥ*	—	*udāttādisvarā-ṇām . . . devatā*	15

Section Headings of the *AS* (Cont.)

No.	Adopted Readings in this Edition	Marginalia Readings	AK Readings	AK Verse No.
63.	jātiḥ	—	udāttādisvarāṇām . . . jātayaḥ	15
64.	guṇalakṣaṇam	—	udāttādisvarāṇām . . . guṇāḥ	15
65.	hastasvaravinyāsalakṣaṇam	—	hastasvaranyāsalakṣaṇam	16
66.	svaravinyāsaphalam	—	tasya tat phalam	16
67.	aṅgādyavasthā	—	—	16
68.	ṣaḍjādisvaranirūpaṇam	—	ṣaḍjādisaptasvaranirūpaṇam	16
69.	udāttādisvarotpattisthānam	—	udāttādisvarotpattiḥ	17
70.	vedādhyayanaphalam	—	x	x
71.	vedamahimā	—	vedasya mahimā	17
72.	adhyayanarahitadoṣaḥ	—	x	x
73.	sāṅgavedādhyayanaphalam	—	vikṛtyaṣṭakasaÿyukta vedasyādhyayane phalam	17

Orthography

There is no orthographic standard for writing Sanskrit. It varies from person to person, time to time, region to region and script to script. The MSS found in different regions in different scripts are orthographically different. The differences mostly occur in the pre-consonantal nasal sounds, the duplication of consonants in certain conditions, the increment of the former unaspirated stop in case the consonant is an aspirated stop that undergoes the conditions required for duplication, the alteration of the *visarga* that precedes a sibilant, a stop that immediately precedes a fricative, the use of *avagraha,* certain euphonic changes, etc. However, nowadays the wide use of Devanāgarī as the standardized script for writing Sanskrit and a close adherence to the Pāṇinian grammar have become effective to some extent in limiting the orthographical varieties of writing Sanskrit. But the Pāṇinian grammar alone cannot eradicate the diversity because the grammar itself recognizes optional rules for the sound changes which are responsible for the orthographical varieties. Therefore, even if we strictly follow the Pāṇinian rules and write in the Devanāgarī script variations are likely to occur. For example, किं च and किञ्च, कर्तुम and कर्त्तुम all these various forms are found even in present-day Sanskrit. Therefore, I feel the necessity of defining the orthography maintained in this critical edition since it is very different from the orthography followed by the scribes of the MSS of the *Ātreyaśīkṣā*. The following principles were adopted during the transcription of the text from Grantha to Devanāgarī script:

- Optional duplication of the consonants and the increment of the previous stop, when the consonant is an aspirated stop, are not considered. E.g., कार्यः, not कार्य्यः; कथ्यते, not कत्थ्यते.

- Final *anusvāra* of a word which is originated from the consonant *m* and precedes the consonant of the succeeding word is not changed into any nasal stop. E.g., परं ज्योतिः, not परञ्ज्योतिः; लक्षाणं तस्य, not लक्षाणन्तस्य.

- Inter-word nasal sounds are altered in accordance with the succeeding stop sound. E.g., अङ्गम्, not अंगम्; कम्पः, not कंपः. It is not altered when the succeeding sound is not a stop. E.g. संयुक्तम्, not सयँयुक्तम् But *anusvāra* is not modified as *ñ* before the consonant-cluster *jñ* as such a kind of change of sound is prohibited in the Śikṣā tradition.[128] E.g., संज्ञा, not सञ्ज्ञा, etc.

---

[128] *jñaghnottare makāraś ced anusvāro 'tra kevalaḥ* । — *Vyāsaśikṣā* 133 (Sastri 1976: 70).

- The final *visarga* of a word followed by a sibilant is not changed into the respective sibilant. E.g., स्वारः सन्धौ, not स्वारस्सन्धौ. But the *visarga,* which does not occur at the final position of a word and is followed by a sibilant, is changed into the respective sibilant. E.g., यजुश्शाखा, not यजुःशाखा.
- A voiceless unaspirated stop is always altered to its voiced counterpart if a voiced sound or a vowel follows it. E.g., त्यजेद् यदि, not त्यजेत् यदि; पृथग्भक्तेः, not पृथक्भक्तेः; यदुक्तम, not यत् उक्तम्.
- All the rules for euphonic changes are properly followed. E.g., विसर्गांश्च, not विसर्गान् च; तयोरेवम् not तयोः एवम्. The euphonic combination between *t* and *ś* is rendered with *cch* though there are other options. तच्छेषः, not तच्छ्शेषः.
- For easy comprehension, words are put separately if there is no significant euphonic change. E.g., तत् तावत्, not तत्तावत्. But it is तन्नेत्यन्तं, not तन् नेत्यन्तं, as there is an euphonic combination. But if the succeeding word starts with a vowel and the preceding one ends with a consonant the words are kept united. E.g., यदित्यन्तम्, not यद् इत्यन्तम्.
- Nasally modified vowels are written with the symbol of *candrabindu.* E.g., तक्राँ, not तक्रां.
- The symbol of *avagraha* is used everywhere in accordance with the convention. E.g., अध्यायान्तेऽनुवाकान्ते, not अध्यायान्तेनुवाकान्ते; योऽनुस्वारः, not योनुस्वारः. It is also used when there is a euphonic combination between *ā* and *a* where *ā* is the former sound and *a* is the latter. E.g., नाम्नाऽसौ, not नाम्नासौ. It is doubled when two *ā*s are euphonically combined. E.g., विवक्षुणाऽऽत्मना, not विवक्षुणात्मना.

ROMAN TRANSCRIPTION

The text of the Roman transcription using IAST is not an exact transliteration of the text that is provided in the 2nd chapter in Devanāgarī script. A slightly different orthography is maintained in this section. First of all, in order to furnish better intelligibility, the words are kept separately in the transcription even though there is a euphonic combination. For example, हलस्त्ववसिता is presented as *halas tv avasitā.* But if the euphonic change of the words is an *ekādeśa* (the substitution of one sound for two) the words are not separated. E.g., *varṇenāpi*. Every euphonic change is accepted in the transcription. Duplication and increment are not considered in this section. E.g., *ūrdhve,* not *ūrddhve; vartate,* not *varttate*. Pre-consonantal nasals, which are not followed by fricatives and *r,* are always changed in accordance with the succeeding consonant. E.g., *pādam pādena,* not *pādaṁ pādena; paṭhanaṅ kuryāt,* not *paṭhanaṁ kuryāt; padadvayay̐ yatra,* not *padadvayaṁ yatra*. Only *ṁ* is not altered into *ñ* when it precedes the consonant cluster *jñ.* E.g., *saṁjñā,* not *sañjñā.* The reason for this has already been mentioned in the previous section. The *visarga* which precedes a sibilant is always modified. It takes the form of the very succeeding sibilant. E.g., *jñeyāṣ ṣoḍaśa,* not *jñeyāḥ ṣoḍaśa; antassthā,* not *antaḥsthā.* The *visarga* that is followed by a voiceless bilabial stop is always changed into *upadhmānīya.* E.g., *sparśāḫ pañcaviṁśatiḥ,* not *sparśāḥ pañcaviṁśatiḥ.* Similarly, it becomes *jihvāmūlīya* when followed by a voiceless velar stop. E.g., *punaẖ kuryāt,* not *punaḥ kuryāt.* But if the *visarga* is followed by the consonant cluster *kṣ* it does not undergo any change.[129] E.g., *antaḥ kṣipati,* not *antaẖ kṣipati.*

TRANSLATION

It is, however, difficult to render the expressions of a particular language into another language as it is. It is even more difficult when the text is in a versified form where many words are used sometimes merely to fulfil the metrical requirements and due to the same reason some words are left with the expectation that the reader would comprehend the complete meaning of the expression from the respective context. Moreover, in many cases the sentence structure of the versified text is so complex that it can hardly be

---

[129] Vide *TP* 9.3 and *AS* 118.

represented in another language without changing the sentence structure. There are many words which cannot be exactly translated into English. And even if they are translated anyhow they lose their precise connotation. For example, the word *śabda* is translated as "sound". However, the word '*śabda*' has a broader meaning which cannot be connoted by the word "sound" entirely. Thus, there are many obstacles in conveying the full meaning of such an old Sanskrit text in English.

I, however, have tried my best to represent the text as nearly, rigorously and accurately as possible. I have closely adhered to the Sanskrit text while translating it. For this, I had to compromise with the stylistic side of English. Therefore the language of the translation is not always elegant.

The parts of the translation kept in the angular bracket "[ ]" indicate that they are not explicitly referred to in the main text but without considering them in the translated version, the sentence cannot be completed. The parts which are not required to complete the sentence but deserve mention for clarifying the meaning of some words are kept in parentheses.

I have tried to give an English equivalent of each Sanskrit word as far as possible. Although all of them may not accurately imply the entire connotations of the Sanskrit words themselves, I felt that it would be favourable to suggest translations of the words that can at least give some near meaning, rather just keeping the Sanskrit word as it is. The readers who are not familiar with the Sanskrit terms would at least get some idea about the Sanskrit words if some English equivalents are provided. The translation may be helpful in reaching the meaning of the text; however it is not a good idea to judge the text merely on the basis of this translation. The accurate sense of the terms can only be grasped by contemplation over the context in which they occur. I therefore have always kept the Sanskrit words in parentheses, beside their English equivalents, when those English terms are introduced for the first time in the translation. I must confess that the translation of the sections dealing with the inner functions of the human body and the activities of five vital airs is based on mere grammatical and lexical knowledge and therefore it requires inspection by the scholars who are authoritative in Yogic knowledge.

2

Critically Edited Text

॥ आत्रेयशीक्षाकारिका ॥ [1]

कारिकां सम्प्रवक्ष्यामि प्रथमं पारिभाषिकम् ।
संहिताविषयं वेदपारायणफलं ततः[2] ॥ १ ॥

पारायणक्रमश्चैव वाग्वृत्तिः पदलक्षणम् ।
क्रमस्याथ जटायाश्च शुद्धवर्णक्रमस्य च[3] ॥ २ ॥

लक्षणं च क्रमात् तत्र यौ च द्वित्वागमौ स्मृतौ ।
तयोरभिनिधानस्य केवलाख्यागमस्य च ॥ ३ ॥

यमानां तन्निषेधानां द्वित्वागमनिषेधयोः ।
लक्षणं स्वरभक्तीनां सोदाहरणसंज्ञकाः ॥ ४ ॥

विवृत्तेर्लक्षणं तस्यां संज्ञोदाहरणानि च ।
व्यक्तिमध्यस्थनासिक्यो रङ्गाख्यप्लुतदीर्घयोः ॥ ५ ॥

लक्षणं स्वरितोदात्तकम्पानां च विशेषतः ।
स्याद् वैकृतप्राकृतयोर्नासिक्यौरस्ययोरपि ॥ ६ ॥

विधिश्च जिह्वामूलीयोपध्मानीयाख्ययोरपि ।
स्थितिसान्धिविधिश्चैव तथा प्रणवलक्षणम् ॥ ७ ॥

स्वरवर्णक्रमस्तत्रोदात्तादीनां निरूपणम् ।
उदाहरणसंयुक्तसप्तस्वरितलक्षणम् ॥ ८ ॥

---

1 T reads हरिः ॐ

2 T था

3 T तु

तत्प्रयत्नप्रभेदा[4]श्च मात्रावर्णक्रमस्तथा ।
मात्रामाननिरूपं च मात्राकालोक्तिविध्यपि ॥ ९ ॥

अङ्गवर्णक्रमस्तत्र परपूर्वाङ्गलक्षणम् ।
अङ्गवर्णक्रमोक्तेश्च सुस्पष्टं लक्षणं ततः ॥ १० ॥

निर्वचनं वर्णसारभूतवर्णक्रमस्य तु ।
सङ्ख्या च वर्णधर्माणां तदुक्तेरानुपूर्विका ॥ ११ ॥

भक्त्यनुस्वारकम्पानां रङ्गस्याप्युक्तिलक्षणम् ।
शब्दोत्पत्तिप्रकारश्च तत्र ध्वनिनिरूपणम् ॥ १२ ॥

शरीरान्तर्गतं तत्र सर्वव्यापारलक्षणम् ।
जाठराग्निस्थितिः पञ्चवायूनां स्थानचेष्टिकाः ॥ १३ ॥

ध्वनिभेदास्तत्र जातवर्णानां च विनिश्चयः ।
तेषां तु स्थानकरणविवेकस्तत्प्रकारकः ॥ १४ ॥

प्रयत्नभेदा वर्णानां देवताजातिसंज्ञ[5]काः ।
उदात्तादिस्वराणां च देवता जातयो गुणाः ॥ १५ ॥

ततो हस्तस्वरन्यासलक्षणं तस्य तत् फलम् ।
अङ्गाद्यवस्था षड्जादिसप्तस्वरनिरूपणम् ॥ १६ ॥

उदात्तादिस्वरोत्पत्तिर्वेदस्य महिमा ततः ।
विकृत्यष्टकसंयुक्त[6]वेदस्याध्ययने फलम् ॥ १७ ॥

इत्येवमानुपूर्व्येण शीक्षा सम्प्रोच्यतेऽधुना ॥
इत्यात्रेयशीक्षाकारिका समाप्ता ।[7]

---

4 T देशा

5 T ज्ञि

6 T क्ते

7 H reads हरिः ॐ

॥ आत्रेयशीक्षामूलम् ॥ [8]

परिभाषा

आम्नाया यस्य निःश्वासाश्चन्द्रसूर्यौ च चक्षुषी।
तत् प्रणम्य परं ज्योतिः शीक्षां वक्ष्यामि निर्मलाम् ॥ १ ॥

अचः स्वरा इति प्रोक्ता व्यञ्जनानि हलः स्मृताः।
ह्रस्वदीर्घप्लुतावर्णेवर्णोवर्णा ऋ ॠ ऌ च ॥ २ ॥

एदैदोदौदिति ज्ञेयाः षोडशेहादितः स्वराः।
कखौ गघौ ङचछजा झञौ टठडढा णतौ ॥ ३ ॥

थदौ धनौ पफबभा मः स्पर्शाः पञ्चविंशतिः।
यरौ लवौ चतस्रोऽन्तस्स्थाश्च ᳵकशषसᳵपहाः ॥ ४ ॥

षडूष्माणो विसर्गोऽनुस्वारो ळो नास्यपञ्चकम्।
इत्येते याजुषा वर्णा एकोनाः षष्टिरीरिताः ॥ ५ ॥

क्रमेण[9] पञ्च पञ्च स्युः स्पर्शानां वर्गसंज्ञिकाः।
वर्गेषु तेषु संज्ञाः स्युश्चतुर्णां प्रथमादयः ॥ ६ ॥

पञ्चमस्योत्तमः प्रोक्तो घोषाघोषौ तु तेषु वै।
हान्योष्मा प्रथमाश्चैव विसर्गश्च द्वितीयकाः ॥ ७ ॥

अघोषाः स्युश्च तेभ्योऽन्ये घोषवन्तो हलः स्मृताः।
परिविन्याभ्युपप्रावप्रत्यधीत्युपसर्गकाः ॥ ८ ॥

कारशब्दोत्तरो वर्णो वर्णाख्या प्रतिपाद्यते।
व्यञ्जनानामकारः स्याच्छषसेत्यादिसङ्ग्रहात् ॥ ९ ॥

ह्रस्वोऽदिदुदृकारश्च तथल्कारः स्वरेषु वै।
वर्गोत्तरस्तु वर्गाख्या[10] प्रथमो भवतीत्यपि ॥ १० ॥ [11]

---

[8] H reads हरिःॐ। शुभमस्तु। अविघ्नमस्तु। T reads ॐ

[9] H The reading found as कादीनां is corrected as क्रमेण

[10] T वर्गाख्य

[11] H and T read इत्यात्रेयशीक्षापरिभाषा समाप्ता।

संहिताविषयम्

आरम्भे यजुषः शाखा या स्यात् सा संहिता स्मृता।
काण्डप्रश्नानुवाकाद्यैः प्रविभक्ताऽन्तराऽन्तरा॥ ११॥

यास्ततोऽन्या यजुश्शाखा न तासां विकृतीः पठेत्।
संहिताग्रन्थमात्रस्य सविशेषौ पदक्रमौ॥ १२॥

जटा वर्णक्रमाश्चैव क्रमाद् विकृतयः स्मृताः।
केवलः स्वरसंयुक्तो मात्रिकासहितस्तथा॥ १३॥

साङ्गश्च वर्णसारश्च पञ्च वर्णक्रमान् विदुः।

वेदपारायणफलम्

सर्वथा[12] नाधिगन्तव्यो वेदो लिखितपाठकः॥ १४॥

अध्येतव्यः सविकृतिर्द्विजैर्यत्नाद् गुरोर्मुखात्।
वेदेष्वक्षरमेकैकमेकैकं हरिनामकम्॥ १५॥

अन्यूना स्वरतश्चैव वर्णतो या च संहिता।
सकृत् पारायणे तस्या यावत् फलमिहोच्यते॥ १६॥

त्रिगुणं तत्पदे तस्मात् क्रमे त्वष्टगुणं भवेत्।
जटाध्याये शतं प्रोक्तं शुद्धवर्णे सहस्रकम्॥ १७॥

स्वरवर्णेऽयुतं विद्यान्नियुतं मात्रिकायुते।
प्रयुतं त्वङ्गवर्णे स्यादनन्तं वर्णसारके॥ १८॥

पारायणक्रमः

प्रायश्चित्तविधौ कृच्छ्रे ब्रह्मयज्ञे क्रियाविधौ।
संहितापठनं कुर्यान्नियमान्न पदादिकान्॥ १९॥

उत्सवार्थं तु देवेशे निर्गते गर्भगेहतः।
क्रमादिकं पठेद् यद् वा तथोपनिषदं पठेत्॥ २०॥

---

12 H सर्वधा

अनध्ययनप्रकरणम्[13]

यस्तु पारायणं हित्वा कालातिक्रमशङ्कया।
कुर्यात् सन्ध्यां स निष्कर्मी विज्ञेयस्तत्र पातकी॥ २१॥

प्राप्ते महाप्रदोषेऽपि तदा देवेशसन्निधौ।
अनध्ययनमानेन न च पारायणं त्यजेत्॥ २२॥

त्यजेद् यदि तदा मोहाद् ब्रह्महत्यां समाविशेत्।

वाग्वृत्तिः

वाचस्तु वृत्तयस्तिस्रो द्रुतमध्यविल[14]म्बिताः॥ २३॥

आवृत्यावृत्य चाभ्यासे द्रुतवृत्या पठेद् द्विजः।
पारायणे प्रयोगार्थे मध्यमां वृत्तिमाचरेत्॥ २४॥

बोधनार्थं तु शिष्याणां वृत्तिं कुर्याद् विल[14]म्बिताम्।

पदलक्षणम्

पदाध्याये पदान्ते यदितिशब्दं प्रयुज्य च॥ २५॥

पुनरुच्चार्यते द्वेधा तद् वेष्टनपदं स्मृतम्।
यत् पदं वेष्टनोपेतं तदिङ्ग्यमिति कथ्यते॥ २६॥

इङ्ग्यते हि पदस्यार्थ इत्यस्मादिङ्ग्यमुच्यते।
विभागवत्पदस्यार्थो विभागेन विचाल्यते॥ २७॥

इत्येवमिङ्ग्यशब्दार्थस्तस्य पूर्वं त्ववग्रहः।
पर्यादीनि दशात्रोक्ता[15]न्युपसर्गपदानि च॥ २८॥

अन्वपात्यपिसूत्सन्निःपरा नव पदानि च।
इत्यन्तानि स्युरेतानि पदान्येकोनविंशतिः॥ २९॥

वाक्यान्तगं द्वयोरादि निहतं त्रिषु मध्यमम्।

---

13 This heading is not there in H.

14 H and T ळ

15 T दश प्रोक्ता

अवग्रहेऽत्र नेत्यन्तं यत् तत् स्यादध्वराव च॥ ३०॥
लक्षणैः प्रग्रहा ये स्युरित्यन्तास्ते पदे सति।

क्रमलक्षणम्

संहितावत् पठेत् पूर्वमनुक्रम्य पदद्वयम्॥ ३१॥
द्वितीयं तत्र पदवदवसाने समापयेत्।
ततस्त्वादिपदं हित्वा द्वितीयं च तृतीयकम्॥ ३२॥
पठेत् ततस्तद् द्वितीयं पदं हित्वा तृतीयकम्।
चतुर्थं च पठेत् पश्चात् क्रमादेवं पठेत् पुनः॥ ३३॥
पूर्वं पूर्व[16]पदं मुक्त्वा संयुज्योत्तरमुत्तरम्।
एवमुच्चार्यते यस्तु क्रमाध्यायः स उच्यते॥ ३४॥
क्रमे तावत् तथोच्चार्ये यदी[17]ङ्घं पूर्विकं पदम्।
पठित्वा वेष्टनं तस्य पठेत् पश्चाद् यथाक्रमम्॥ ३५॥
पूर्ववाक्यान्तगं[18] यच्च परवाक्यादिकं तथा।
तयोर्नानुक्रमेत् तद्वदन्तमाद्यनुवाकयोः॥ ३६॥
प्रग्रहानिङ्घयुक्तं च यदि स्यादादिमं पदम्।
अखण्डवेष्टनं तस्य वाक्यान्ते यदनिङ्घकम्॥ ३७॥
पदे तु यद् यदित्यन्तं तन्नेत्यन्तं पठेत् क्रमे।
षणत्वटत्वविधिना सह नित्यमनुक्रमेत्॥ ३८॥
आदन्तं यदुदात्तान्तं पूर्वं यच्चोपसर्गतः।
तस्योर्ध्वेन त्रिक्रमः स्यान्नःपरं षुपदं त्वधः॥ ३९॥
पदत्रयमनुक्रम्य हित्वा चादिपदं पुनः।
मध्यमान्तिममुच्चार्य त्रिक्रमे क्रमशो वदेत्॥ ४०॥

---

16 T पूर्वपूर्व

17 T दि

18 T कं

जटालक्षणम्

क्रमवत् पूर्वमुच्चार्य प्रतिलोमं पठेच्च तत्।
सन्धितश्च पुनः कुर्यात् क्रमपाठं पदद्वयम्॥ ४१॥

एवं पाठक्रमो यस्तु सा जटेति प्रकीर्तिता।
अखण्डवेष्टनेङ्ग्यादि यद् यदुक्तं क्रमे यथा॥ ४२॥

तत्र तत्र तथा सर्वं जटायां च पठेद् बुधः[19]।
त्रिक्रमे त्रिपदस्यापि जटामुक्त्वा यथाविधि॥ ४३॥

ततस्तत्र द्वितीयादिपदानां पूर्ववत् पठेत्।
तुल्यं पदद्वयं यत्र स्वरतो वर्णतोऽपि वा॥ ४४॥

न पठेत् तु जटां तत्र क्रममात्रं पठेत् सदा।
लोपालोपादयो ये च षत्वणत्वादयश्च ये॥ ४५॥

जटायां लक्षणैरुक्तास्तान् पठेत् तु यथाविधि।

केवलवर्णक्रमलक्षणम्

ये अत्र[20] सांहिता वर्णाः समाम्नाताश्च शास्त्रतः॥ ४६॥

तान् सर्वान् कारशब्दान्तान् वदेद् वर्णक्रमोक्तिषु।
अकारेण व्यवेतः स्यात् कारशब्दो हलामिह॥ ४७॥

अनुस्वारे च नासिक्ये जिह्वामूल्यविसर्गयोः।
उपध्मानीयवर्णे च कारशब्दस्तु नेष्यते॥ ४८॥

रस्य त्वेफस्त्रयाणां च ह्रस्वो वर्णोत्तरो भवेत्।
स्वरात् कारपरादर्वाङ् न सन्धिर्वर्णपाठके॥ ४९॥

तान् सदीर्घविसर्गांश्च वदेदुक्तिसमापने।
पूर्वं वर्णक्रमोक्तेस्तु तत् तावत् संहितां पठेत्॥ ५०॥

यस्तु संहितया हीनाञ्छुष्कान् वर्णक्रमान् वदेत्।
निष्फलं स्याद् यथा भित्तिहीनं चित्रविलेखनम्॥ ५१॥

---

19 T पुनः

20 T येऽत्र

येनावसीयते वाक्यं वर्णेनापि स्वरेण च।
तमेव वर्णपाठेषु प्रवदेन्न च सांहितम्॥ ५२॥
एतेन विधिना विद्वान् क्रमाद् वर्णक्रमान् वदेत्।

द्वित्वप्रकरणम्

अच्पूर्वं व्यञ्जनोर्ध्वं यद् व्यञ्जनं द्वित्वमाप्नुयात्॥ ५३॥
स्पर्शश्च लवपूर्वो यो यत् तु रेफात् परं च तत्[21]।
ह्रस्व[22]पूर्वौ पदान्तस्थौ ङनौ द्वित्वं परेऽप्यचि[23]॥ ५४॥
योऽनुस्वारो यजुष्यत्र स स्यादर्धगकारयुक्।
यद्यात्माधः सरूर्ध्वे च शान्तिः शोर्ध्वे न गो भवेत्॥ ५५॥
योगात् पूर्वमनुस्वारो ह्रस्वाद् यश्च परस्थितः।
स एव द्वित्वमाप्नोति तस्य स्यादेकमात्रता॥ ५६॥

आगमः

व्यञ्जनं यन्निमित्तेन द्वित्वमाप्नोति तेन वै।
पूर्वागमः क्रमात् तत्र स्याद् द्वितीयचतुर्थयोः॥ ५७॥
अखण्डे स्वरयोर्मध्ये यदि द्वित्वागमौ पदे।
लक्ष्यानुसारसंज्ञौ तौ भवेतां लक्षणैः पृथक्॥ ५८॥
पाथएषोऽतिधामातिभूतेपरमपूर्विकाः।
तथोपसर्गपूर्वाश्चागमं छखिभुजा इयुः॥ ५९॥
प्रथमस्योष्मणि परे द्वितीयादेशकः पदे।
समे वर्ण[24]द्वयं भिन्ने............................॥ ६०॥[25]
तैत्तिरीये शपूर्वस्य नस्य ञः स्यान्न काठके।

---

[21] T यत्

[22] T द्वित्व

[23] T च्यपि

[24] T वर्णे

[25] This hemistich is missing in both H and T.

अभिनिधानम्

अघोषादूष्मणः स्पर्शपराद् यत्र परस्थितः॥ ६१॥

प्रथमोऽभिनिधानः स्यात् तस्य सस्थान एव च।
शसौ यत्रागमौ स्यातां प्रथमः परतो यदि॥ ६२॥

न तत्राभिनिधानोक्तिः प्रथमं द्विर्वदेद् बुधः।

केवलागमः

नीचापूर्वस्तथोच्चोर्ध्वो दकारः केवलागमः॥ ६३॥

तथोत्तरे ङतोऽनन्त्यादागमौ स्तः कगौ क्रमात्।

यमाः

स्याद् य[26]त्रानुत्तमात् स्पर्शादुत्तमः परतो यदि॥ ६४॥

क्रमेण स्युर्यमास्तत्र नान्तस्स्था[27] परतो यदि।

यमनिषेधः[28]

स्पर्शो यद्यूष्मविकृतिर्न तत्र स्याद् यमागमः॥ ६५॥

यत्र यस्माद् यमप्राप्तिस्तत्रोष्मा वर्तते यदि।
नैव तत्र यमावाप्तिरप्यूष्मा द्वित्वमाप्नुयात्॥ ६६॥

योऽपदान्ते पदान्ते वा प्रथमः स्यात् सषोत्तरे।
स द्वितीयमवाप्नोति शोर्ध्वेऽनन्त्यः स चेत्तथा॥ ६७॥

नादः

ह्रस्वात् परस्तु यो नादो भवत्यत्र द्विरूपवत्।
तं च वर्णक्रमाध्याये सकृदेव वदेद् बुधः॥ ६८॥

---

26 T स्याद

27 T स्थाः

28 H धाः

द्वित्वागमनिषेधः

प्राप्ते पूर्वागमद्वित्वलक्षणे[29] यस्य वै हळः।
द्वित्वं पूर्वागमश्चैव[30] निवर्तेत तदुच्यते॥ ६९॥

द्विरूपं नाप्नुयादूष्मा प्रथमोर्ध्वेऽच्परेऽपि वा।
वकारश्च परे स्पर्शे विसर्गो रेफ एव च॥ ७०॥

ळकार ऊष्मणि स्पर्शे पर ईदैदधश्च यः।
सवर्गीयानुत्तमोर्ध्वे सवर्णोर्ध्वे च हळ् तथा॥ ७१॥

मः स्पर्शयवळोर्ध्वश्चेत् तेषामेत्यनुनासिकम्।
दीर्घात् परोऽन्तगो वोर्ध्वे न द्विर्नो न व्य वृ ण्व्र च॥ ७२॥

परोऽपि ह्रस्वदीर्घाभ्यां न च द्वित्वं यहो[31]त्तरे।

स्वरभक्तिविषयम्

आप्नुतो रळयोर्यस्मादूर्ध्वे सत्यच्परोष्मणि॥ ७३॥

ऋॡस्वरार्धावादेशौ तस्मात् स्यात् स्वरभक्तिता।
चतुर्भिरेव सा श्लिष्टा[32] पादैरज्व्यञ्जनात्म[33]का॥ ७४॥

आद्यन्तौ तेषु पादेषु पादौ स्यातां स्वरात्मकौ[34]।
स्थितौ मध्ये तु यौ पादौ तौ ज्ञेयौ व्यञ्जनात्मकौ॥ ७५॥

पादं द्वितीयं पादेन प्रथमेनैव योजयेत्।
तृतीयं च चतुर्थेन पादं पादेन योजयेत्॥ ७६॥

एवं तत्र क्रमात् पादौ द्वौ द्वौ तु विभजेत् पृथक्।
हळन्ता स्यात् पूर्वभागस्वरभक्तिस्तु संवृता॥ ७७॥

भक्तिरुत्तरभागा स्याद् विवृता च स्वरोदया।

---

29 T णं

30 T द्वित्वपूर्वागमो यस्तु

31 T हयो

32 The reading can be साऽऽश्लिष्टा

33 T त्मि

34 T स्थितौ

पूर्वभागो हकारे स्याच्छषसेषूत्तरस्तथा॥ ७८॥

अत्वमित्वं तथोत्वं च भक्तेरूर्ध्वस्वरस्य[35] च।
त्रयमेतदनुच्चार्य स्वरभक्तिं समुच्चरेत्॥ ७९॥

स्वरभक्तीनां सोदाहरणसंज्ञाः[36]

बर्हिः करेणुसंज्ञा स्याद् योगे तु रहयोर्यदि।
सा मल्हा कर्विणी ज्ञेया संयोगे लहकारयोः॥ ८०॥

वर्षं हंसपदा ज्ञेया योगे तु रषयोरपि।
शोत्तरे हरिणी रेफो दर्शः पर्शुरुदाहृतः[37]॥ ८१॥

सपरे यत्र रेफः स्याद्धस्तिनी बर्समित्यपि।
तस्य धूर्षदमित्यादौ सा स्वतन्त्रा प्रचक्षते॥ ८२॥

हारिता लशयोर्योगे शतवल्शमुदाहृतम्।
क्रमेणैवं सुविज्ञेयाः सप्तैताः स्वरभक्तयः॥ ८३॥

विवृत्तिलक्षणं तस्याः संज्ञाश्च[38]

स्वरयोरुभयोः सन्धिर्विवृत्तिरिति कथ्यते।
अत्र सैव विवृत्तिस्तु व्यक्तिरित्यपि चोच्यते॥ ८४॥

वत्सानुसृतिराख्याता तथा वत्सानुसारिणी।
वैशेषिका पाकवती मध्यमा च पिपीलिका॥ ८५॥

तथा सवर्णदीर्घी चोभयदीर्घी तथा स्मृता।
इत्येवमष्ट संज्ञाः स्युर्विवृत्तीनां तु भेदतः॥ ८६॥

ह्रस्वपूर्वा च या व्यक्तिस्तथैवोत्तरदीर्घिका।
सा वत्सानुसृतिः प्रोक्ता समात्राकालतस्तथा॥ ८७॥

---

35 T रूर्ध्वं परस्य

36 H स्वरभक्तिसंज्ञा

37 H तं

38 H and T विवृत्तिलक्षणम्

ह्रस्वात् पूर्वे विवृत्तिः स्यात् प्लुताद् दीर्घात् परा[39] च या।
वत्सानुसारिणी सेयमेकमात्रेण संयुता॥ ८८॥

व्यक्तेराद्यन्तयोर्यस्या दीर्घौ यद्यसवर्णकौ।
यदि मध्ये विसर्गः स्यात् तदभावोऽथवा यदि॥ ८९॥

सा तु वैशेषिकाख्या स्यादेकमात्रा च तत्र वै।
पूर्वे यत्रोत्तरे चैव ह्रस्वो यदि भवेत् तदा॥ ९०॥

पादोनमात्रिका तत्र सा च पाकवती स्मृता।
यस्याः सवर्णदीर्घौ स्त उभयत्रोच्चनीचकौ॥ ९१॥

विसर्गस्तत्र च स्वारः सन्धौ मात्रा च मध्यमा।
मध्यमालक्षणे तत्र विसर्गो न भवेद्यदि॥ ९२॥

पिपीलिकेति विज्ञेया सा व्यक्तिः पादमात्रिका।
सवर्णदीर्घौ यद्यादावन्ते भिन्ने विसर्गकः॥ ९३॥

सवर्णदीर्घ्येकमात्रा न सन्धौ स्वरितो यदि।
तस्याः सवर्णदीर्घ्यास्तु सम्पूर्णे लक्षणे सति॥ ९४॥

विसर्गस्तत्र नो चेत् सा समात्रोभयदीर्घ्यथ।

विवृत्त्युदाहरणम्

उदाह्रियन्ते वत्सानुसृत्यादिव्यक्तयः क्रमात्॥ ९५॥

वत्सानुसृतिसंज्ञा स्यात् त एनं भि स आयुरा।
वत्सानुसारिणी प्रोक्ता सेदग्ने अस्तु वा इयम्॥ ९६॥

वैशेषिका स्यात् ता एव कक्षीवाँ[40] औशिजस्तथा।
सा तु पाकवती ज्ञेया प्रउगं च स इज्जने॥ ९७॥

मध्यमा या आविविशुर्वेद्या आदन् यदीत्यपि।
पिपीलिका तु ते एनं वा आरण्यमुदाहृतम्॥ ९८॥

सवर्णदीर्घी संयत्ता आसन्नित्यादिदर्शनात्।

---

[39] T परे

[40] H and T वां

इयं तूभयदीर्घी साद्‌ वा आपस्त तथेत्यपि ॥ ९९ ॥

व्यक्तिमध्यस्थनासिक्यः

नासिक्यो व्यक्तिमध्ये[41] यः स भवेत् साणुमात्रिकः ।
व्यक्तेश्च साणुमात्रत्वं नाम पूर्वोक्तमेव हि ॥ १०० ॥

रङ्गप्लुताः

यशो ममोपह्वताँ च सुश्लोकाँ च सुमङ्गलाँ ।
एते रङ्गप्लुता ज्ञेयास्तथा यद्‌ ग्राँ इतीत्यपि ॥ १०१ ॥

रङ्गप्लुते द्विमात्रं स्यादादौ व्याघ्ररुतोपमम् ।
अनास्यं हृदयोत्पन्नं मन्द्रध्वनियुतं भवेत् ॥ १०२ ॥

अथ मध्यमभागे स्यात् तृतीयो मूर्धसम्भवः ।
कांस्यघण्टानादसमः स कम्पस्त्वेकमात्रिकः ॥ १०३ ॥

अथान्त्यभागे नासिक्यरन्ध्रद्वयविनिस्स्रुतः[42] ।
एकमात्रस्तुरीयांशः स तु काकलि[43]को भवेत् ॥ १०४ ॥

यथा सौराष्ट्रिका गोपी मधुरेण स्वरेण वै ।
तक्राँ इत्युच्चरेदुच्चैस्तथा रङ्गं समुच्चरेत् ॥ १०५ ॥

रङ्गदीर्घाः

देवाँ उ ताँ इम्यमृवाँ अव स्वाँ अह काठके ।
रङ्गदीर्घा इति प्रोक्तास्ते सपादत्रिमात्रिकाः ॥ १०६ ॥

हृज्जातो मात्रिकस्तस्मिन् स्यात् सपादत्रिमात्रिके ।
मूर्धजस्त्वर्धमात्रः स्यात् तच्छेषो मुखनासिकात् ॥ १०७ ॥

---

41 T मध्यो

42 T निस्सृतः

43 H and T ळि

स्वरितोदात्तकम्पविषयम्

नित्याभिनिह[44]तक्षैप्रप्रश्लिष्टाः स्वरिता इमे।
सन्धौ तत्र प्रकम्पन्ते यत्रोच्चस्वरितोदयाः ॥ १०८ ॥

नीचं पूर्वस्वरस्यान्ते कुर्यात् स्यात् कम्प एव सः।
ह्रस्वमप्यत्र कम्पेऽस्मिन् यथा दीर्घं तमुच्चरेत् ॥ १०९ ॥

स च कम्पोऽत्र विज्ञेयः स्वार उच्च इति द्विधा।
स्वारकम्पः संहितायामुच्चस्त्वारण्यके भवेत् ॥ ११० ॥

पुनश्च तत्र तौ कम्पौ ह्रस्वदीर्घाविति स्मृतौ।
आदौ तु तस्य कम्पस्य स्वारः स त्र्यणुमात्रिकः ॥ १११ ॥

अन्त्यभागे तु निहतः पादमात्रः प्रकीर्तितः।
उदात्तश्च तथैवादौ त्रिपादाधिकमात्रिकः ॥ ११२ ॥

तस्यान्ते चानुदात्तः स्यादणुमात्रो भवेत् तथा[45]।
सम्मेल[46]ने द्विमात्रः स्यात् तयोरेवं सुनिश्चितः ॥ ११३ ॥

वैकृतप्राकृते[47]

शषसेष्वच्परेष्वत्र विसर्गो यत्र दृश्यते।
वैकृतत्वं प्राकृतत्वं क्रमात् स्याच्छ्लिष्ट एव हि ॥ ११४ ॥

नासिक्यत्वोरस्यत्वे[48]

हकारान्नणमा यत्र दृश्यन्ते परतस्तदा।
नासिक्यत्वमुरस्यत्वं हस्तु तत्र द्विरुच्यते ॥ ११५ ॥

व्यक्तिमध्यस्थविसर्गः*

विवृत्तिमध्ये यत्र स्याद् विसर्गः सोऽर्धमात्रिकः।

---

44 H हि
45 T दा
46 H and T ळ
47 H वैकृतप्राकृतादि
48 H नासिक्यत्वोरस्यत्वादि

विरामश्चैकमात्रः स्यात् तस्याः संज्ञा यथाविधि॥ ११६॥

जिह्वामूलीयोपध्मानीयविधिः[49]

प्राग् यद्यघोषवर्णाभ्यां विसर्गः कपवर्गयोः।
क्रमात् स जिह्वामूलीय उपध्मानीय उच्यते॥ ११७॥

स्थितिसन्धिः

ककारः षपरो यत्र भवेत् तस्मिन् परे सति।
पूर्वस्थितो विसर्गः स्यात् स्थितिसन्धिरिति स्मृतः॥ ११८॥

स्वरहीनस्य वर्णस्य वाचकं नाम*

वर्णस्य स्वरहीनस्य नाम वाचकमुच्यते।
वर्णक्रमस्याध्ययने न वदेदन्यसंज्ञिकाम्॥ ११९॥

केवलानुस्वारः*

योऽनुस्वारः केवलाख्यः स मध्यस्थो विधेरपि।
तत्परस्य योगादेर्न जातु द्वित्वमिष्यते॥ १२०॥

प्रणवलक्षणम्[50]

आदौ प्रारम्भकोङ्कारे त्वकारः पादमात्रिकः।
स त्रिपादद्विमात्रः स्यादुकारो मस्तुमात्रिकः॥ १२१॥
अध्यायान्तेऽनुवाकान्ते मकारस्त्वर्धमात्रिकः।

सन्धिनिषेधः

वर्णक्रमप्रपाठेषु स्वरात् कारपरादधः॥ १२२॥

---

49 H जिह्वामूलीयादि

* The starred headings are found neither in the MSS leaves nor in the आत्रेयशीक्षाकारिका.

50 H प्रारम्भकोङ्कारादि

हरिप्रणवमध्येऽपि सन्धिर्न स्यात् प्लुतेषु च।

स्वरवर्णक्रमलक्षणम्

शुद्धवर्णक्रमे तस्मिन्नुच्यमाने यथाक्रमम्॥ १२३॥

तत्रोदात्तानुदात्तौ च प्रचयश्च त्रयः स्वराः।
तथैव सप्त स्वरिताः सप्रयत्नाः सनामकाः॥ १२४॥

दशैतांस्तत्र तत्रैव स्वरेभ्योऽर्वाक् प्रयो[51]ज्य च।
प्रवदेद्यदि नाम्नाऽसौ स्वरवर्णक्रमो भवेत्॥ १२५॥

व्यञ्जनानामुदात्तादीन् वर्णोक्तौ न वदेत् स्वरान्।

उदात्तादीनां संज्ञा

तत्र तावदुदात्ताद्याः स्वरास्तन्नामवाचकः॥ १२६॥

प्रयत्नाश्च क्रमेणैव निरूप्यन्ते यथाविधि।
उच्चैरुदात्तो नीचैस्तु निहतश्चानुदात्तकः॥ १२७॥

स्वरितः स्यात् समाहारः स्वार इत्यपि चोच्यते।
परेषामनुदात्तानां स्वरितात् पदवर्तिनाम्॥ १२८॥

संहितायां तु प्रचय उदात्तश्रुतिरिष्यते।
धृतप्रचयशब्दौ च पर्यायौ स्तः परस्परम्॥ १२९॥

सप्तस्वरितलक्षणानि सोदाहरणानि

स्वाराः सप्तविधा ज्ञेयास्तत्प्रयत्नाश्चतुर्विधाः।
क्षैप्रः प्राथमिकः स्वारो द्वितीयो नित्यसंज्ञकः॥ १३०॥

तृतीयः स्यात् प्रातिहतश्चतुर्थो नामतो द्विधा।
तत्राभिनिह[52]तश्चैक इतरोऽभिहतः स्मृतः॥ १३१॥

प्रश्लिष्टः पञ्चमः षष्ठो वृत्तः स्यात् पादवृत्तकः।
तैरोव्यञ्जनसंज्ञो यः स्वरितः सप्तमो भवेत्॥ १३२॥

---

[51] T यु

[52] H हि

इवर्णौतोर्यवत्वे सत्युच्चयोः स्वर्यते च यः।
स च क्षैप्राभिधः स्वारस्त्र्यम्बकं ब्यन्न इत्यपि॥ १३३॥

पदे स्थितेऽप्यपूर्वे वा नीचपूर्वे यवाक्षरम्॥
स्वर्यते यत्र नित्यः स्यान्न्यञ्चं कुह्वा उदाहृतम्॥ १३४॥

उच्चे नानापदस्थेऽपि श्लिष्टेन स्वर्यते च यः।
स प्रातिहत एव स्यात् स इधानः सतेजसम्॥ १३५॥

नानापदे ह्युच्चपूर्वं नीचं यत् स्वर्यते यदि।
व्यक्तेरभावे भावेऽपि स प्रातिहत इष्यते॥ १३६॥

तस्मिन्नकारलोपश्चेत् पृथग्भूतपदे तदा[53]।
स्वारोऽभिनिहतो ज्ञेयः सोऽब्रवीत् तेऽब्रुवन्नपि॥ १३७॥

उदात्तपूर्वे तस्मिन् स्यादूभावः स्वर्यते यदि।
प्रश्लिष्टाख्यः स सूद्गाता सून्नीयमिव यस्तथा॥ १३८॥

या त्वखण्डपदे व्यक्तिः सा भवेदर्धमात्रिका।
यस्तस्याः परतः स्वारः पादवृत्तः स कथ्यते॥ १३९॥

मध्ये पदस्य या व्यक्ति[54]स्तस्यां च स्वरितश्च यः।
स एव पादवृत्तः स्यात् प्रउगं नान्यदिष्यते॥ १४०॥

तिरस्तिर्यगिति प्रोक्तं हल् व्यञ्जनमिति स्मृतम्।
तेन व्यवेतो यः स्वारस्तैरोव्यञ्जनसंज्ञकः॥ १४१॥

व्यञ्जनेन व्यवहितः पदे तूदात्तपूर्वकः।
स्वरितो यः स एव स्यात् तैरोव्यञ्जन उच्यते॥ १४२॥

यः समानपदे स्वारः स्वर्यते ह्युच्चपूर्वकः।
स तैरोव्यञ्जनो ज्ञेय आपो वाचमुपायवः॥ १४३॥

---

53 T था

54 T वृत्ति

स्वरितानां प्रयत्नभेदाः

क्षैप्रे नित्ये प्रयत्नः स्यात् स्वारे दृढतरो भवेत्।
नीचपूर्वेऽभिनिहते प्रयत्नोऽतिदृढः स्मृतः॥ १४४॥

उच्चपूर्वेऽप्यपूर्वे च प्रयत्नो दृढ इष्यते।
प्रश्लिष्टप्रातिहतयोः स वै मृदुतरः स्मृतः॥ १४५॥

स तैरोव्यञ्जने पादवृत्ते चाल्पतरः स्मृतः।
एवं स्वरितभेदानां प्रयत्नानां च भेदतः॥ १४६॥

विवक्षया लक्षणानि तेषामुक्तानि शास्त्रतः।
एतत् सर्वं विदित्वैव स्वरवर्णक्रमं वदेत्॥ १४७॥

मात्रावर्णक्रमलक्षणम्[55]

[56]अथातः संहिताध्याये लक्षणैरानुपूर्व्यशः।
भवन्ति यद्यद्वर्णानां यद्यत्कालाः सुनिश्चिताः॥ १४८॥

तत्र तत्र च ते सर्वे स्वरवर्णे यथाविधि।
उदात्तादिस्वरेभ्योऽर्वाक् प्रयुज्यन्ते तथा यदि॥ १४९॥

एवं पाठक्रमो यः स्यान्मात्रिकावर्ण उच्यते।

मात्राकाललक्षणम्

मात्राणां कालनियमा उच्यन्ते हेतुभिः पृथक्॥ १५०॥

ब्राह्मणी नकुलश्चाषो वायसश्च शिखी क्रमात्।
अण्वर्धैकद्वित्रिमात्रान् ब्रुवते कालतः सुखम्॥ १५१॥

इन्द्रियाविषयो योऽसावणुरित्युच्यते बुधैः।
चतुर्भिरणुभिर्मात्रापरिमाणमिति स्मृतम्॥ १५२॥

एकमात्रो भवेद्ध्रस्वो दीर्घः स्यात् तु द्विमात्रिकः।
त्रिमात्रिकः प्लुतो ज्ञेयो ह्रस्वार्धं त्वर्धमात्रिकम्॥ १५३॥

---

55 H मात्राकालवर्णक्रमलक्षणम्

56 H reads ॐ

तत्र रङ्गप्लुतो यः स्याच्चातुर्मात्रः स कथ्यते।
तं तु व्याघ्ररुतान्ते यो घण्टानादोऽनुवर्तते॥ १५४॥

मात्राकालोक्तिविवेकः

संयुक्तं वाऽप्यसंयुक्तं व्यञ्जनं सस्वरं यदि।
स्वरकालं वदेत् तत्र न पृथग् व्यञ्जनस्य तु॥ १५५॥

सिद्धेऽप्यर्धाणुमात्रत्वे सस्वरे वा पृथग्घलि।
तथाऽपि न वदेत् तस्य कालं वर्णक्रमेषु वै॥ १५६॥

हलस्त्ववसिता यत्र तत्रैषां काल इष्यते।
अनुत्तमे त्वर्धमात्रो विरामस्थे विधीयते॥ १५७॥

विरामस्थेषूत्तमेषु कालाधिक्यं प्रदृश्यते।
पूर्वेऽनुनासिकं ह्रस्वाद् द्विमात्रं यत् तदुच्यते॥ १५८॥

दीर्घात् प्लुताच्च तन्मात्र[57]मेकमात्रमिति श्रुतिः।
अवसाने विशेषोऽयमन्येषां च न विद्यते॥ १५९॥

संहितायां तु तन्मात्रः प[58]दकालेऽधिको भवेत्।
ह्रस्वात् परोऽवसानस्थः पदाध्यायेऽनुनासिकः॥ १६०॥

द्विमात्रो मात्रिकस्त्वन्यः संहितायां तथाखिलः।
तत्तत्कालान् विदित्वैवं मात्रिकावर्णमुच्चरेत्॥ १६१॥

अङ्गवर्णक्रमलक्षणम्

अङ्गवर्णे हलामादावङ्गं संज्ञां च नाम च।
अचां संज्ञां च मात्रां च स्वरं नाम वदेत् क्रमात्॥ १६२॥

अङ्गलक्षणम्

वर्णानामङ्गवर्णेऽस्मिन् सुव्यक्तं चाङ्गलक्षणम्।
पूर्वत्वेन परत्वेन विधिना वा सहोच्यते॥ १६३॥

---

57 H and T तन्नाद

58 T पा

राजतेऽसौ स्वयं यस्मात् तस्मात् तु स्वर उच्यते।
उपरिस्थायिना तेन व्यङ्ग्यं व्यञ्जनमुच्यते॥ १६४॥

न शक्यं केवलं स्थातुं व्यञ्जनं तु स्वरं विना।
सापेक्षं व्यञ्जनं नित्यं स्वरस्तु निरपेक्षकः॥ १६५॥

व्यञ्जनानि च सर्वाणि स्वराङ्गानि भवन्ति हि।

पराङ्गपूर्वाङ्गलक्षणम्

भवेत् परस्वरस्याङ्गं व्यञ्जनं प्रायशोऽपि हि॥ १६६॥

तत्र पूर्वस्वराङ्गं स्यादवसाने स्थितं च यत्।
परायुक्तमनुस्वारो विसर्गो भक्तिरेव च॥ १६७॥

योगाद्यसंयुतो ङो नो रेफः स्याद्दपरे सति।
पूर्वाङ्गं न भवेत् स्पर्श ऊष्मणो विकृतिर्यदि॥ १६८॥

सा पराङ्गं भवत्येव या भक्तिः प्रचयात् परा।
धृते ह्युकारे परतो रेफश्च स्यात् पराङ्गभाक्[59]॥ १६९॥

पराङ्गमसवर्णं स्यादन्तस्स्थापरमेव यत्।
पराङ्गे चोष्मणि परे पराङ्गं स्पर्शको यमाः॥ १७०॥

अङ्गवर्णक्रमोक्तिलक्षणम्

पौर्वापर्यक्रमेणैव विदित्वाङ्गं प्रयोजयेत्।
हलां तु पूर्वशब्दं वा परशब्दमथापि वा॥ १७१॥

उक्त्वा ततोऽङ्गशब्दं तु भूतशब्दोत्तरं क्रमात्।
हल्संज्ञकेति संज्ञां च नाम कारोत्तरं वदेत्॥ १७२॥

अचामच्संज्ञकेत्युक्त्वा तन्मात्रांश्च ततः स्वरान्।
उदात्तादींस्ततो नामान्यानुपूर्व्येण संवदेत्॥ १७३॥

संयोगो यत्र पूर्वाङ्गं स्यात् सवर्णात्मको यदि।
सकृदेव वदेत् तत्र पूर्वाङ्गादि पठेत् ततः॥ १७४॥

---

59 T ता. H keeps the reading पराङ्गता but suggests भाक् at the place of ता of पराङ्गता.

योगो यत्रोभयाङ्गं स्याद् यद्येकव्यञ्जनात्मकः।
पौर्वापर्यक्रमात् तत्र पृथगङ्गं प्रयोजयेत्॥ १७५॥

यद् यदुक्तं शुद्धवर्णे द्वित्वागमयमादिकम्।
अङ्गवर्णे तु तत् सर्वं तत्र तत्र वदेत् क्रमात्॥ १७६॥

स्वरवर्णे स्वरा यद्वल्लक्षणैः प्रतिपादिताः।
मात्राश्च मात्रिकावर्णे यथा[60] यत्र विनिश्चिताः॥ १७७॥

तान् सर्वानङ्गवर्णोक्तौ तथा[61] तत्र वदेत् सुधीः।

वर्णसारभूतवर्णक्रम इत्यस्य नाम्नो निर्वचनम्

सर्वेषामेव वर्णानां सारा ध्वन्यादयः स्मृताः॥ १७८॥

ध्वनिस्थानादयो ये स्युस्ते धर्मा इति कीर्तिताः।
तैर्भूतो भूतशब्देन प्रापि[62]तार्थ इहोच्यते॥ १७९॥

स तथोक्तश्च वर्णानां क्रमो वर्णक्रमः स च।
असौ वर्णक्रमश्चेति विग्रहो विशदीकृतः॥ १८०॥

तस्मादयं वर्णसारभूतवर्णक्रमः स्मृतः।

वर्णधर्मक्रमः

एकस्योच्चादियुक्तस्याप्यचः सव्यञ्जनस्य च॥ १८१॥

धर्माः षड्विंशतिः प्रोक्ताः क इतीत्थमुदाहृतः।
लक्षणैः शब्द एवात्र ध्वनिरित्युच्यते तथा॥ १८२॥

ध्वनिः प्राथमिको धर्मो द्वितीयः स्थानमुच्यते।
तृतीयः करणं विद्यात् प्रयत्नः स्यात् तुरीयकः॥ १८३॥

देवता पञ्चमो ज्ञेयः षष्ठो जातिरिहोच्यते।
अङ्गं तु सप्तमः प्रोक्तो वर्णसंज्ञाऽष्टमो भवेत्॥ १८४॥

---

60 T त्र

61 T दा

62 T प्य

एते धर्माः क्रमेणैव विधीयन्ते हलामिह।
अचां धर्माष्टकेऽप्यस्मिन्नुच्यमाने सति क्रमात्॥ १८५॥

मात्राकालश्च वक्तव्यो मध्ये देवप्रयत्नयोः।
स्वराणां निहतादीनां दश धर्माः समीरिताः॥ १८६॥

तत्रादौ देवता ज्ञेया ततो जातिस्ततो गुणः।
ततो रेखादर्शनं स्यादङ्गावस्थात्रयं पुनः॥ १८७॥

ततः षड्जादिहेतुः स्यादुत्पत्तिस्थानकं ततः।
तत्संज्ञा च ततश्चैतान् दश धर्मान् वदेत् क्रमात्॥ १८८॥

केवलस्वरमात्राङ्गवर्णेषु चतृषूदिताः।
ये ये धर्माश्च तान् सर्वान् प्रयुज्यास्मिन् क्रमात् पठेत्॥ १८९॥

अनुस्वारभक्तिकम्पविषये रङ्गप्लुतविषये च

यो धर्मः पञ्चमत्वेन स्यादचां वर्णसारके।
स्वरभक्त्यंशभूतानामचां स्यात् सप्तमो हि सः॥ १९०॥

अनुस्वारस्य भक्तीनामंशभूताज्झलामपि।
धर्मान् यथावद् ध्वन्यादीन् वर्णसारे वदेत् सदा॥ १९१॥

अनुस्वारस्य वर्णेऽस्मिन्नज्ञात् पूर्वं तु मात्रिकाम्।
अप्यनुस्वारभक्त्यंशे व्यञ्जान् धर्मान् क्रमाद् वदेत्॥ १९२॥

कम्पे तद्धेतुकस्वारधर्मानादौ पठेत् तथा।
तस्मादुत्पन्नकम्पस्य य आद्यंशश्च तस्य तु॥ १९३॥

त्रिपादाधिकमात्रस्य धर्मान् स्वारस्य नोच्चरेत्।
तदन्त्यांशस्य नीचस्य ब्रूयाद् धर्मान् यथाविधि॥ १९४॥

शुद्धवर्णो यथा तत्र तथैवात्रापि योजयेत्।
रङ्गप्लुते त्ववर्णोच्चप्लुतानामानुपूर्व्यशः॥ १९५॥

वदेद् धर्मान् वर्णसारे तदन्ते वर्णसंज्ञकाम्।
सर्वत्राभिनिधानाख्यो यस्तस्याङ्गं तथैव च॥ १९६॥

वर्णसंज्ञामपि ब्रूयान्नान्यधर्मान् पठेत् सदा।
न ध्वन्यादीन् यमे ब्रूयात् स्थानान्न निषिध्यते॥ १९७॥

शब्दोत्पत्तिप्रकरणम्

अथात्र सर्ववर्णानां याजुषाणां विशेषतः।
उच्चारणप्रसिद्ध्यर्थं शब्दस्योत्पत्तिरुच्यते॥ १९८॥

तत्प्रकारः

नित्यः कार्य इति द्वेधा शब्दः सामान्यतो भवेत्।
नित्योऽव्यक्तो विभुः शब्दो यो ब्रह्मव्यपदेशभाक्॥ १९९॥

तस्माद् व्यक्तः कार्यशब्दः कार्यादुत्पद्यते श्रुतिः।
श्रुतेर्नादस्ततो नाली[63] नाल्या[64] उच्चावचस्वराः॥ २००॥

एते क्रमात् प्रजायन्ते शब्दोच्चारणमात्रतः।
मिथो[65]ऽपृथक्त्वमेतेषां दीपतत्प्रभयोरिव॥ २०१॥

भवन्ति नादप्रमुखा वर्णोच्चारणहेतवः।

ध्वनिनिरूपणप्रकरणे शरीरान्तर्गतजाठराग्निस्थितिः

उपनाभ्युदये सूक्ष्मधमनीघुटिबन्धनम्॥ २०२॥

आधारं सर्वधातूनामिन्द्रियाणां भवत्यपि।
तत्प्रत्यगाढकस्थूलाप्यर्धाङ्गुलि[66]समुच्छ्रि[67]ता॥ २०३॥

निश्चला सततं[68] दीप्ता ज्वाला वह्नेस्तु जाठरी।
पराणुसूक्ष्मावरणा धमनी तत्परिस्थिता॥ २०४॥

वायुना पूरिता वृत्ता द्रुतं सञ्चर[69]ताऽनिशम्।

---

63 H and T ळी

64 H and T ळ्या

65 T थः

66 T ळि

67 H छ्र्श्र

68 T ता

69 T ञ्चारि

प्राणादीनां पञ्चानां वायूनां स्थानस्थित्यादिकम्

प्राणोदानापानसमा हृत्कण्ठगुदनाभिषु ॥ २०५ ॥
चत्वारः संस्थिता देहे व्यानः सर्वाङ्गसंश्रितः ।

तेषां स्थूलसूक्ष्मरूपचेष्टाविशेषः

एते पञ्चांशकास्तत्र स्थित्वैवांशैस्त्रिभिस्त्रिभिः ॥ २०६ ॥

द्वाभ्यां द्वाभ्यां शरीरेऽस्मिन् स्वस्वचेष्टां प्रकुर्वते ।
समः सुषीरचक्रस्थस्तौन्दं बर्हिषमावति ॥ २०७ ॥

नाडीलताश्रितोऽपानः शिक्यमूले त्रिकोपरि ।
विभज्योच्चारशमलौ पुरः पश्चात् क्षिपत्यधः ॥ २०८ ॥

सर्वनाडीः समाश्रित्य व्यानः सर्वत्र सञ्चरन् ।
सदा वितनुते सर्वं नमनोन्नमनादिकम् ॥ २०९ ॥

उदानो गल[70]गर्तस्थो व्यानदत्तं रसादिकम् ।
आजिह्वामूलमुत्प्लुत्य गृहीत्वाऽन्तः क्षिपत्यधः ॥ २१० ॥

हृत्पद्मकोशपृष्ठस्थे नाडीनाल[71]निरन्तरे ।
स्थित्वा स्थाने बली[72] प्राणो ह्रासैर्विकसनैरपि ॥ २११ ॥

यथाक्रमं स्वयं दत्ते भुक्तिमुक्त्योः सृतिं पराम् ।
प्राणादीनामिमाश्चेष्टाः स्थूलाः[73] सूक्ष्मा तु कथ्यते ॥ २१२ ॥

प्राणो हृदिस्थस्वांशेन कण्ठस्थोदानमंशतः ।
अन्तराकर्षति बहि[74]स्तदंशोऽस्यांशकं क्रमात् ॥ २१३ ॥

उभाभ्यां श्वासरूपाभ्यामंशाभ्यां धार्यते वपुः ।
विवक्षुणाऽऽत्मना नुन्नं मनो रुद्ध्वा गला[75]निलम् ॥ २१४ ॥

---

70 H and T ळ

71 T ळ

72 T लि

73 T ल

74 T र्हि

75 H and T ळा

सह तेन पतित्वाऽग्नौ जाठरे तत्समुत्थया।
ज्वालया भेदयत्याशु समानावरणं ततः॥२१५॥

भिन्नावृतौ समे कण्ठवायुना मनसा सह।
कण्ठोरोमध्यदेशस्थे प्राणोंऽशं स्वं नियच्छति॥२१६॥

श्रुत्यादिप्रकृतिः कार्यो नित्याच्छब्दोऽत्र जायते।
स्थानं कण्ठोरसोम[76]ध्यं करणं तु समोऽनिलः॥२१७॥

मनःप्रयोगो यत्नोऽस्य स्याच्छब्दोत्पत्तिरीदृशी।
इत्थमुच्चार्यमाणेषु शब्देषु श्वासरोधिषु॥२१८॥

तदर्थं सममच्छिन्नमाकृष्योदानसंयुते।
मनस्यभ्युत्थिते तस्मिन्नैश्लेष्यं सोढुमक्षमः॥२१९॥

सममध्ये पुनः प्राणः स्वांशेनैव पतत्यसौ।
तस्माद् विच्छिद्यते तत्र प्राणसङ्घट्टनात् समः॥२२०॥

छिन्नधारो भवत्याशु स्वस्थानान्तर्गतश्च सः।
सद्यस्तत्त्वक् तिरोधत्ते प्राणोदानौ तु पूर्ववत्॥२२१॥

विचेष्टेते तदा ताभ्यां महाञ्छ्वासः प्रजायते।
भूयो मनःप्रयोगेन शब्दः सम्पद्यते तथा॥२२२॥

ध्वनिभेदाः

कण्ठाकाशगतः कार्यः शब्द एव ध्वनिः स्मृतः।
नादः श्वासो हकारश्चेत्येवं त्रेधा ध्वनिर्भवेत्॥२२३॥

कण्ठे तु संवृते नादः श्वासः स्याद् विवृते सति।
मध्यस्थे तु हकारः स्याद् वर्णप्रकृतयश्च ताः॥२२४॥

तज्जातवर्णाः

नादजाः स्वरघोषाः स्युर्हचतुर्था हकारजाः।
अघोषाः श्वासजास्तत्र श्वासो द्वेधाऽल्पको महान्॥२२५॥

---

76 T र्म

प्रथमाश्च तदन्ये च वर्णा अल्पमहद्ध्वाः।

वर्णानां स्थानकरणविवेकः[77]

अचां स्थानमुपश्लेषो यत्रान्याङ्गस्य तन्यते॥ २२६॥

तदङ्गं करणं स्थानसमीपे नीयते च यत्।
यदङ्गं स्पृश्यतेऽङ्गेन हलां स्थानं तदिष्यते॥ २२७॥

अङ्गेन स्पृश्यते स्थानं येन तत् करणं हलाम्।
संहितायामचो नित्यं यत्राव्यञ्जनपूर्वकाः॥ २२८॥

भवन्ति तेषां स्थानोक्तौ पूर्वं कण्ठेति संवदेत्।
अकारोच्चारणे चौ[78]ष्ठौ हनू नात्युपसंहृतौ॥ २२९॥

कार्यौ तु दीर्घप्लुतयोर्न चातिविवृता इमे।
उपश्लेष्यमिवर्णोक्तौ जिह्वामध्यं तु तालुनि॥ २३०॥

ओष्ठावुवर्णे दीर्घौ स्त उपश्लेषयुतौ तथा।
पृथगोष्ठोपसंहारो नार्धमात्रान्तरे भवेत्॥ २३१॥

एकमात्रान्तरत्वस्य स्यात् तु सर्वत्र सम्भवे।
ऋवर्णे ऌति च स्यातामोष्ठौ नात्युपसंहृतौ॥ २३२॥

हनू अत्युपसंहार्ये जिह्वाग्रं बर्स्वके भवेत्।
एकारेऽव्यञ्जने जिह्वाप्रान्तावीषद्युतोष्ठकौ॥ २३३॥

करणं तालु तु स्थानमतिश्लिष्टहनूर्ध्वयुक्।
सव्यञ्जनेऽस्मिन् करणमीषच्छ्लिष्टोष्ठयुग् भवेत्॥ २३४॥

जिह्वामध्यं स्थानमतिश्लेषवद्धनुतालुकम्।
हनू अनतिविश्लेषे ओष्ठौ चात्यु[79]पसंहृतौ॥ २३५॥

दीर्घौ च भवतस्तत्र त्वो[80]कारोच्चारणे सति।

---

77 H वर्णानां स्थानकरणविवेकलक्षणम्

78 H and T चो

79 T प्यु

80 T त्वे

अणुस्त्वादावदेदोतोरन्त्ये[81] स त्र्यणुकस्त्विदुत्॥ २३६ ॥

ऐकारौकारयोरादावकारस्त्वर्धमात्रिकः।
इवर्णोवर्णयोः शेषौ स्यातामध्यर्धमात्रिकौ॥ २३७॥

ऐकारौकारावयवेष्वदिदुत्सु यथाक्रमम्।
अदिदुत्स्थानकरणप्रयत्ना एव नान्यथा॥ २३८॥

एदोतोरदिदुत् स्वल्पोऽप्यत्र न श्रूयते पृथक्।
नातोऽस्ति तेषां धर्मोऽस्य किन्त्वेत्वं त्वोत्वमेव हि॥ २३९॥

ऐदौतोराद्यकारस्य करणीभवदोष्ठकः।
संवृताख्य इति प्राहुर्वर्णक्रमविचक्षणाः॥ २४०॥

उच्चारणे कवर्गस्य हनूमूलं स्पृशेद् बुधः।
जिह्वामूलेन चोरुक्तौ जिह्वामध्येन तालु च॥ २४१॥

जिह्वाग्रेण टवर्गे तु प्रतिवेष्ट्य शिरः स्पृशेत्।
जिह्वाग्रतस्तवर्गे च दन्तमूलेष्वधस्तथा॥ २४२॥

अधरेणोत्तरोष्टं तु पवर्गोच्चारणे स्पृशेत्।
जिह्वामध्यस्य पार्श्वाभ्यां तालु योच्चारणे स्पृशेत्॥ २४३॥

जिह्वाञ्चलस्य मध्येन दन्तमूलोपरि क्रमात्।
आसन्नमत्यासन्नं च प्रदेशं रलयोः स्पृशेत्॥ २४४॥

अधरोष्ठाग्रभागेन बाह्येनोर्ध्वदतः स्पृशेत्।
ओष्ठ्यस्वरान्तरस्थे वे तद्भिन्ने त्वान्तरेण चेत्॥ २४५॥

जिह्वामूलीयपूर्वाणां हभिन्नानां तथोष्मणाम्।
कवर्गादिषु यत् स्थानं तदेव स्युर्य[82]थाक्रमम्॥ २४६॥

करणानां तु यत् तेषां मध्यं तु विवृतं भवेत्।
विसर्गस्य च हस्य स्यात् स्थानं च करणं गलः[83]॥ २४७॥

उरो हस्योत्तमान्तस्स्थापरत्वे स्यात् तु तद्वयम्।

---

[81] न्ते (?)

[82] स्याद् य (?)

[83] H and T ळः

वर्गान्त्या नासिकामात्रस्थानका हात् परेऽपरे ॥ २४८ ॥
मुखावयवनासिक्या नासिका नस्विकासतः ।[84]

वर्णानां प्रयत्नभेदाः

प्रयत्नाः पञ्चधा ज्ञेया वर्णानां संवृतादयः ॥ २४९ ॥

संवृतो विवृतः स्पृष्ट ईषत्स्पृष्टोऽतिपूर्वकः ।
संवृतोऽकारमात्रस्य प्रयत्नः परिकीर्तितः ॥ २५० ॥

प्रयत्नो विवृतोऽन्येषां स्वराणामूष्मणामपि ।
स्पर्शेषु स्पृष्टताऽन्तस्स्थास्वीषत्स्पृष्टत्वमीरितम् ॥ २५१ ॥

द्वितीयाश्च चतुर्थाश्चाप्यतिस्पृष्टप्रयत्नजाः ।
अतिस्पृष्टे चतुर्थानां न्यूनत्वं किञ्चिदिष्यते ॥ २५२ ॥

देवतालक्षणम्

देवता वेदवर्णानां वाय्वग्निक्ष्मेन्दुभानवः ।
यषकारावेदवर्णौ प्रथमा वायुदेवकाः ॥ २५३ ॥

आग्नेया ऐदिवर्णौ च द्वितीयाश्च रसावपि ।
उवर्ण ओत् तृतीयाश्च हळौ स्युर्भूमिदेवकाः ॥ २५४ ॥

ऋवर्ण औच्चतुर्थाश्च वळौ चान्द्रमसाः स्मृताः ।
ऌकारोत्तमशाः सौर्या नेतरेषां तु देवताः ॥ २५५ ॥

जातिलक्षणम्

वर्गप्रथमवर्णाश्च स्वराः स्युर्ब्रह्मजातयः ।
क्षात्रा द्वित्रितुरीयाः स्युर्विशोऽन्तस्स्थोत्तमा अपि ॥ २५६ ॥
शूद्रा ऊष्मविसर्गानुस्वाराः स्युरिति निश्चिताः ।

वर्णसंज्ञा

अचः स्वरा व्यञ्जनानि स्पर्शान्तस्स्थोष्मणो हलः ॥ २५७ ॥

---

84 H reads इति स्थानकरणविवेकप्रकरणम् ।

अघोषघोषवद्वर्गप्रथमाद्युत्तमादयः।
ह्रस्वदीर्घप्लुता भक्तिकम्परङ्गप्लुता यमः॥ २५८॥

विसर्गजिह्वामूलीयोपध्मानीयादयस्तथा।
अनुस्वारादयश्चैते वर्णसंज्ञा इति स्मृताः॥ २५९॥

उदात्तादीनां देवतानियमः

सूर्याग्निचन्द्रवसुधाश्चत्वारश्च क्रमादिह।
धृतानुदात्तस्वारोच्चस्वराणां देवताः स्मृताः॥ २६०॥

जातिः

उच्चनीचस्वारधृताः स्वराश्चत्वार एव च।
ब्रह्मक्षत्रियविट्शूद्रा आसन् जात्या क्रमादिह॥ २६१॥

गुणलक्षणम्

सात्त्विकः स्याद् गुणेनोच्चः स्वरितो राजसः स्मृतः।
द्वौ तामसगुणौ स्यातामनुदात्तधृतावपि॥ २६२॥

हस्तस्वरविन्यासलक्षणम्

यः स्वरन्यासकृद् विद्वान् स आसीनस्त्वतन्द्रितः।
कृत्वा गोकर्णवद्धस्तं दक्षिणं दक्षजानुनि॥ २६३॥

क्रमात् स्वरेषु हस्ते च मनो दृष्टिं निवेश्य च।
यथाशास्त्रं स्वरन्यासमङ्गुष्ठाग्रेण विन्यसेत्॥ २६४॥

तदा यद्यागतः पूज्यो गुरुर्वा देवताऽपि वा।
प्रणम्याथ न्यसेत् तिष्ठन् कृत्वा नाभिसमं करम्॥ २६५॥

यदि तैरभ्यनुज्ञातः सोऽभ्यासकरणे सति।
आसीन एव कुर्वीत स्वरन्यासं यथाविधि॥ २६६॥

उदात्तं निर्दिशेन्न्यासे तर्जनीमध्यपर्वणि।
नीचं कनिष्ठिकादौ च मध्यमामध्यमे धृतम्॥ २६७॥

स्वारं चानामिकान्त्ये तु सर्वत्रैवं विनिर्दिशेत्।
यः स्वरः स्यात् पृथग्भक्तेः स्वरेखास्थानमाप्नुयात्॥ २६८॥

स्याद् यत्रोच्च इव स्वारः स्यात् तदूर्ध्वस्थितश्च यः।
क्रमादनामिकायास्तौ विन्यसेन्मध्यमान्त्ययोः॥ २६९॥

आद्यन्त्यांशौ स्वारकम्पे यौ स्यातां स्वारनीचकौ।
अनामिकान्त्यादिमयोस्तौ न्यसेद् द्वावपि क्रमात्॥ २७०॥

ततश्चोदात्तकम्पे तु यावुच्चनिहतौ च तौ।
मध्याद्ययोः प्रदेशिन्याः क्रमात् सन्निर्दिशेदपि॥ २७१॥

विरामे व्यञ्जनं यत् तदुच्चारणवशात् क्वचित्।
स्वरान्तरश्रुतिं सम्यक् स्वतन्त्रमिव चाप्नुयात्॥ २७२॥

तथाऽपि तस्य विन्यासे पृथक् स्थानं न निर्दिशेत्।

स्वरविन्यासफलम्

य एवं स्वरवर्णार्थाञ्छास्त्रदृष्ट्याऽनुचिन्तयन्॥ २७३॥

स्वरन्यासक्रमेणैव सह वेदमिमं पठेत्।
स पूतः सर्ववेदैश्च परं ब्रह्माभिगच्छति॥ २७४॥

अङ्गाद्यवस्था

गात्रदैर्घ्यं ध्वनेर्दार्ढ्यं कण्ठाकाशाणुता तथा।
तिस्रोऽवस्था इमाः शब्दमुच्चैः कुर्वन्ति तत्र तु॥ २७५॥

ह्रस्वता या च देहस्य मृदुता च ध्वनेश्च या।
महत्ता कण्ठखस्यैता नीचैः कुर्वन्ति शब्दकम्॥ २७६॥

षड्जादिस्वरनिरूपणम्

नीचात् षड्जर्षभौ जातावुच्चाद् गान्धारमध्यमौ।
निषादः पञ्चमश्चैव धैवतश्च त्रयः स्वराः॥ २७७॥

स्वरितप्रभवास्तेषां पुनस्तत्कारणक्रमः।
नित्याभिनिहतक्षैप्रा निषादस्वरहेतवः॥ २७८॥

हतश्लिष्टावुभौ स्यातां पञ्चमस्वरहेतुकौ।
तैरोव्यञ्जनवृत्ताभ्यां जायते धैवतस्वरः[85] ॥ २७९ ॥

दीर्घह्रस्वानुदात्ताभ्यां जातौ षड्जर्षभावुभौ।
उदात्तप्रचयाभ्यां तु गान्धारो मध्यमस्तथा ॥ २८० ॥

रौति क्वणत्यजा क्रौ[86]ञ्चो गान्धारं मध्यमं क्रमात्।
केकारुतसमः षड्ज उक्षा रौत्यृषभस्वरम् ॥ २८१ ॥

निषादं बृंहते कुम्भी पिकः कूजति पञ्चमम्।
हयहेषातुल्यरूपं संविद्याद् धैवतस्वरम् ॥ २८२ ॥

उदात्तादिस्वरोत्पत्तिस्थानम्

अनुदात्तो हृदि ज्ञेयो मूर्ध्न्युदात्त उदाहृतः।
स्वरितः कर्ण[87]मूलीयः सर्वाङ्गे प्रचयः स्मृतः ॥ २८३ ॥

वेदाध्ययनफलम्

अङ्गमात्रादयो धर्माः पूर्वमेवोदिताश्च ये।
तान् सर्वान् वर्णसारेऽस्मिन् तत्र तत्र प्रयोजयेत् ॥ २८४ ॥

एवं सलक्षणं वेदं योऽधीतेऽध्यापयत्यपि।
न तत् कल्पसहस्रैश्च गदितुं शक्यते फलम् ॥ २८५ ॥

वेदमहिमा

वेद एव परो धर्मो वेद एव परं तपः।
वेद एव परं ब्रह्म सर्वं वेदमयं जगत् ॥ २८६ ॥

तस्माच्छ्रेयः परं प्राप्तुं विधिनैव गुरोर्मुखात्।
अध्येतव्योऽखिलैर्विप्रैरेष धर्मः सनातनः ॥ २८७ ॥

धर्मेण य इमां ब्राह्मीं विद्यां शिष्याय बोधयेत्।

---

85 The reading can be धैवतः स्वरः.

86 T क्रो

87 T ण्ठ

नन्दन्ति देवताः सर्वास्तं विप्रं नाविशेद् भयम्॥ २८८॥

अध्ययनरहितदोषः

यो हित्वा ब्राह्मणो वेदानन्यग्रन्थे प्रवर्तते।
ब्रह्मत्यागी स विज्ञेयः कर्मशूद्र इति स्मृतः॥ २८९॥

वेदहीनस्य विप्रस्य सर्वशास्त्रप्रगल्भता।
वस्त्रहीनस्य देहस्य सर्वभूषणता यथा॥ २९०॥

यो निराकृतिना विप्रः स जग्धिं कुरुते यदा।
स विप्रस्तु तदाऽऽप्नोति सुरापानफलं ध्रुवम्॥ २९१॥

तदाऽनिराकृतिः सोऽयं लभते पावनं परम्।
तस्मान्निराकृतेः पापं न कुर्यात् पङ्क्तिभोजनम्॥ २९२॥ [88]

वेदांश्च श्रोत्रियं ब्रह्म ये के दूष्यन्ति मानवाः।
ते घोरं नरकं प्राप्य जायन्ते भुवि सूकराः॥ २९३॥

साङ्गवेदाध्ययनफलम्

वेदरूपविलसत् परात् परं
ये पठन्ति विधिना द्विजोत्तमाः।
ते त्रिवर्गमिह चानुभूय तच्-
छाश्वतं पदमवाप्नुयुः परम्॥ २९४॥ [89]

॥ इत्यात्रेयशीक्षामूलं सम्पूर्णम्॥ [90]

---

88 H and T read निराकृतिरध्ययनरहित इत्यर्थः।

89 H reads हरिः ॐ

90 H reads श्लोकसङ्ख्या—२९४। शुभमस्तु। श्रीमते हयग्रीवपरब्रह्मणे नमः। ऊरुतिटिचक्रमय्य-ङ्गारूस्वहस्तलिखितम्।
T reads हरिः ॐ। श्रीवेदव्यासाय नमः। श्रीनिवासराघवमहागुरवे नमः॥

3

Transliteration and Translation

ĀTREYAŚĪKṢĀKĀRIKĀ

kārikāṁ sampravakṣyāmi prathamaṁ pāribhāṣikam ।
saṁhitāviṣayav̄ vedapārāyaṇaphalan tataḥ ॥ 1 ॥

pārāyaṇakramaś caiva vāgvṛttiḫ padalakṣaṇam ।
kramasyātha jaṭāyāś ca śuddhavarṇakramasya ca ॥ 2 ॥

lakṣaṇañ ca kramāt tatra yau ca dvitvāgamau smṛtau ।
tayor abhinidhānasya kevalākhyāgamasya ca ॥ 3 ॥

yamānān tanniṣedhānān dvitāgamaniṣedhayoḥ ।
lakṣaṇaṁ svarabhaktīnāṁ sodāharaṇasaṁjñakāḥ ॥ 4 ॥

vivṛtter lakṣaṇan tasyāṁ saṁjñodāharaṇāni ca ।
vyaktimadhyasthanāsikyo raṅgākhyaplutadīrghayoḥ ॥ 5 ॥

lakṣaṇaṁ svaritodāttakampānāñ ca viśeṣataḥ ।
syād vaikṛtaprākṛtayor nāsikyaurasyayor api ॥ 6 ॥

vidhiś ca jihvāmūlīyopadhmānīyākhyayor api ।
sthitisandhividhiś caiva tathā praṇavalakṣaṇam ॥ 7 ॥

svaravarṇakramas tatrodāttādīnān nirūpaṇam ।
udāharaṇasay̆yuktasaptasvaritalakṣaṇam ॥ 8 ॥

tatprayatnaprabhedāś ca mātrāvarṇakramas tathā ।
mātrāmānanirūpañ ca mātrākāloktividhy api ॥ 9 ॥

aṅgavarṇakramas tatra parapūrvāṅgalakṣaṇam ।
aṅgavarṇakramokteś ca suspaṣṭav̄ lakṣaṇan tataḥ ॥ 10 ॥

nirvacanaṁ varṇasārabhūtavarṇakramasya tu |
saṅkhyā ca varṇadharmāṇān tadukter ānupūrvikā || 11 ||

bhaktyanusvārakampānāṁ raṅgasyāpy uktilakṣaṇam |
śabdotpattiprakāraś ca tatra dhvaninirūpaṇam || 12 ||

śarīrāntargatan tatra sarvavyāpāralakṣaṇam |
jāṭharāgnisthitiḥ pañcavāyūnāṁ sthānaceṣṭikāḥ || 13 ||

dhvanibhedās tatra jātavarṇānāñ ca viniścayaḥ |
teṣān tu sthānakaraṇavivekas tatprakārakaḥ || 14 ||

prayatnabhedā varṇānān devatājātisaṁjñakāḥ |
udāttādisvarāṇāñ ca devatā jātayo guṇāḥ || 15 ||

tato hastasvaranyāsalakṣaṇan tasya tat phalam |
aṅgādyavasthā ṣaḍjādisaptasvaranirūpaṇam || 16 ||

udāttādisvarotpattir vedasya mahimā tataḥ |
vikṛtyaṣṭakasaṁyuktavedasyādhyayane phalam || 17 ||

ity evam ānupūrvyeṇa śīkṣā samprocyate 'dhunā ||
ity ātreyaśīkṣākārikā samāptā ||

I am going to declare the concise versified statements (*kārikā*). There should be at first the explanatory rule and then the topic related to the Saṁhitā, the fruit of the Vedic recitation (1); the order in recitation, the modes of speech, the definitions of the word-reading, the sequential reading, the tangled reading and the simple phonic sequence (2); the definitions of both of them which are termed duplication and increment respectively, [the definitions] of their adjacent imposition and insertion (3); [the definitions] of the twin-phones and their prevention and that of the prevention of duplication and increment; the definitions of the anaptyxes along with the examples and the appellations (4); the definitions of the hiatus and its examples and appellations, the intermediate nasal within the hiatus; the definitions of the protracted and long nasally modified *a*-vowel (5); the definitions of the circumflex tremulous and the acute tremulous and specially those of the modified and original [sibilants] as well as [those] of the nasal and the pulmonic [aspirate] (6); the rule regarding the sound produced by the root of the tongue and the blowing sound and also the rule for stability in juncture and the definition of Om (7); the accentual phonic sequence, the determination of the acutes, etc. therein, the definitions of the seven circumflexes along with examples (8), and the varieties of their manners of articulation and the moraic phonic sequence, the determination of the duration of mora and also the rule for the utterance of the moraic time duration (9); the adjunctive phonic sequence and the definitions of the adjuncts of succeeding and preceding [vowels] therein; and then the very clear definition of the utterance of the adjunctive phonic sequence (10); the etymology of the [word] *varṇasārabhūtavarṇakrama*, the sequential number of the phonic attributes [which are pronounced in] its (phonic sequence of the phonic attributes) utterance (11); the features of the utterances of anaptyxis, *ṁ*, tremulous and also of the nasally modified protracted *a*-vowel; the origin of sound and its varieties; the determination of speech sound therein (12); the features of all activities in the body; the location of the stomach fire therein; the locations and activities of the five vital airs (13); the varieties of speech sounds and the assertion of the phones [that originate from them], discussion of their various places of articulation and articulators (14); the types of the manners of articulation, deities, classes and appellations of the phones; deities, classes and qualities of the accents beginning with the acute (15); then the characteristics of the manual demonstration of the accents, the fruit of that, conditions of organs etc. and determination of the notes beginning with sa (16); the origin of the accents such as acute, then the magnificence of the Veda, the fruit of the study of the Veda along with its eight artificial readings (17) — in this order the science of proper pronunciation is being explicated now.

Thus the *Ātreyaśīkṣākārikā* is concluded.

ĀTREYAŚĪKṢĀMŪLA

PARIBHĀṢĀ

Explanatory Rules and Terms

āmnāyā yasya niśśvāsāś candrasūryau ca cakṣuṣī |
tat praṇamya parañ jyotiś śīkṣāṽ vakṣyāmi nirmalām || 1 ||

Having bowed to the highest light, whose breaths are the Vedas and eyes are the sun and the moon, I am going to speak the pure science of proper pronunciation (*śīkṣā*).

acas svarā iti proktā vyañjanāni halas smr̥tāḥ |

The vowels (*ac*) are called *svara*s and the consonants (*hal*) are declared as *vyañjana*s.

hrasvadīrghaplutāvarṇevarṇovarṇā r̥ r̥̄ l̥ ca || 2 ||
ed aid od aud iti jñeyāṣ ṣoḍaśehāditas svarāḥ |

The short (*hrasva*), long (*dīrgha*) and protracted (*pluta*) phones of *a, i* and *u;* the short vocalic *r* (*r̥*), the long vocalic *r* (*r̥̄*), the short vocalic *l* (*l̥*), *e, ai, o* and *au* — these are first sixteen [of the sound inventory] known as vowels herein.

kakhau gaghau ṅacachajā jhañau ṭaṭhaḍaḍhā ṇatau || 3 ||
thadau dhanau paphababhā mas sparśāḫ pañcaviṁśatiḥ |

The stops (*sparśa*) are twenty-five, viz. *k, kh, g, gh, ṅ, c, ch, j, jh, ñ, ṭ, ṭh, ḍ, ḍh, ṇ, t, th, d, dh, n, p, ph, b, bh* and *m.*

yarau lavau catasro 'ntassthāś ca ẖkaśaṣasaḫpahāḥ || 4 ||

ṣaḍ ūṣmāṇo visargo 'nusvāro ḷo nāsyapañcakam |[1]
ity ete yājuṣā varṇā ekonāṣ ṣaṣṭir īritāḥ || 5 ||

---

[1] This portion from the last line of the second verse up to the first line of the fifth verse is identical with *Āpiśaliṣikṣā* 7-9 (Vira 1981: 347) and the *Pāriśikṣā* (Chandra 1981: 319). This portion, with a slight change, is also quoted by *Vaidikābharaṇa* (Sastri and Rangacarya 1906: 9) on *TP* 1.1.

The semi-vowels (*antassthā*) are four, viz. *y, r, l* and *v;* six are fricatives (*ūṣman*), viz. *ẖ, ś, ṣ, s, ḫ* and *h; ḥ, ṁ, ḷ* and five nose-sounds[2] (*nāsikya*) — these fifty-nine phones are said to be the sound [inventory] of *Yajurveda.*

kramena pañca pañca syus sparśānāṽ vargasaṁjñikāḥ ।

The five [sets, each consisting of] five of the stops, are, one by one, designated as series (*varga*).

vargeṣu teṣu saṁjñās syuś caturṇām prathamādayaḥ ।। 6 ।।
pañcamasyottamaḫ prokto ghoṣāghoṣau tu teṣu vai ।

The designations of the [first] four [phones] in each of those series should be the "First" (*prathama*),[3] etc. but the [designation] of the fifth is said to be the "Last" (*uttama*). But indeed, there are voiced and voiceless [phones in the sound inventory].

hānyoṣmā prathamāś caiva visargaś ca dvitīyakāḥ ।। 7 ।।
aghoṣās syuś ca tebhyo 'nye ghoṣavanto halas smr̥tāḥ ।

The fricatives other than *h,* the firsts, *ḥ* and the seconds (*dvitīya*s) are voiceless while all the consonants except these are declared as voiced.

pari vi ny ā 'bhy upa prāva praty adhīty upasargakāḥ ।। 8 ।।

The prefixes (*upasarga*) are *pari, vi, ni, ā, abhi, upa, pra, ava, prati* and *adhi.*

kāraśabdottaro varṇo varṇākhyā pratipādyate ।
vyañjanānām akāras syāc chaṣasetyādisaṅgrahāt ।। 9 ।।

---

2 In order to render distinctly the term *nāsikya* in English, Whitney (1868: 384) uses the word nose-sound for *nāsikya.* Though the accurate translation of the word *nāsikya* would be "nasal", the word "nasal" may also refer to the five nasal stops, namely *ṅ, ñ, ṇ, n* and *m.*

3 *prathama* (voiceless unaspirated stop); *dvitīya* (voiceless, aspirated stop); *tr̥tīya* (voiced unaspirated stop); *caturtha* (voiced aspirated stop); *uttama* (voiced unaspirated nasal).

A phone, with the word *kāra* after it, attains the appellation of that phone. [In the appellations of] the consonants there should be an *a* [after them] as there is a reference to *śa, ṣa, sa,* etc.

hrasvo 'd id ud ṛkāraś ca tathalkāras svareṣu vai ।

Among the vowels *a, i, u, ṛ* and *ḷ* are short, indeed.

vargottaras tu vargākhyā prathamo bhavatīty api ।। 10 ।।[4]

Also, however, the first, with [the word] *varga* after it, is the designation of the series.

SAṀHITĀVIṢAYAM

The Topic Related to Saṁhitā

ārambhe yajuṣaś śākhā yā syāt sā saṁhitā smṛtā ।
kāṇḍapraśnānuvākādyaiḥ pravibhaktā 'ntarā 'ntarā ।। 11 ।।

That, which was the branch of *Yajurveda* at the outset, is mentioned as Saṁhitā, being duly divided into *kāṇḍa, praśna, anuvāka,* etc. internally.

yās tato 'nyā yajuśśākhā na tāsāṽ vikṛtīḥ paṭhet ।

One should not read the artificial readings of the branches of *Yajurveda* other than that (the Saṁhitā).

saṁhitāgranthamātrasya saviśeṣau padakramau ।। 12 ।।

The word-reading (*pada*) and the sequential reading (*krama*) are nothing but special varieties of the Saṁhitā text itself.

jaṭā varṇakramāś caiva kramād vikṛtayas smṛtāḥ ।

The tangled reading (*jaṭā*) and the readings of phonic sequence (*varṇakramas*) are mentioned as the artificial readings.

kevalas svarasaỹyukto mātrikāsahitas tathā ।। 13 ।।
sāṅgaś ca varṇasāraś ca pañca varṇakramān viduḥ ।

The five phonic sequences are called — the simple (*kevala-varṇakrama*), the accentual (*svara-varṇakrama*), the moraic (*mātrā-*

4 This half-verse is also found in *Pāriśikṣā* (Chandra 1981: 325).

varṇakrama), the adjunctive (*aṅga-varṇakrama*) and the phonic attributive (*varṇasārabhūta-varṇakrama*).

VEDAPĀRĀYAṆAPHALAM

Fruit of Vedic Recitation

sarvathā nādhigantavyo vedo likhitapāṭhakaḥ || 14 ||
adhyetavyas savikṛtir dvijair yatnād guror mukhāt |

In no way the Veda is to be approached as a written text; [rather it] should be studied by the brāhmaṇas carefully along with [its] artificial readings from the *guru*'s lips.

vedeṣv akṣaram ekaikam ekaikaṁ harināmakam || 15 ||

Each syllable in the Vedas is one of the names of Hari.

anyūnā svarataś caiva varṇato yā ca saṁhitā |
sakṛt pārāyaṇe tasyā yāvat phalam ihocyate || 16 ||

triguṇan tatpade tasmāt krame tv aṣṭaguṇam bhavet |[5]

[As compared to the fruit obtained] during one-time recitation (*pārāyaṇa*) of the continuous reading (*saṁhitā*), intact in terms of the accents and the phones; the fruit is said to be as much as triple from that in the word-reading of that (the continuous reading). However it would be eightfold in the sequential reading.

jaṭādhyāye śatam proktaṁ śuddhavarṇe sahasrakam || 17 ||

It (the fruit) is said to be hundredfold in the tangled reading [and] thousandfold in the [reading of] the simple phonic sequence.

svaravarṇe 'yutaṽ vidyān niyutam mātrikāyute |

One should consider the ten thousandfold [and] the hundred thousandfold [fruit] in the [readings of] accentual phonic sequence [and] in the moraic phonic sequence [respectively].

5 *Sarvalakṣaṇamañjarī* refers to some similar verses and ascribes them to *Skanda Purāṇa*: *saṁhitāpāpāṭhamātreṇa yat phalam procyate budhaiḥ* | *pade tu dviguṇaṽ vidyāt krame tu ca caturguṇam* || *varṇakrame śataguṇañ jaṭāyān tu sahasrakam* || (Sastri 1976: 186)

prayutan tv aṅgavarṇe syād anantaṽ varṇasārake ||18||

[The fruit] would be one millionfold in the adjunctive phonic sequence and infinite times in the [phonic sequence of] the phonic attributes.

PĀRĀYAṆAKRAMAḤ

System of Vedic Recitation

prāyaścittavidhau kṛcchre brahmayajñe kriyāvidhau |
saṁhitāpaṭhanaṁ kuryān niyamān na padādikān ||19||

During the painstaking expiation, Vedic studies and performance of any rite, one should necessarily pursue the continuous reading but not the [other readings] such as the word-reading etc.

utsavārthan tu deveśe nirgate garbhagehataḥ |
kramādikam paṭhed yad vā tathopaniṣadam paṭhet ||20||

But when the chief of the gods has been taken out from the innermost sanctum for festive purposes one should read the sequential reading, etc. or similarly read the Upaniṣad.

ANADHYAYANAPRAKARAṆAM

Discussion on Intermission in Vedic Recitation

yas tu pārāyaṇaṁ hitvā kālātikramaśaṅkayā |
kuryāt sandhyāṁ sa niṣkarmī vijñeyas tatra pātakī ||21||

However he who performs the daily junctional rituals (*sandhyā*), desisting the Vedic recitation [and] apprehending the wastage of time, is then an idle and is known as a sinner.

prāpte mahāpradoṣe 'pi tadā deveśasannidhau |
anadhyayanamānena na ca pārāyaṇan tyajet ||22||

Even on the day of *mahāpradoṣa* (the thirteenth day of every fortnight which occurs on Mondays and Saturdays) in the presence of the chief of the gods; one should not give up the Vedic recitation with the idea of intermission of studies.

tyajed yadi tadā mohād brahmahatyāṁ samāviśet |

If one leaves it due to ignorance one enters into the [crime] of killing a brāhmaṇa.

VĀGVR̥TTIḤ

Mode of Speech

vācas tu vr̥ttayas tisro drutamadhyavilambitāḥ ॥23॥

There are, however, three modes of speech — fast, intermediate [and] slow.

āvr̥tyāvr̥tya cābhyāse drutavr̥ttyā paṭhed dvijaḥ ।

And while practising repetitively, a brahmaṇa should recite in the fast mode.

pārāyaṇe prayogārthe madhyamāṁ vr̥ttim ācaret ॥24॥

[He] should use the intermediate mode for an applicative purpose during recitation

bodhanārthan tu śiṣyāṇāv̐ vr̥ttiṅ kuryād vilambitām ।

[He] should, however, use the slow mode for instructing the pupils.

PADALAKṢAṆAM

Definition of Word-Reading

padādhyāye padānte yad itiśabdam prayujya ca ॥25॥
punar uccāryate dvedhā tad veṣṭanapadaṁ smr̥tam ।

The word (*pada*) that is uttered again for a second time, having used the word *iti* at the end of the [first] word [used], is termed as entwining word (*veṣṭanapada*) in the word-reading.

yat padav̐ veṣṭanopetan tad iṅgyam iti kathyate ॥26॥

A word which is accompanied by the entwining word is called separable word (*iṅgya*).

iṅgyate hi padasyārtha ity asmād iṅgyam ucyate ।

Therefore, it is called a separable word because the meaning of the word is being separated.

vibhāgavatpadasyārtho vibhāgena vicālyate ||27||
ity evam iṅgyaśabdārthas tasya pūrvan tv avagrahaḥ |

The meaning of the word that has division is put apart through the division — in this way the meaning of the term *iṅgya* is [understood]. Its former [member] is [called] separative word (*avagraha*).[6]

paryādīni daśātroktāny upasargapadāni ca ||28||

Ten prefixes starting with *pari* have been mentioned here.

anv apāty api sūt san niḫ parā nava padāni ca |

And there are nine [more] words — *anu, apa, ati, api, su, ut, sam, niḥ* and *parā.*

ityantāni syur etāni padāny ekonaviṁśatiḥ ||29||

These nineteen words should end with *iti.*

vākyāntagan dvayor ādi nihatan triṣu madhyamam |
avagrahe 'tra netyantaỹ yat tat syād adhvarā 'va ca ||30||

Here [in the word reading when] this (one of the nineteen words) is the final word of a sentence or the former between two (of the nineteen words) or entirely graved (*nihata*) or the middle one among the three (of the nineteen words) or a separative word it should not end with *iti* nor the [*ava* in] *adhvarā 'va.*[7]

lakṣaṇaiḫ pragrahā ye syur ityantās te pade sati |

Those which are *pragraha* (final detachable vowels)[8] by the definitions should end with *iti* in the word-reading.

KRAMALAKṢAṆAM

Definition of Sequential Reading

saṁhitāvat paṭhet pūrvam anukramya padadvayam ||31||

One should first read two words sequentially as in the continuous reading.

---

6 The first part of a separable word in the word-reading.

7 *TS* 4.1.4.

8 *Pragraha* does not undergo euphonic changes.

dvitīyan tatra padavad avasāne samāpayet |

At the point of termination [of the second word one] should put an end to the second [word] like in the word-reading.

tatas tv ādipadaṁ hitvā dvitīyañ ca tṛtīyakam || 32 ||

Then [one] should [read] the second and the third [words] leaving aside the first word.

paṭhet tatas tad dvitīyam padaṁ hitvā tṛtīyakam |
caturthañ ca paṭhet paścāt kramad evam paṭhet punaḥ || 33 ||

And then [one] should read the third and the fourth [words] leaving aside the second word. After that in this way one should read on sequentially.

pūrvam pūrvam padam muktvā saỹyujyottaram uttaram |
evam uccāryate yas tu kramādhyāyas sa ucyate || 34 ||

That is called sequential reading which is uttered thus, i.e. leaving aside each former word, having joined the latter word after.

krame tāvat tathoccārye yadīṅgyam pūrvikam padam |
paṭhitvā veṣṭanan tasya paṭhet paścād yathākramam || 35 ||

Meanwhile in the sequential reading which is to be uttered in that manner, if a separable word is the former word, one should read [it] in proper sequence after reading its entwining word.

pūrvavākyāntagaỹ yac ca paravākyādikan tathā |
tayor nānukramet tadvad antam ādy anuvākayoḥ || 36 ||

In that way, one should not combine the final [word] of the previous sentence and the initial [word] of the subsequent sentence sequentially and so for the last and first [words] of the two *anuvāka*s.

pragrahāniṅgyayuktañ ca yadi syād ādimam padam |
akhaṇḍaveṣṭanan tasya vākyānte yad aniṅgyakam || 37 ||

In the sequential reading, if the first word is an inseparable word (*aniṅgya*) with a final detachable vowel (*pragraha*) one should read its undivided entwining word. [The undivided entwining word should also be read] when the inseparable word occurs at the end of a sentence.

pade tu yad yad ityantan tan netyantam paṭhet krame ।

In the sequential reading one should not read the words with the ending *iti,* which end with *iti* in the word-reading.

ṣaṇatvaṭatvavidhinā saha nityam anukramet ॥38॥

One should proceed sequentially always with the rules of *ṣ*-substitution (*ṣa-tva*), *ṇ*-substitution (*ṇa-tva*) and *ṭ*-substitution (*ṭa-tva*).

ādantaỹ yad udāttāntam pūrvaỹ yady opasargataḥ ॥
tasyordhvena trikamas syān naḫparaṁ ṣupadan tv adhaḥ ॥39॥

If an *ā*-ending oxytone (*udāttānta*) precedes the prefix *ā* there should be a tri-sequence (*tri-krama*) with the succeeding [word]. [There should be a tri-sequence with the preceding word] even [when] the word *ṣu* followed by *naḥ* occurs after [the preceding word].

padatrayam anukramya hitvā cādipadam punaḥ ।
madhyamāntimam uccārya trikrame kramaśo vadet ॥40॥

Combining the three words successively and again pronouncing the middle and the final [words] excluding the first word, one should sequentially utter [the words] in the tri-sequence.

JAṬĀLAKṢAṆAM

Definition of Tangled Reading

kramavat pūrvam uccārya pratilomam paṭhec ca tat ।
sandhitaś ca punaḫ kuryāt kramapāṭham padadvayam ॥41॥

First having uttered the [pair of words] like in the sequential reading, one should read that [pair of words] in reverse and euphonically and [then] again one should carry out the sequential reading of that pair of words.

evam pāṭhakramo yas tu sā jaṭeti prakīrtitā ।

Such a kind reading sequence is stated as tangled reading.

akhaṇḍaveṣṭaneṅgyādi yad yad uktaṅ krame yathā ॥42॥
tatra tatra tathā sarvañ jaṭāyāñ ca paṭhed budhaḥ ।

And a knowledgeable person should read everything, i.e. the undivided entwining words, the separable words, etc. there in the tangled reading according to the manner stated in the sequential reading.

trikrame tripadasyāpi jaṭām uktvā yathāvidhi ॥43॥
tatas tatra dvitīyādipadānām pūrvavat paṭhet ।

After uttering the tangled reading of the three words in tri-sequence in accordance with the rules, one should read the second word onwards in the previous manner therein.

tulyam padadvayay̐ yatra svarato varṇato 'pi vā ॥44॥
na paṭhet tu jaṭān tatra kramamātram paṭhet sadā ।

One should not, however, recite the tangled reading where two words are [exactly] similar in terms of accents as well as phones; [one] should always recite only the sequential reading therein.

lopālopādayo ye ca ṣatvaṇatvādayaś ca ye ॥45॥
jaṭāyāl̐ lakṣaṇair uktās tān paṭhet tu yathāvidhi ।

One should, however, read those which are stated with definitions — elision, non-elision, etc. and *ṣ*-substitution, *ṇ*-substitution, etc. in accordance with the rules in the tangled reading.

KEVALAVARṆAKRAMALAKṢAṆAM

Definition of the Phonic Sequence

ye atra sāṁhitā varṇās samāmnātāś ca śāstrataḥ ॥46॥
tān sarvān kāraśabdāntān vaded varṇakramoktiṣu ।

Here in the reading of phonic sequence, one should utter all those phones of the continuous reading, which are traditionally handed down in accordance with the theoretical system with [each of the phones] ending with the word *kāra*.

akāreṇa vyavetas syāt kāraśabdo halām iha ॥47॥

Here the word *kāra* should be separated [from its] consonant with an *a*.

anusvāre ca nāsikye jihvāmūlyavisargayoḥ ।
upadhmānīyavarṇe ca kāraśabdas tu neṣyate ।।48।।

But the word *kāra* is not required in *ṁ*, the nose-sound[s], *ẖ*, *ḥ* and *ḫ*.

rasya tv ephas trayāṇāñ ca hrasvo varṇottaro bhavet ।

However, there should be *epha*[9] of *r* and a short [vowel] with *varṇa*[10] after it should belong to the three [vowels].

svarāt kāraparād arvāṅ na sandhir varṇapāṭhake ।।49।।

There is no euphonic change before a vowel which is followed by *kāra* in the reading of phonic sequence.

tān sadīrghavisargāṁś ca vaded uktisamāpane ।

While concluding a sentence one should utter them [i.e. the phones with the final phone] lengthened and [followed] by *ḥ*.

pūrvaṽ varṇakramoktes tu tat tāvat saṁhitām paṭhet ।।50।।

But before the reading of phonic sequence, one should, meanwhile read the continuous reading there.

yas tu saṁhitayā hīnāñ chuṣkān varṇakramān vadet ।
niṣphalaṁ syād yathā bhittihīnañ citravilekhanam ।।51।।

[The reading of one] who would utter the dry phonic sequences devoid of the continuous reading would be futile like the drawing of a picture without a frame.

yenāvasīyate vākyaṽ varṇenāpi svareṇa ca ।
tam eva varṇapāṭheṣu pravaden na ca sāṁhitam ।।52।।

[While concluding] one should enunciate that very phone and accent

---

9 *Epha* is to be added to *r* (instead of *kāra*) to get *repha.*

10 The word *varṇa* when added to a short vowel designates short, long and protracted forms of the same vowel. Therefore, the *varṇa* can be added exclusively to those vowels which have all the three moraic forms — short, long and protracted.

with which a sentence is concluded but not one which is produced by the continuous reading.

etena vidhinā vidvān kramād varṇakramān vadet ।

By this method, a knowledgeable person should sequentially utter the phonic sequences.

DVITVAPRAKARAṆAM

Discussion on Duplication

acpūrvaṽ vyañjanordhvaỹ yad vyañjanan dvitvam āpnuyāt ॥53॥
sparśaś ca lavapūrvo yo yat tu rephāt parañ ca tat ।

A consonant which is preceded by a vowel and followed by a consonant and a stop which is preceded by *l* or *v* and [also] that (consonant) which is after *r* should attain duplication.

hrasvapūrvau padāntasthau ṅanau dvitvam pare 'py aci ॥54॥

Also *ṅ* and *n* preceded by a short vowel and occurring at the end of a word and followed by a vowel [should attain] duplication.

yo 'nusvāro yajuṣy atra sa syād ardhagakārayuk ।

The *ṁ* which is here in *Yajurveda* should be joined with a half *g*.

yady ātmādhas sarūrdhve ca śāntiś śordhve na go bhavet ॥55॥

If occurring after *ātmā* and before *sarū*[11] and [also before] *śāntiḥ* that is followed by *ś* (as in ***oṁ*** *śāntiś śāntiḥ*) there would be no *g* [in *ṁ*].

yogāt pūrvam anusvāro hrasvād yaś ca parasthitaḥ ।
sa eva dvitvam āpnoti tasya syād ekamātratā ॥56॥

That *ṁ* itself which occurs before a conjunct and after a short vowel attains duplication. It should be of one mora.

---

11 . . . *paramā́tmaṁ sarūpám* . . . *TA* 10.33.

ĀGAMAḤ

Increment[12]

vyañjanaỹ yannimittena dvitvam āpnoti tena vai ।
pūrvāgamaḫ kramāt tatra syād dvitīyacaturthayoḥ ॥ 57 ॥

There should be an increment (*āgama*) [consisting] of the previous [phones] of the second and the fourth respectively [instead of duplication, going] by the very reason (conditions) by which a consonant [usually] attains duplication.

akhaṇḍe svarayor madhye yadi dvitvāgamau pade ।
lakṣyānusārasaṁjñau tau bhavetāl̃ lakṣaṇaiḫ pr̥thak ॥ 58 ॥

If there is duplication or increment [of a consonant] between two vowels in a single word, they (the duplication and the increment) are distinct by [their own] definitions should be termed as definable-according[13] (*lakṣyānusāra*).

pāthaeṣo'tidhāmātibhūteparamapūrvikāḥ ।
tathopasargapūrvāś cāgamañ chakhibhujā iyuḥ ॥ 59 ॥

Ch, khi and *bhuja* should obtain increment when preceded by *pātha, eṣaḥ, ati, dhāma, āti, bhūte* and *parama,* and similarly while preceded by the prefixes.

prathamasyoṣmaṇi pare dvitīyādeśakaḫ pade ।
same varṇadvayam bhinne .... ॥ 60 ॥[14]

There would be a substitution of the second at the place of a first [that is] followed by a fricative in the same word.

taittirīye śapūrvasya nasya ñas syān na kāṭhake ।

In the Taittirīya School, *n* preceded by *ś* should be *ñ*, but not in the Kāṭhaka School.

---

12 Whitney (1868: 37) renders the term *āgama* as "increment".

13 According to that which is to be defined.

14 This line is left untranslated because its meaning is incomprehensible due to the unavailability of the final hemistich.

ABHINIDHĀNAM

Adjacent Imposition[15]

aghoṣād ūṣmaṇas sparśaparād yatra parasthitaḥ ॥61॥
prathamo 'bhinidhānas syāt tasya sasthāna eva ca ।

There should be[16] an adjacent imposition (*abhinidhāna*) of a first where it (the adjacent imposition of a first) occurs after a voiceless fricative that is followed by a stop and it has the same place of articulation which it [the stop] has.

śasau yatrāgamau syātām prathamaḫ parato yadi ॥62॥
na tatrābhinidhānoktiḫ prathaman dvir vaded budhaḥ ।

If followed by a first where *ś* and *s* are the increments there is no utterance of adjacent imposition. A knowledgeable person should utter the first twice.

KEVALĀGAMAḤ

Insertion

nīcāpūrvas tathoccordhvo dakāraẖ kevalāgamaḥ ॥63॥

Similarly, after [the word] *nīcā*, followed by [the word] *uccā* there is an insertion (*kevalāgama*) of *d.*[17]

tadhottare ṅato 'nantyād āgamau staẖ kagau kramāt ।

There are insertions of *k* and *g* respectively after a non-final *ṅ* followed by *t* and *dh.*

YAMĀḤ

Twin Phones

syād yatrānuttamāt sparśād uttamaḫ parato yadi ॥64॥
krameṇa syur yamās tatra nāntassthā parato yadi ।

---

[15] Varma (1929: 137) mentions that the etymological meaning of the word is "adjacent imposition".

[16] The adjacent imposition takes place between a voiceless fricative and a subsequent stop.

[17] . . . *nīcā́uccā́* . . . — *TS* 2.3.14.

Where a stop which is not the last is followed by a last, there should be the twin phones[18] in accordance with the order [of the twin phones] if no semivowel follows.

YAMANIṢEDHAḤ

Prevention of Twin Phones

sparśo yady ūṣmavikr̥tir na tatra syād yamāgamaḥ ||65||

If the stop is an alteration of a fricative there would be no increment of a twin phone.

yatra yasmād yamaprāptis tatroṣmā vartate yadi |
naiva tatra yamāvāptir apy ūṣmā dvitvam āpnuyāt ||66||

Where the attainment of a twin phone [is expected], after which if there is a fricative, never would the attainment of the twin phone take place; instead the fricative should attain duplication.

yo 'padānte padānte vā prathamas syāt saṣottare |
sa dvitīyam avāpnoti śordhve 'nantyas sa cet tathā ||67||

Followed by *s* or *ṣ*, a first, whether it is at the end of a word or not at the end of a word and likewise if that (the first) which is non-final occurs before *ś*, would transform into the [corresponding] second.

NĀDAḤ

Final Nasal Stop

hrasvāt paras tu yo nādo bhavaty atra dvirūpavat |
tañ ca varṇakramādhyāye sakr̥d eva vaded budhaḥ ||68||

Here in the reading of phonic sequence, a knowledgeable person should utter the final nasal stop (*nāda*), which resembles [its] duplicated form after a short vowel, but once only.

---

18 Transition sounds between an oral stop and a subsequent nasal (Scharf 2013: 230).

DVITVĀGAMANIṢEDHAḤ

Prevention of Duplication and Increment

prāpte pūrvāgamadvitvalakṣaṇe yasya vai halaḥ |
dvitvam pūrvāgamaś caiva nivarteta tad ucyate || 69 ||

The consonant[s], whose characteristic of preceding increment and duplication is attained, indeed [but] the preceding increment and the duplication is still ruled out, are being referred to.

dvirūpan nāpnuyād ūṣmā prathamordve 'cpare 'pi vā |

Also, a fricative followed by a first or followed by a vowel should not attain duplication.

vakāraś ca pare sparśe visargo repha eva ca || 70 ||

V, when followed by a stop, and also *r* and *ḥ* [should never attain duplication].

lakāra ūṣmaṇi sparśe para īdaidadhaś ca yaḥ |

L followed by a fricative or a stop and *y* occurring after *ī* or *ai* [should never attain duplication].

savargīyānuttamordhve savarṇordhve ca hal tathā || 71 ||

Similarly, a consonant either followed by one of the same series (*savargīya*) which is not the last (*anuttama*) or followed by a homogeneous phone (*savarṇa*) [should never attain duplication].

mas sparśayavalordhvaś cet teṣām ety anunāsikam |

M when followed by either a stop or *y* or *v* or *l* turns into their [corresponding] nasalized forms (*anunāsika*).

dīrghāt paro 'ntago vordhve na dvir no na vya vr̥ ṇvra ca || 72 ||

After a long vowel, a final *n* [if] followed by *v*, [but] not *vya*, *vr̥* and *ṇvra*, is not doubled.

paro 'pi hrasvadīrghābhyān na ca dvitvaỹ yahottare |

Also, there is no duplication [of a final *n* occurring] after a short or a long vowel and before *y* or *h*.

SVARABHAKTIVIṢAYAM

The Topic Related to Anaptyxis[19]

āpnuto ralayor yasmād ūrdhve saty acparoṣmaṇi ||73||
r̥l̥svarārdhāv ādeśau tasmāt syāt svarabhaktitā |

Because of which [*r* and *l*] receive the substitutions of half *r̥* and [half] *l̥* [respectively], there should be vowel-fragmentation of *r* and *l* while followed by a fricative that is [in turn] followed by a vowel.

caturbhir eva sā śliṣṭā pādair ajvyañjanātmakā ||74||

Integrated by four quarters, it (the anaptyxis) is vocalic as well as consonantal.

adyantau teṣu pādeṣu pādau syātāṁ svarātmakau |

The initial and final quarters among these quarters should be vocalic.

sthitau madhye tu yau pādau tau jñeyau vyañjanāt makau ||75||

But those two quarters which are located in the middle are to be known as consonantal.

pādan dvitīyam pādena prathamenaiva yojayet |

One should join the second quarter with the first quarter only.

tr̥tīyañ ca caturthena pādam pādena yojayet ||76||

And one should join the third quarter with the fourth quarter.

evan tatra kramāt pādau dvau dvau tu vibhajet pr̥thak |

Thus, one should gradually segregate each two quarter [pairs] separately therein.

halantā syāt pūrvabhāgasvarabhaktis tu sav̐vr̥tā ||77||
bhaktir uttarabhāgā syād vivr̥tā ca svarodayā |

The first part anaptyxis which ends with the consonant should be closed and the latter part anaptyxis which has vocalic ending

19 Whitney (1879: 72) and Monier-Williams (1899: 1285) translate the term *svarabhakti* respectively as vowel-fragment and vowel-separation.

should be open.

pūrvabhāgo hakāre syāc chaṣaseṣūttaras tathā ǁ 78 ǁ

The first part [anaptyxis] should be in *h* and likewise the latter should be in *ś*, *ṣ* and *s*.

atvam itvan tathotvañ ca bhakter ūrdhvasvarasya ca ।
trayam etad anuccārya svarabhaktiṁ samuccaret ǁ 79 ǁ

One should enunciate the anaptyxis without pronouncing the three tendencies of *a*, *i* and *u* of the final vowel of the anaptyxis.

SVARABHAKTĪĀṀ SODĀHARAṆASAṀJÑĀḤ

Appellations of the Anaptyxes along with Examples

barhiḫ kareṇusaṁjñā syād yoge tu rahayor yadi ।
sā malhā karviṇī jñeyā saẏyoge lahakārayoḥ ǁ 80 ǁ

Kareṇu should be the appellation [of the anaptyxis] in the conjunct of *r* and *h* as in *bar**hi**ḥ*[20] while it is to be known as *karviṇī* in the conjunct of *l* and *h* as in *mal**hā**.*[21]

varṣaṁ haṁsapadā jñeyā yoge tu raṣayor api ।

Also, it (the anaptyxis) should be known as *haṁsapadā* while there is a conjunct of *r* and *ṣ* as in *var**ṣ**am.*[22]

śottare hariṇī repho darśaḫ parśur udāhṛtaḥ ǁ 81 ǁ

It is *hariṇī* while *r* is followed by *ś*. For example, *dar**ś**aḥ,*[23] *par**ś**uḥ.*[24]

sapare yatra rephas syād dhastinī barsam ity api ।

Furthermore, it should be *hastinī* where *r* is followed by *s* as in

---

[20] *TS* 1.1.2, 11, 13, 4.1.8; *TB* 1.6.3, 6, 8, 9, 1.7.3, 2.1.4-5, 2.3.2, 2.4.3, 5-6, 8, 2.5.5, 2.6.4, 7.10-12, 14, 17-18, 20, 2.7.12, 2.8.2, 6, 3.2.2-3, 10, 3.3.6, 8, 3.5.2, 5, 3.6.2, 6, 13-14, 3.7.4-6; *TA* 6.64.

[21] *TB* 1.8.3.

[22] *TS* 1.1.2, 5; *TB* 2.7.12, 3.1.4, 3.2.2, 3.6.13.

[23] *TS* 2.5.4, 3.1.11, 3.2.5, 3.3.11; *TB* 2.2.2, 2.8.9, 3.2.3, 3.4.4, 3.4.16, 3.9.23.

[24] *TB* 3.2.2.

barsam.[25]

tasya dhūrṣadam ityādau sā svatantrā pracakṣate ।

It is called discrete (*svatantrā*) as in *tasya dhūrṣadam,*[26] etc.

hāritā laśayor yoge śatavalśam udāhṛtam ।

It is *hāritā* in the conjunct of *l* and *ś*. For example, *śatavalśam.*[27]

krameṇaivaṁ suvijñeyās saptaitās svarabhaktayaḥ ॥ 83 ॥

Thus, gradually these seven anaptyxes are to be thoroughly understood.

VIVṚTTILAKṢAṆAN TASYĀS SAṀJÑĀŚ CA

Definition of Hiatus and Its Appellations

svarayor ubhayos sandhir vivṛttir iti kathyate ।

The juxtaposition of two vowels is called hiatus (*vivṛtti*).

atra saiva vivṛttis tu vyaktir ity api cocyate ॥ 84 ॥

And, however, the very hiatus is also called *vyakti* herein.

vatsānusṛtir ākhyātā tathā vatsānusāriṇī ।
vaiśeṣikā pākavatī madhyamā ca pipīlikā ॥ 85 ॥

tathā savarṇadīrghī cobhayadīrghī tathā smṛtā ।
ity evam aṣṭa saṁjñās syur vivṛttīnān tu bhedataḥ ॥ 86 ॥

[Hiatuses] are termed as *vatsānusṛti, varsānusāriṇī, vaiśeṣikā, pākavatī, madhyamā, pipīlikā, savarṇadīrghī* and *ubhayadīrghī.* In this way there should be eight appellations of the hiatuses according to their varieties.

hrasvapūrvā ca yā vyaktis tathaivottaradīrghikā ।
sā vatsānusṛtiḥ proktā samātrākālatas tathā ॥ 87 ॥

The hiatus where the former [vowel] is short and the latter is long is called *vatsānusṛti* and it is of one mora of time.

---

[25] *TS* 5.7.11.

[26] *TB* 1.2.1.

[27] *TS* 1.1.2, 1.3.5, 6.3.3.

hrasvāt pūrve vivṛttis syāt plutād dīrghāt parā ca yā ।
vatsānusāriṇī seyam ekamātreṇa saỹyutā ॥ 88 ॥

That very hiatus, which would occur before a short vowel and after a protracted or a long vowel, is [called] *vatsānusāriṇī* which is comprised of one mora.

vakter ādyantayor yasyā dīrghau yady asavarṇakau ।
yadi madhye visargas syāt tadabhāvo 'thavā yadi ॥ 89 ॥

sā tu vaiśeṣikākhyā syād ekamātrā ca tatra vai ।

But if the hiatus comprises of two heterogeneous long vowels as its beginning and end, and if *ḥ* is in-between [them while separated] or its absence is there, it is termed as *vaiśeṣikā* and there should be definitely one mora.

pūrve yatrottare caiva hrasvo yadi bhavet tadā ॥ 90 ॥
pādonamātrikā tatra sā ca pākavatī smṛtā ।

If there is a short vowel before as well as after [the hiatus], it is termed as *pākavatī* and there should be three quarters of a mora.

yasyās savarṇadīrghau sta ubhayatroccanīcakau ॥ 91 ॥
visargas tatra ca svāras sandhau mātrā ca madhyamā ।

It (hiatus) is *madhyamā,* [the vowels] of which are long and homogeneous, one of them is acute and other one is grave [i.e. consequently] circumflex (*svāra* or *svarita*) in the juncture. There is a *ḥ* [when separated].[28] And it is of one mora.

madhyamālakṣaṇe tatra visargo na bhaved yadi ॥ 92 ॥
pipīliketi vijñeyā sā vyaktiḥ pādamātrikā ।

If there is no *ḥ* in the definition of *madhyamā* it is to be known as *pipīlikā.* This hiatus comprises a quarter of a mora.

savarṇadīrghau yady ādāv ante bhinne visargakaḥ ॥ 93 ॥
savarṇadīrghy ekamātrā na sandhau svarito yadi ।

If there are two homogeneous long vowels at the beginning

---

[28] *Ḥ* is dropped because of the euphonic change.

[and] at the end [and] there is *ḥ* when separated, if there is no circumflex accent (*svarita*) at the juncture it is *svarṇadīrghī* which is monomoraic.

tasyās savarṇadīrghyās tu sampūrṇe lakṣaṇe sati ||94||
visargas tatra no cet sā samātrobhayadīrghy atha |

Now, if there is no *ḥ* but all [other] characteristics of that *savarṇadīrghī* exist, it is *ubhayadīrghī* that comprises one mora.

VIVṚTTYUDĀHARAṆAM

Examples of Hiatus

udāhriyante vatsānusṛtyādivyaktayaḥ kramāt ||95||

Gradually the hiatus *vatsānusṛti,* etc. are being exemplified.

vatsānusṛtisaṁjñā syāt ta enam bhi sa āyur ā |

The appellation *varsānusāriṇī* should be there in ***tá e**nam bhi*[29] [and] ***sá ā́**yur ā́'.*[30]

vatsānusāriṇī proktā sed agne astu vā iyam ||96||

Vatsānusāriṇī is said to be there in *séd agn**e a**stu*[31] [and] *v**ā́ i**yám.*[32]

*vaiśeṣikā syāt **tā e**va kakṣīvā̃ auśijas tathā* |

Vaiśeṣikā should be there in ***tā́ e**vá*[33] (also *'**tā e**vá'*[34]) and in *kakṣī́v**ā̃ a**uśijáḥ.*[35]

sā tu pākavatī jñeyā praügañ ca sa ij jane ||97||

---

29 *TS* 2.3.11.

30 *TS* 1.3.14.

31 *TS* 1.2.14.

32 *TS* 6.5.6.

33 *TS* 1.5.4, 2.1.2, 2.3.5, 7, 2.4.2, 10, 3.4.3, 9, 5.3.9, 5.6.4, 5.7.2, 7.3.7, 7.4.3; *TB* 1.6.4, 9-10, 1.7.10, 1.8.7, 2.7.1, 3.7.1, 3.8.17, 3.9.4; *TA* 2.15.

34 *TS* 1.7.4, 2.5.5, 9, 5.1.4, 5.4.1, 5.4.8, 6.1.11, 6.2.5, 6.3.9, 7.3.6, 7.3.8, 7.4.1-2, 6, 7.5.1, 7; *TB* 1.1.9, 1.2.2, 5, 1.5.6, 1.6.6, 2.7.1, 3.2.4, 3.8.7, 3.9.16.

35 *TS* 5.6.5.

It is, however, to be known as *Pākavatī* as in *práü̇gam*[36] (also *praü̇gam*[37]) and *sá íj jáne*.[38]

madhyamā yā āvivisur vedyā ādan yad ity api ।

Madhyamā — *yā́ āviviśúḥ*[39] and also *vedā́ ādan yád*.[40]

pipīlikā tu te enaṁ vā āraṇyam udāhṛtam ॥ 98 ॥

However, *té enam*[41] [and] *vā́ āraṇyám*[42] are given as examples of *pipīlikā*.

savarṇadīrghī sayyattā āsann ityādidarśanāt ।

Savarṇadīrghī [is to be known] from the examples like *sáyyattā āsan*[43] etc.

iyan tūbhayadīrghī syād vā āpas ta tathety api ॥ 99 ॥

Moreover, it should be *ubhayadīrghī* as well in *vā́ ā́pas tá*[44] (also *vā ā́pas tá*[45])

VYAKTIMADHYASTHANĀSIKYAḤ

Intermediate Nasal within a Hiatus

nāsikyo vyaktimadhye yas sa bhavet sāṇumātrikaḥ ।
vyakteś ca sāṇumātratvan nāma pūrvoktam eva hi ॥ 100 ॥

The nasal which occurs within a hiatus should be of minute (*aṇu*) mora.[46] And the hiatus, whose appellation has been already said

36 *TS* 4.4.2.

37 *TS* 5.4.11; *TB* 2.8.6.

38 *TS* 2.3.14; *TB* 2.8.5.

39 *TS* 4.2.6.

40 *TS* 6.2.7.

41 *TS* 2.5.6.

42 *TS* 1.6.7.

43 *TS* 1.5.1, 2.3.7, 2.4.3, 3.4.4, 5.3.11, 5.4.1, 5.4.6, 5.5.3, 5.7.3, 6.2.2, 6.3.10; *TB* 1.1.6, 1.3.1.

44 *TS* 5.6.2.

45 *TS* 6.1.1, 6.4.2.

46 One-fourth part of a mora.

before, also consists of a minute mora.

RAṄGAPLUTĀḤ

Nasally Modified Protracted *a*-Vowel

yaśo mamopahūtā ca suślokā ca sumaṅgalā |
ete raṅgaplutā jñeyās tathā yad ghrā̃ itīty api || 101 ||

Yáśo mamā́$_3$[47], *úpahūtā́*$_3$[48], *súślokā́*$_3$[49], *súmaṅgalā́*$_3$[50] and also *yád ghrā́*$_3$[51] — these should be known as nasally modified protracted *a*-vowels (*raṅgapluta*).

raṅgaplute dvimātraṁ syād ādau vyāghrarutopamam |
anāsyaṁ hṛdayotpannam mandradhvaniyutam bhavet || 102 ||

The first two morae would be like the roar of a tiger, i.e. they should be non-nasal, comprising a deep sound and produced from the heart.

atha madhyamabhāge syāt tṛtīyo mūrdhasambhavaḥ |
kāṁsyaghṇṭānādasamas sa kampas tv ekamātrikaḥ || 103 ||

Then, in the middle part, however, the third single mora produced from the roof of the oral cavity (*mūrdhan*) should be tremulous, resembling the gong of a bell made of bell metal.

athāntyabhāge nāsikyarandhradvayavinissrutaḥ |
ekamātras turīyāṁśas sa tu kākaliko bhavet || 104 ||

Then, during the final part, i.e. the fourth quarter that consists of one mora, should, however, be a humming sound exuding from both the nostrils.

yathā saurāṣṭrikā gopī madhureṇa svareṇa vai |
takrā̃ ity uccared uccais tathā raṅgaṁ samuccaret || 105 ||

One should enunciate the nasally modified *a*-vowel as a Saurashtrian milkmaid would indeed pronounce [the word] *takrā̃* (buttermilk),

---

47 *TS* 7.4.20.

48 *TS* 2.6.7.

49 *TS* 1.8.16; *TB* 1.7.10, 2.6.5.

50 *TS* 1.8.16; *TB* 1.7.10, 2.6.5.

51 *TA* 5.1.

loudly in a sweet voice.

RAṄGADĪRGHĀḤ

Nasally Modified Long *a*-Vowel

devā̃ u tā̃ imy amṛvā̃ ava svā̃ aha kāṭhake ।
raṅgadīrghā iti proktās te sapādatrimātrikāḥ ॥ 106 ॥

hṛjjāto mātrikas tasmin syāt sapādatrimātrike ।
mūrdhajas tv ardhamātras syāt taccheṣo mukhanāsikāt ॥ 107 ॥

In the *Kāṭhaka*[52] these, consisting of three and a quarter mora are called nasally modified long *a*-vowel (*raṅgadīrgha*) — *devā̃́ ú*[53], *tā̃́ imi*[54], *amṛvā̃́ áva*[55], *svā̃́ ahá*[56]. In this [nasally modified long *a*-vowel constituting] three and a quarter morae, one mora should be produced from the heart, the half-mora should be produced from roof of the oral cavity whereas the rest of it [should be produced] from the mouth and the nose [respectively].

SVARITODĀTTAKAMPAVIṢAYAM

Topic Related to Circumflex and Acute Tremulous[57]

nityābhinihatakṣaipraprāśliṣṭās svaritā ime ।
sandhau tatra prakampante yatroccasvaritodayāḥ ॥ 108 ॥[58]

---

52 The term *Kāṭhaka* refers to *Kāṭhaka Āraṇyaka* (8 *Kāṭhaka* sections) which are the first two *praśnas* of *Taittirīya Āraṇyaka*. These eight *Kāṭhaka* sections are not native to the tradition of the Taittirīya recension. They were adopted from the Kāṭhaka recension. Cf. *Sarvasammataśikṣā* 47 (Franke 1886: 40).

53 *TA* 1.13.

54 *TA* 1.12.

55 *TA* 1.10.

56 *TA* 2.5.

57 In this translation, the term "tremulous" which is used as an English rendering of the Sanskrit term *kampa* should be taken as a noun though it is actually an adjective in English.

58 In their comments on *TP* 19.3 a very similar verse is quoted in both the *Tribhāṣyaratna* and *Vaidikābharaṇa* (Sastri and Rangacarya →

These circumflex accents, viz. innate (*nitya*), absorbed (*abhinihata*), hastened (*kṣaipra*) and coalesced (*praśliṣṭa*) tremble at the juncture where an acute accent or a circumflex accent appears after [them].

nīcam pūrvasvarasyānte kuryāt syāt kampa eva saḥ ।

One should produce a grave accent at the end of the previous vowel. This should be a tremulous (*kampa*) indeed.

hrasvam apy atra kampe 'smin yathādīrghan tam uccaret ॥109॥

One should pronounce even the short vowel here in this tremulous as a long vowel.

sa kampo 'tra vijñeyas svāra ucca iti dvidhā ।

The tremulous is to be known here as of two types, viz. circumflex tremulous (*svārakampa*) and acute tremulous (*uccakampa*).

svārakampas saṁhitāyām uccas tv āraṇyake bhavet ॥110॥

The circumflex tremulous would be in the *Saṁhitā* whereas the acute tremulous [would be] in the *Āraṇyaka*.

punaś ca tatra dvau kampau hrasvadīrghāv iti smṛtam ।

Furthermore, there are two [kinds of] tremulous mentioned as short and long.

ādau tu tasya kampasya svāras sa tryaṇumātrikaḥ ॥111॥
antyabhāge tu nihataḥ pādamātraḥ prakīrtitaḥ ॥

At first the circumflex accent of the tremulous vowel is of one and three minute morae whereas the grave accent is mentioned as consisting of quarter of a mora at the final stage.

udāttaś ca tathaivādau tripādādhikamātrikaḥ ॥112॥
tasyānte cānudāttas syād aṇumātro bhavet tathā ।

← 1906: 457-58) *nityo 'bhinihataś caiva kṣaipraḥ praśliṣṭa eva ca* । *ete svārāḥ prakampante yatroccasvaritodayāḥ* ॥ Similar verse is found in the *Ṛgveda Prātiśākhya* — *jātyo 'bhinihitaś caiva kṣaipraḥ praśliṣṭa eva ca* । *ete svārāḥ prakampante yatroccasvaritodayāḥ* ॥ (Shastri 1931: 125).

Similarly at first the acute accent comprises one and three quarters of a mora. And in that manner there should be a grave accent which should be of a minute mora.

sammelane dvimātras syāt tayor evaṁ suniścitaḥ || 113 ||

It is properly determined that [the tremulous] should be of two morae in such a combination of them (the above-mentioned circumflex accent and another circumflex or an acute).

VAIKR̥TAPRĀKR̥TE

Modification and Originality

śaṣaseṣv acpareṣv atra visargo yatra dr̥śyate |
vaikr̥tatvam prākr̥tatvaṅ kramāt syāc chliṣṭa eva hi || 114 ||

Here, where *ḥ* is seen (before it takes the form of the subsequent sibilant) preceding *ś, ṣ* or *s* which are followed by a vowel, there should respectively be modification and originality [of the two concurrent sibilants] only in the connected [reading].

NĀSIKYATVORASYATVE

Nasalization and Pulmonic-ness

hakārān naṇamā yatra dr̥śyante paratas tadā |
nāsikyatvam urasyatvaṁ has tu tatra dvir ucyate || 115 ||

Where a *n, ṇ* or *m* is seen after *h, h* comprising [the qualities] of nasalization (*nāsikyatva*) and pulmonic-ness (*urasyatva*) is then pronounced twice.[59]

VYAKTIMADHYASTHAVISARGAḤ

Intermediate *ḥ* within a Hiatus

vivr̥ttimadhye yatra syād visargas so 'rdhamātrikaḥ |
virāmaś caikamātras syāt tasyās saṁjñā yathāvidhi || 116 ||

Where there is a *ḥ* within a hiatus, it should be semi-moraic and the

[59] The first *h* is pulmonic and the latter, which is the fifth nose-sound reckoned as one of the phones constituting the sound inventory of *Kr̥ṣṇa-Yajurveda*, is nasalized.

pause should be monomoraic. The appellation of that (the hiatus) would be in accordance with the rule.

JIHVĀMŪLĪYOPADHMĀNĪYAVIDHIḤ

Rule for ẖ and ḫ

prāg yady aghoṣavarṇābhyāṽ visargaẖ kapavargayoḥ ।
kramāt sa jihvāmūlīya upadhmānīya ucyate ॥ 117 ॥

If there is *ḥ* before the voiceless phones of the *ka*-series (velar stops) and the *pa*-series (bilabial stops) it is called sound produced by the root of the tongue[60] (*jihvāmūlīya=ẖ*) [and] blowing sound[61] (*upadhmānīya=ḫ*), respectively.

STHITISANDHIḤ

Stability in Juncture

kakāraṣ ṣaparo yatra bhavet tasmin pare sati ।
pūrvasthito visargas syāt sthitisandhir iti smṛtaḥ ॥ 118 ॥

Where *k* would be followed by *ṣ* while it is occurring after [a *ḥ*], the previously existing *ḥ* should be [retained] — this is termed stability in juncture (*sthitisandhi*).

SVARAHĪNASYA VARṆASYA VĀCAKAN NĀMA

Proper Names of the Phones [designated] without Vowel

varṇasya svarahīnasya nāma vācakam ucyate ।
varṇakramasyādhyayane na vaded anyasaṁjñikām ॥ 119 ॥

In the reading of phonic sequence, the proper names of the phones[62] [designated] without a vowel is uttered. One should not speak of [any] other appellation.

---

60 Velar fricative.

61 Bilabial fricative.

62 Unlike the other consonants these are not designated with an *a*-vowel. E.g., *visarga, anusvāra, upadhmānīya, svarabhakti.*

KEVALĀNUSVĀRAḤ

Pure *ṁ*

yo 'nusvāraḫ kevalākhyas sa madhyastho vidher api ।
tatparasya yogāder na jātu dvitvam iṣyate ।।120।।

After a pure *ṁ* (*kevalānusvāra*) which occurs even in the middle of a precept,[63] the duplication of the initial [consonant] of the subsequent conjunct is never required.

PRAṆAVALAKṢAṆAM

Definition of Om

ādau prārambhakoṅkāre tv akāraḫ pādamātrikaḥ ।
sa tripādadvimātras syād ukāro mas tu mātrikaḥ ।। 121 ।।

In the initial *om*, at first the *a*-vowel is of quarter mora. That *u*-vowel should, however, be of three quarter and two morae. But *ṁ* is monomoraic.

adhyāyānte 'nuvākānte makāras tv ardhamātrikaḥ ।

However, at the end of a chapter [or] an *anuvāka m* [should be] semi-moraic.

SANDHINIṢEDHAḤ

Prevention of Euphonic Change

varṇakramaprapāṭheṣu svārāt kāraparād adhaḥ ।। 122 ।।

---

63 In the Prātiśākhya tradition of the Taittirīya School, a rule cannot be overridden in the presence of *ṁ* that occurs in between the phones for which the rule is stated. Therefore, the precept that mandates the duplication of the first member of a consonant cluster after a vowel (*AS* 53; *TP* 14.1) cannot be precluded if *ṁ* occurs in between the vowel and the first member of the subsequent consonant cluster. Such a *ṁ* is referred to as *vidher madhyasthaḥ*. Cf. *vidher madhyasthanāsikyo na virodho bhavet smr̥taḥ* । *tasmāt kurvanti kāryāṇi varṇānān dharma eva tu* ।। —*Śambhuśikṣā* (Chandra 1981: 534) also, *Tribhāṣyaratna* on *TP* 8.15 (Sastri and Rangacarya 1906: 239). The present verse states an exceptional rule in this context.

haripraṇavamadhye 'pi sandhir na syāt pluteṣu ca ।

There should not be euphonic change between [the words] *hari* and *oṁ*, neither in the protracted vowels and nor after the final vowel of the [word] *kāra* in readings of the phonic sequence.

SVARAVARṆAKRAMALAKṢAṆAM

Definition of Accentual Phonic Sequence

śuddhavarṇakrame tasminn ucyamāne yathākramam ॥ 123 ॥
tatrodāttānudāttau ca pracayaś ca trayas svarāḥ ।

tathaiva sapta svaritās saprayatnās sanāmakāḥ ॥ 124 ॥
daśaitāṁs tatra tatraiva svarebhyo 'rvāk prayojya ca ।

pravaded yadi nāmnā 'sau svaravarṇakramo bhavet ॥ 125 ॥

It should be accentual phonic sequence (*svaravarṇakrama*) by name if one would recite after applying these ten [accents, that comprise] the three accents, acute (*udātta*), grave (*anudātta*) and accumulated[64] (*pracaya*) and also especially the seven circumflex accents (*svarita*s) [which are in turn pronounced] along with their appellations and manner of articulation, in the [properly designated] places before each vowel in the simple phonic sequence [that is] being uttered sequentially.

vyañjanānām udāttādīn varṇoktau na vadet svarān ।

One should not utter the accents like acute, etc. of the consonants in the reading of [accentual] phonic sequence.

UDĀTTĀDĪNĀṀ SAṀJÑĀḤ

Appellations of [the Accents that] Begin with Acute

tatra tāvad udāttādyās svarās tannāmavācakaḥ ॥ 126 ॥
prayatnāś ca krameṇaiva nirūpyante yathāvidhi ।

Meanwhile, the accents therein such as acute, their proper names and the manners of articulation are truly being determined in accordance with the rules, gradually.

---

[64] Whitney (1879: 30) renders the term *pracaya* as "accumulated".

uccair udātto nīcais tu nihataś cānudāttakaḥ || 127 ||
svaritas syāt samāhāraḥ svāra ity api cocyate |

The high-[pitch] is *udātta* (acute), the low [pitch] is, however, *nihata* or *anudātta* (grave) and the combination [of the high and the low-pitch] should be *svarita* (circumflex) which is also called *svāra.*

pareṣām anudāttānāṁ svaritāt padavartinām || 128 ||
saṁhitāyān tu pracaya udāttaśrutir iṣyate |

In the continuous reading, an acute tone (*udāttaśruti*) [called] *pracaya* (accumulated) is prescribed for the subsequent grave accents occurring in the word/words after a circumflex accent.

dhr̥tapracayaśabdau ca paryāyau staḥ parasparam || 129 ||

The words *dhr̥ta* (held) and *pracaya* (accumulated) are synonyms of each other.

SAPTASVARITALAKṢAṆĀNI SODĀHARAṆĀNI

Definitions of the Seven Circumflex Accents with Examples

svārās saptavidhā jñeyās tatprayatnāś caturvidhāḥ |

The circumflexes are known to be of seven types [and] their manners of articulation are of four types.

kṣaipraḥ prāthamikas svāro dvitīyo nityasaṁjñakaḥ || 130 ||

The first circumflex accent is *kṣaipra* (hastened). The second is designated as *nitya* (innate).

tr̥tīyas syāt prātihataś caturtho nāmato dvidhā |
tatrābhinihataś caika itaro 'bhihatas smr̥taḥ || 131 ||

The third one should be *prātihata* (obstructive). The fourth is of two types in terms of [its] names: one [of them] is termed as *abhinihata* (absorbed) and the other as *abhihata*[65] therein.

praśliṣṭaḥ pañcamaṣ ṣaṣṭho vr̥ttas syāt pādavr̥ttakaḥ |

---

65 *Abhihata* is the alternative designation of the same circumflex accent *abhinihata.*

Praśliṣṭa (coalesced) is the fifth. The sixth one should be *vṛtta* (hiatal) [or] *pādavṛtta* (same-word hiatal).

tairovyañjanasaṁjño yas svaritas saptamo bhavet || 132 ||

The circumflex accent which is designated as *tairovyañjana* (consonant-interventional) should be the seventh.

ivarṇotor yavatve saty uccayos svaryate ca yaḥ |
sa ca kṣaiprābhidhas svāras tryambakan drvanna ity api || 133 ||

The circumflex accent which is circumflexed when an acute *i*-vowel or an acute *u*-vowel becomes *y* or *v* [respectively] is designated as hastened. E.g., *tryàmbakam,*[66] also *drvànnaḥ.*[67]

pade sthite 'py apūrve vā nīcapūrve yavākṣaram |
svaryate yatra nityas syān nyañcaṅ kuhvā udāhṛtam || 134 ||

Where a syllable [containing] a *y* or a *v* is circumflexed in a fixed word, being preceded by a grave or not preceded by anything, it should be innate. *Nyàñcam*[68] [and] *kuhvà*[r69] are given as examples.

ucce nānāpadasthe 'pi śliṣṭena svaryate ca yaḥ |
sa prātihata eva syāt sa idhānas satejasam || 135 ||

Also, that, which is circumflexed through the connectedness [where] an acute occurs in another word, should be obstructive indeed. E.g., *sá idhānáḥ,*[70] *sátejasam.*[71]

nānāpade hy uccapūrvan nīcaȳ yat svaryate yadi |
vyakter abhāve bhāve 'pi sa prātihata iṣyate || 136 ||

If a grave, which is preceded by an acute that occurs in another word, is circumflexed in the absence of a hiatus or even in the presence of [the same], it is proclaimed as obstructive.

---

66 *TS* 1.8.6.

67 *TS* 4.1.9.

68 *TS* 3.1.11, 5.5.3.

69 *TS* 3.4.9.

70 *TS* 4.4.4.

71 *TS* 5.3.5, 6.1.7, 6.3.3-4.

tasminn akāralopaś cet pr̥thagbhūtapade tadā ।
svāro 'bhinihato jñeyas so 'bravīt te 'bruvann api ॥ 137 ॥

If there is an elision of a short *a* in a separate word the circumflex is to be known as absorbed. E.g., ***sò*** *'bravīt,*[72] also ***tè*** *'bruvan.*[73]

udāttapūrve tasmin syād ūbhāvas svaryate yadi ।
praśliṣṭākhyas sa sūdgātā sūnnīyam iva yas tathā ॥ 138 ॥

If there is [a grave] preceded by an acute [and consequently] a resultant *ū* is circumflexed, it should be designated as coalesced as in ***sū̀****dgātā*[74] and similarly in ***sū̀****nnīya.*[75]

yā tv akhaṇḍapade vyaktis sā bhaved ardhamātrikā ।
yas tasyāḫ paratas svāraḫ pādavr̥ttas sa kathyate ॥ 139 ॥

The hiatus which [occurs] in a single word should, however, be semi-moraic. The circumflex, which occurs after that (hiatus), is called same-word hiatal.

madhye padasya yā vyaktis tasyāñ ca svaritaś ca yaḥ ।
sa eva pādavr̥ttas syāt praügan nānyad iṣyate ॥ 140 ॥

The very circumflex accent which is there in a hiatus that [occurs] in the middle of a word should be same-word hiatal. E.g., *práǜgam;* nothing else is prescribed.

tiras tiryag iti proktaṁ hal vyañjanam iti smr̥tam ।
tena vyaveto yas svāras tairovyañjanasaṁjñkaḥ ॥ 141 ॥

Tiryak (intervention) is mentioned as *tiras*. Consonant is termed as *vyañjana.* The circumflex accent, which is separated by that (a consonant), is designated as consonant-interventional.

vyañjanena vyavahitaḫ pade tūdāttapūrvakaḥ ।
svarito yas sa eva syāt tairovyañjana ucyate ॥ 142 ॥

That very circumflex which would be separated by a consonant

---

[72] *TS* 2.1.2; *TB* 2.1.2, 2.2.3, 10.

[73] *TS* 2.5.1-2, 2.6.8, 3.2.2, 6.2.3, 6.4.6, 6.5.6; *TB* 3.9.11, 21.

[74] *TS* 7.1.8.

[75] *TS* 6.2.4.

[and] preceded by an acute in a [single] word is called consonant-interventional.

yas samānapade svāras svaryate hy uccapūrvakaḥ ।
sa tairovyañjano jñeya āpo vācam upāyavaḥ ॥ 143 ॥

In a same word, the circumflex, which is circumflexed, preceded by an acute, is to be known as consonant-interventional. E.g., *ā́pa**ḥ**,*[76] *vā́**ca**m,*[77] *upāyáv**a**ḥ.*[78]

SVARITĀNĀM PRAYATNABHEDĀḤ

Varieties of the Manners of Articulation of the Circumflexes

kṣaipre nitye prayatnas syāt svāre dṛḍhataro bhavet ।

The manner of articulation should be firmer (*dṛḍhatara*) in the hastened and innate circumflexes.

nīcapūrve 'bhinihate prayatno 'tidṛḍhas smṛtaḥ ॥ 144 ॥

The manner of articulation is proclaimed as very firm (*atidṛḍha*) in the absorbed circumflex that is preceded by a grave.

uccapūrve 'py apūrve ca prayatno dṛḍha iṣyate ।

The manner of articulation is required to be firm (*dṛḍha*) in the [absorbed circumflex] when it is either preceded by an acute or preceded by nothing.

praśliṣṭaprātihatayos sa vai mṛdutaras smṛtaḥ ॥ 145 ॥

It is indeed proclaimed as gentler (*mṛdutara*) in the coalesced and obstructive circumflexes.

sa tairovyañjane pādavṛtte cālpataras smṛtaḥ ।

It is proclaimed as feebler (*alpatara*) in the consonant-interventional and the same-word hiatal circumflexes.

---

[76] *TS* 1.3.12, 2.2.12, 3.3.4, 4.1.8, 4.2.3, 5.5.10, 5.6.1-2, 6.1.2, 6.3.8, 6.4.3; *TB* 2.5.8, 2.8.9, 3.2.5, 3.3.6, 3.7.4, 3.7.7, 3.7.14, 3.8.2.

[77] *TS* 1.1.10, 1.3.2, 1.6.8, 1.7.8, 3.1.8, 3.2.10, 4.3.6, 4.4.12, 7.3.14; *TB* 1.3.2, 1.3.6, 2.6.20, 3.1.2, 3.6.1.

[78] *TS* 1.1.1.

evaṁ svaritabhedānām prayatnānāñ ca bhedataḥ ।। 146 ।।
vivakṣayā lakṣaṇāni teṣām uktāni śāstrataḥ ।

Thus, according to [their] varieties, the definitions of the circumflex accents and their manners of articulations are stated from the theoretical system with the intention of expressing [them].

etat sarvaṽ viditvaiva svaravarṇakramaṽ vadet ।। 147 ।।

Only after knowing all this, one should enunciate the accentual phonic sequence.

MĀTRĀVARṆAKRAMALAKṢAṆAM

Definition of Moraic Phonic Sequence

athātas saṁhitādhyāye lakṣaṇair ānupūrvyaśaḥ ।
bhavanti yadyadvarṇānāỹ yadyatkālās suniścitāḥ ।। 148 ।।

tatra tatra ca te sarve svaravarṇe yathāvidhi ।
udāttādisvarebhyo 'rvāk prayujyante tathā yadi ।। 149 ।।

evam pāṭhakramo yas syān mātrikāvarṇa ucyate ।

Now, therefore, if all those time durations of the phones which are properly asserted in terms of the characteristics [of those phones] and which occur successively in the continuous reading, are used in their properly designated places before the accents such as *udātta*, etc. in the accentual phonic sequence and also in accordance with the rule [that continues being elaborated] such a sequence of reading is called moraic phonic sequence (*mātrāvarṇakrama*).

MĀTRĀKĀLALAKṢAṆAM

Definitions of Moraic Time Durations

mātrāṇāṅ kālaniyamā ucyante hetubhiḫ pr̥thak ।। 150 ।।

The rules for the different time periods of the morae are being stated with reasons.

brāhmaṇī nakulaś cāṣo vāyasaś ca śikhī kramāt ।
aṇvardhaikadvitrimātrān bruvate kālatas sukham ।। 151 ।।

A red-tailed skink, a mongoose, a jay, a crow and a peacock respectively cry [for the duration of] a minute mora, a half mora, a single mora, two morae and three morae in terms of time periods, with ease.

indriyāviṣayo yo 'sāv aṇur ity ucyate budhaiḥ ।

That which is not perceptible by the sense-organ is called minute by knowledgeable persons.

caturbhir aṇubhir mātrāparimāṇam iti smṛtam ॥ 152 ॥[79]

It is proclaimed that the duration of one mora is constituted by four minute morae.

ekamātro bhaved dhrasvo dīrghas syāt tu dvimātrikaḥ ।

A short vowel should be monomoraic whereas a long should be bimoraic.

trimātrikaḫ pluto jñeyo hrasvārdhan tv ardhamātrikam ॥ 153 ॥

A protracted vowel is to be known as trimoraic whereas the half of a short vowel is semi-moraic.

tatra raṅgapluto yas syāc cāturmātras sa kathyate ।
tan tu vyāghrarutānte yo ghaṇṭānādo 'nuvartate ॥ 154 ॥

That, which would be a nasally modified protracted *a*-vowel which the bell-gong[-like sound] follows at the end of the tiger-roar[-like sound], is considered as tetramoraic therein.

MĀTRĀKĀLOKTIVIVEKAḤ

Discussion on the Recitation of Moraic [Phonic Sequence]

saỹyuktaṽ vā 'py asaỹyuktaṽ vyañjanaṁ sasvaraỹ yadi ।
svarakālaṽ vadet tatra na pṛthag vyañjanasya tu ॥ 155 ॥

If a consonant, either conjoined or not conjoined [with another consonant] is [attached] with a vowel one should utter the time duration of the vowel there but not of the consonants.

---

[79] This verse is also found in *Śambhuśikṣā* (Chandra 1981: 535).

siddhe 'py ardhāṇumātratve sasvare vā pr̥thag ghali |
tathā 'pi na vadet tasya kālaȳ varṇakrameṣu vai || 156 ||

Although the semi-moraic or the quarter-moraic quality (*ardhamātratva*) is proved in a consonant that occurs either with a vowel or separately, one should never utter its time duration in the phonic sequences.

halas tv avasitā yatra tatraiṣāṅ kāla iṣyate |

But where the consonants are terminal their time duration is required.

anuttame tv ardhamātro virāmasthe vidhīyate || 157 ||

However, half of a mora in a non-nasal sound that occurs at a pause is mandated.

virāmastheṣūttameṣu kālādhikyam pradr̥śyate |

In the lasts that occur at pauses, excess of time is perceived.

pūrve 'nunāsikaṁ hrasvād dvimātraȳ yat tad ucyate || 158 ||
dīrghāt plutāc ca tanmātram ekamātram iti śrutiḥ |[80]

At the onset, it is being stated that a nasal preceded by a short vowel is bimoraic. It is the saying that after a long or a protracted vowel its mora is monomoraic.

avasāne viśeṣo 'yam anyeṣāñ ca na vidyate || 159 ||
saṁhitāyān tu tanmātraḫ padakāle 'dhiko bhavet |[81]

---

80 An almost identical verse is quoted in *Vaidikābharaṇa* (Sastri and Rangacarya 1906: 39):
hrasvāt paran tu nāsikyan dvimātraȳ yat tad ucyate |
dīrghāt plutāc ca tan mātram ekamātram iti śrutiḥ ||

81 This verse is also quoted in *Vaidikābharaṇa* (ibid.). *Vaidikābharaṇa* further goes on to paraphrase the verse as follows: *atra pūrvārdhena anavasānastheṣv atiprasaṅgaḫ parihr̥taḥ* | *saṁhitāyān tanmātra iti hrasvāt parasyāpi saṁhitāprayogakāle mātrikatvam evety ucyate* | *yas tu hrasvāt parasyādhikakāla uktas sa padādhyāya evety uktam, 'padakāle 'dhiko bhaved' iti* |

This speciality that occurs in termination (*avasāna*) does not take place elsewhere. In the continuous reading it (the terminal nasal preceded by a short vowel) is monomoraic. However, it should be more in the word-reading.

hrasvāt paro 'vasānasthaḥ padādhyāye 'nunāsikaḥ ।। 160 ।।
dvimātro mātrikas tv anyas saṁhitāyān tathā 'khilaḥ ।[82]

In the word-reading, the terminal nasal that occurs after a short vowel is bimoraic. [It is] monomoraic in the continuous reading. However, all other [nasals, which are preceded by long or protracted vowels] are likewise [monomoraic].

tattatkālān viditvaivam mātrikāvarṇam uccaret ।। 161 ।।

Thus, after knowing the time durations of each [of the phones], one should enunciate the moraic phonic sequence.

AṄGAVARṆAKRAMALAKṢAṆAM

Definition of Adjunctive Phonic Sequence

aṅgavarṇe halām ādāv aṅgaṁ saṁjñāñ ca nāma ca ।
acāṁ saṁjñāñ ca mātrāñ ca svaran nāma vadet kramāt ।। 162 ।।

In the adjunctive phonic sequence, one should first utter the adjunction, the designation and the appellation of the consonants [and then] the designation, the mora, the accent and the appellation of the vowels respectively.

AṄGALAKṢAṆAM

Definition of Adjunct

varṇānām aṅgavarṇe 'smin suspaṣṭañ cāṅgalakṣaṇam ।
pūrvatvena paratvena vidhinā vā sahocyate ।। 163 ।।

---

82 *Vaidikābharaṇa* quotes an identical verse (Sastri and Rangacarya 1906: 39). It is *akhilam* in the printed edition of *Vaidikābharaṇa* whereas in this text I found it to be *akhilaḥ*. The same verse occurs in *Āpiśaliṣikṣā* 14 (Vira 1981: 348) where it is exactly identical with *AS*.

The characteristic of adjunct that is uttered according to the precept of antecedence or succession is very clear in the adjunctive phonic sequence of the phones.

rājate 'sau svayaỹ yasmāt tasmāt tu svara ucyate ।

Since it subsists by itself (*svayam*) [i.e. independently] it is, therefore, called *svara* (vowel).

uparisthāyinā tena vyaṅgyaṽ vyañjanam ucyate ॥ 164 ॥

Being manifested (*vyaṅgya*) by the predominant one [i.e. the vowels], it is called *vyañjana* (consonant).

na śakyaṅ kevalaṁ sthātuṽ vyañjanan tu svaraṽ vinā ।

A consonant, however, is unable to stand alone without a vowel.

sāpekṣaṽ vyañjanan nityaṁ svaras tu nirapekṣakaḥ ॥ 165 ॥
vyañjanāni ca sarvāṇi svarāṅgāni bhavanti hi ।

A consonant is always dependent whereas a vowel is independent as all the consonants become adjuncts of the vowels.

PARĀṄGAPŪRVĀṄGALAKṢAṆAM

Definition of Adjuncts of Subsequent and Antecedent [Vowel]

bhavet parasvarasyāṅgaṽ vyañjanam prāyaśo 'pi hi ॥ 166 ॥
tatra pūrvasvarasyāṅgaṁ syād avasāne sthitañ ca yat ।

Mostly, a consonant should be the adjunct of the succeeding vowel indeed and [the consonant] which is situated at the end should be the adjunct of the preceding vowel.

parāyuktam anusvāro visargo bhaktir eva ca ॥ 167 ॥
yogādy asaỹyuto ṅo no rephas syād r̥pare sati ।

Also [the consonant] uncombined with the succeeding [vowel], *ṁ*, *ḥ*, the anaptyxis, the initial [consonant] of a conjunct, uncombined *ṅ* and *n* and *r* followed by *r̥* [should be the adjunct of the preceding vowel].

pūrvāṅgan na bhavet sparśa ūṣmaṇo vikr̥tir yadi ॥ 168 ॥

A stop does not become the adjunct of the preceding [vowel] if it is an alteration of a fricative.

sā parāṅgam bhavaty eva yā bhaktiḫ pracayāt parā ।

That very anaptyxis which follows an accumulated accent becomes the adjunct of the succeeding [vowel].

dhr̥te hy r̥kāre parato rephaś ca syāt parāṅgabhāk ।। 169 ।।

And of course, when followed by an accumulated *r̥, r* should be the adjunct of the succeeding [vowel].

parāṅgam asavarṇaṁ syād antassthāparam eva yat ।

A heterogeneous [consonant] which is followed by a semi-vowel should certainly be the adjunct of the succeeding [vowel].

parāṅge coṣmaṇi pare parāṅgaṁ sparśako yamāḥ ।। 170 ।।

Stops and twin phones, followed by a fricative that is an adjunct of the succeeding [vowel], become adjuncts of the succeeding [vowel].

AṄGAVARṆAKRAMOKTILAKṢAṆAM

Accurate Description of the Recitation of Adjunctive Phonic Sequence

paurvāparyakrameṇaiva viditvā 'ṅgam prayojayet ।

One should use [the word] *aṅga* after knowing [it] through the sequence of antecedence and succession.

halān tu pūrvaśabdaṽ vā paraśabdam athāpi vā ।। 171 ।।
uktvā tato 'ṅgaśabdan tu bhūtaśabdottaraṅ kramāt ।

halsaṁjñaketi saṁjñāñ ca nāma kārottaraṽ vadet ।। 172 ।।

However, [in the case] of the consonants, having enunciated either the word *pūrva* or the word *para,* one should utter the word *aṅga* before the word *bhūta,* the designation *halsaṁjñaka* and then the appellation followed by *kāra*, respectively.

acām acsaṁjñakety uktvā tanmātrāṁś ca tatas svarān ।
udāttādīṁs tato nāmāny ānupūrvyeṇa saṽvadet ।। 173 ।।

Having uttered the designations of the vowels as *acsaṁjñaka* one should properly utter their morae, then the accents such as *udātta* (acute), etc. and afterwards the appellations in due order.

saÿyogo yatra pūrvāṅgaṁ syāt savarṇātmako yadi ।
sakṛd eva vadet tatra pūrvāṅgādi paṭhet tataḥ ।। 174 ।।

One should utter [the words] *pūrva, aṅga,* etc. only once where a conjunct that consists of homogeneous [consonants] is the adjunct of the preceding [vowel] and then one should read on.

yogo yatrobhayāṅgaṁ syād yady ekavyañjanātmakaḥ ।
paurvāparyakramāt tatra pṛthag aṅgam prayojayet ।। 175 ।।

If a conjunct consisting of the same consonant would be the adjunct of both [vowels] one should use [the word] *aṅga* separately in due sequence of antecedence and succession therein.

yad yad uktaṁ śuddhavarṇe dvitvāgamayamādikam ।
aṅgavarṇe tu tat sarvan tatra tatra vadet kramāt ।। 176 ।।

One should, however, sequentially utter each of these there in the adjunctive phonic sequence — the duplication, twin phones, etc. which are stated in simple phonic sequence.

svaravarṇe svarā yadval lakṣaṇaiḥ pratipāditāḥ ।
mātrāś ca mātrikāvarṇe yathā yatra viniścitāḥ ।। 177 ।।

tān sarvān aṅgavarṇoktau tathā tatra vadet sudhīḥ ।

As the accents are explained through [their] characteristics in the accentual phonic sequence and as the morae are asserted in the moraic phonic sequence, an intelligent one should utter all those accordingly there in the reading of adjunctive phonic sequence.

VARṆASĀRABHŪTAVARṆAKRAMA ITYASYA NĀMNO NIRVACANAM

Etymology of the Term *Varṇasārabhūtavarṇakrama*

sarveṣām eva varṇānāṁ sārā dhvanyādayas smṛtāḥ ।। 178 ।।

The speech sounds (*dhvani*), etc. are proclaimed as the very ingredients (*sāra*) of all phones.

dhvanisthānādayo ye syus te dharmā iti kīrtitāḥ ।

Those [ingredients] which begin with speech sounds and the places of articulation are called attributes (*dharma*).

tair bhūto bhūtaśabdena prāpitārtha ihocyate ।। 179 ।।

(The phonic sequence) is produced (*bhūta*) by them (attributes of the phones). Here, "the attainment of significance" is conveyed by the word "produced".

sa tathokaś ca varṇānāṅ kramo varṇakramas sa ca ।
asau varṇakramaś ceti vigraho viśadīkr̥taḥ ।। 180 ।।

And, the sequence of phones (*varṇānāṅ kramaḥ*) is *varṇakrama* (phonic sequence) [as] it is uttered in that manner. This is [how] the compound word *varṇakrama* is illustrated.

tasmād ayaṽ varṇasārabhūtavarṇakramas smr̥taḥ ।

Therefore, this is proclaimed as *varṇasārabhūtavarṇakrama* (phonic sequence of the phonic attributes).

VARṆADHARMAKRAMAḤ

Order of Attributes of the Phones

ekasyoccādiyuktasyāpy acas savyañjanasya ca ।। 181 ।।
dharmāṣ ṣaḍviṁśatiḫ proktāẖ ka itīttham udāhr̥taḥ ।

Twenty-six attributes even of a single vowel comprising accents like acute and accompanied by a consonant are mentioned, as *ká* is [cited] as an example.

lakṣaṇaiś śabda evātra dhvanir ity ucyate tathā ।। 182 ।।

So, by definitions, sound (*śabda*)[83] itself is called speech sound.

dhvaniḫ prāthamiko dharmo dvitīyas sthānam ucyate ।

[83] Although *śabda* is translated as "sound" the word *śabda* has some higher significance that cannot be entirely connotated by its so-called English equivalent "sound".

Speech sound is the first attribute. The second is called place of articulation.

tr̥tīyaḫ karaṇaṽ vidyāt prayatnas syāt turīyakaḥ || 183 ||

One should know the articulator (*karaṇa*)[84] as the third. The manner of articulation should be the fourth.

devatā pañcamo jñeyaṣ ṣaṣṭho jātir ihocyate |

Deity (*devatā*) is to be known as fifth. The sixth is called class (*jāti*) herein.

aṅgan tu saptamaḫ prokto varṇasaṁjñā 'ṣṭamo bhavet || 184 ||

The seventh is called adjunct. The eighth should be the designation of the phone (*varṇasaṁjñā*).

ete dharmāḫ krameṇaiva vidhīyante halām iha |

Here, these attributes of the consonants are arranged in due order.

acān dharmāṣṭake 'py asminn ucyamāne sati kramāt || 185 ||
mātrākālaś ca vaktavyo madhye devaprayatnayoḥ |

The moraic time duration (*mātrākāla*) should be uttered between the deity and the manner of articulation while these eight attributes, which also belong to the vowels, are enunciated sequentially.

svarāṇān nihatādīnān daśa dharmās samīritāḥ || 186 ||

Of the accents such as grave ten attributes are mentioned.

tatrādau devatā jñeyā tato jātis tato guṇaḥ |

At first the deity is to be known, then class [and] then quality therein.

tato rekhādarśanaṁ syād aṅgāvasthātrayam punaḥ || 187 ||

Then there should be indication [of the accents] through the [interphalangeal] lines (*rekhādarśana*) [and] then the three physical conditions.

---

84 The accurate English rendering of the word *karaṇa* would be "instrument". In this discipline the term *karaṇa* is equivalent to articulator or especially active articulator.

tataṣ ṣaḍjādihetus syād utpattisthānakan tataḥ ।
tatsaṁjñā ca tataś caitān daśa dharmān vadet kramāt ॥ 188 ॥

Then there should be the cause of [the musical notes that] begin with *ṣaḍja* (*ṣaḍjādihetu*), then there should be the original abode and then its designation. One should utter these ten attributes respectively.

kevalasvaramātrāṅgavarṇeṣu catṛṣū[85] *ditāḥ* ।
ye ye dharmāś ca tān sarvān prayujyāsmin kramāt paṭhet ॥ 189 ॥

After applying all those attributes which are stated in the four phonic [sequences], viz. the simple, the accentual, the moraic and the adjunctive in this [phonic sequence produced by phonic attributes], one should read on, sequentially.

ANUSVĀRABHAKTIKAMPAVIṢAYE RAṄGAPLUTAVIṢAYE CA

[Order of Attributes] in the Contexts of ṁ, Anaptyxis, Tremulous and Nasally Modified Protracted a-Vowel

yo dharmaḥ pañcamatvena syād acāṽ varṇasārake ।
svarabhaktyaṁśabhūtānām acāṁ syāt saptamo hi saḥ ॥ 190 ॥

In the [phonic sequence of] the phonic attributes, that, which would be the fifth attribute of the vowels, should be the seventh [attribute] of those vowels which are constituents of the anaptyxes.

anusvārasya bhaktīnām aṁśabhūtājjhalām api ।
dharmān yathāvad dhvanyādīn varṇasāre vadet sadā ॥ 191 ॥

One should always utter even the vowels' and the consonants' attributes that start with speech sound, [wherein the vowels and the consonants] are the constituents of *ṁ* and the anaptyxes, accordingly in the [phonic sequence of] the phonic attributes.

anusvārasya varṇe 'smінn aṅgāt pūrvan tu mātrikām ।
apy anusvārabhaktyaṁśe vyaṅgyān dharmān kramād vadet ॥ 192 ॥

---

85 The form *catṛṣu* seems to be ungrammatical. The customary form is *caturṣu*. However, the form *catṛṣu* can be traced to *TB* 1.5.6, 3.8.9.

However, in this [phonic sequence of] phonic [attributes] of *ṁ*, one should [utter] the mora before the adjunct. Also, one should sequentially speak of the attributes that are implied in the portions of the anaptyxes and *ṁ*.

kampe tu taddhetukasvāradharmān ādau paṭhet tathā |
tasmād utpannakampasya ya ādyaṁśaś ca tasya tu || 193 ||

tripādādhikamātrasya dharmān svārasya noccaret |
tadantyāṁśasya nīcasya brūyād dharmān yathāvidhi || 194 ||

In the tremulous, first one should read accordingly the attributes of the circumflex that is the cause of that (the tremulous), but one should not pronounce the attributes of that circumflex which constitutes one and three quarter morae and which is the first part of the tremulous produced from that (the circumflex). But one should methodically speak of the attributes of the grave that is the final part of that (the tremulous).

śuddhavarṇo yathā tatra tathaivātrāpi yojayet |

One should thus add [the tremulous] here [in the phonic sequence of phonic attributes] as [it is] there [in] the simple phonic reading.

raṅgaplute tv avarṇoccaplutānām ānupūrvyaśaḥ || 195 ||
vaded dharmān varṇasāre tadante varṇasaṁjñakām |

In the [phonic sequence of] the phonic attributes [of] a nasally modified protracted *a*-vowel, one should, however, utter the attributes of the phone *a*, the acute and the protracted vowel in due order with the designation of the phone at its end.

sarvatrābhinidhānākhyo yas tasyāṅgan tathaiva ca || 196 ||
varṇasaṁjñām api brūyān nānyadharmān paṭhet sadā |

One should always exclusively speak of the designation of the phone whose appellation is "adjacent imposition" and also of that which is a part of it. One should never read the other attributes.

na dhvanyādīn yame brūyāt sthānān na niṣidhyate || 197 ||

In a twin-phone, one should not utter [some of the attributes] such as speech sound. [But] it is not restricted from the place of articulation.

ŚABDOTPATTIPRAKARAṆAM

Section on the Origin of Sound

athātra sarvavarṇānāỹ yājuṣāṇaṽ viśeṣataḥ ।
uccāraṇaprasiddhyarthaṁ śabdasyotpattir ucyate ॥ 198 ॥

Now, the origination of sound is being stated for the perfection in the articulation of all phones especially that of *Yajurveda.*

TATPRAKĀRAḤ

Its Types

nityaẖ karya iti dvedhā śabdas sāmānyato bhavet ।

Universally, the sound should be of two types, viz. eternal (*nitya*) [and] producible (*kārya*).

nityo 'vyakto vibhuś śabdo yo brahmavyapadeśabhāk ॥ 199 ॥

The eternal sound is unmanifested (*avyakta*) and omnipresent (*vibhu*), which attains the designation *Brahman.*

tasmād vyaktaẖ kāryaśabdaẖ kāryād utpadyate śrutiḥ ।
śruter nādas tato nālī nālyā uccāvacasvarāḥ ॥ 200 ॥

ete kramāt prajāyante śabdoccāraṇamātrataḥ ।

The producible sound is manifested from that. *Śruti*[86] originates from the producible sound. Resonance (*nāda*)[87] from *śruti,* from

[86] Though the word *śruti* literally means "audible" here it certainly does not refer to that range of sound which is audible to the listener. It is much subtler than the gross audible sound. It is perhaps the non-resonant primary manifestation of the sound. Cf. Shringy and Sharma (1978: 119).

[87] *Saṅgītaratnākara* 1.3.6 (Shringy and Sharma 1978: 113) suggests an interesting etymology for the word *nāda* — *nakāram prāṇanāmānan dakāram analaṽ viduḥ* । *jātaẖ prāṇāgnisaỹyogāt tena nādo 'bhidhīyate* ॥ (It is understood that the syllable *na* [of *nāda*] represents the vital force and *da* represents fire; thus being produced →

that (resonance) *nālī*,[88] from *nālī* the high and the low tunes — these are gradually produced just from the articulation of the sound.[89]

mitho 'pṛthaktvam eteṣān dīpatatprabhayor iva ।। 201 ।।

Their mutual inseparability is like that of the lamp and its light.

bhavanti nādapramukhā varṇoccāraṇahetavaḥ ।

The *nāda*, etc. become the causes of the articulation of the phones.

DHANINIRŪPAṆAPRAKARAṆE
ŚARĪRĀNTARGATAJĀṬHARĀGNISTHITIḤ

Situation of Stomach Fire Inside the Body in the Section on Determination of Speech Sound

upanābhy udaye sūkṣmadhamanīghuṭibandhanam ।। 202 ।।
ādhāraṁ sarvadhātūnām indriyāṇām bhavaty api ।

← by the interaction of the vital force and fire it is called *nāda*.) This etymological explanation entirely fits with the description of the production of sound discussed in the subsequent section where the detailed process of sound production in the astral body is elucidated.

88 The connotation of the word *nālī* is not clear to me. In the MSS, this word is written as *nāḷī*. There could be two possible explanations: *nālī* could be one of the twenty-two pitch-wise variations of the resonance recognized in the scale. According to the Indian yogic tradition, there are twenty-two minor *nāḍi*s which branch off crosswise from the central *nāḍī*, i.e. *suṣumṇā*. Cf. *Saṅgītaratnākara* 1.3.8 (Shringy and Sharma 1978: 115). These are responsible for producing speech sounds of different frequencies. *Nālī* may refer to that very sound whose frequency level is determined but has not yet been uttered from the mouth. Hence it is subtler than *svara* but grosser than *nāda*. The other explanation may suggest that the word *nālī* is related to the *śvāsanālī* (windpipe or trachea). *Nālī* may refer to that level of sound that has been produced in the trachea but which has not come out from the mouth and therefore, it is not audible to the listener. However, these are mere conjectures.

89 *Kārya, śruti, nāda, nālī* and *svara* are the sequential levels in the process of sound production. This text, however, does not give any explanation of *śruti, nāda* and *nālī*.

The subtle plexus (*ghuṭibandhana*) of arteries[90] (*dhamanī*) above the place close to the navel (*upanābhi*) is the base of all constituents of the body (*dhātu*) and also of the sense-organs (*indriya*).

tatpratyag āḍhakasthūlā 'py ardhāṅgulisamucchritā ।। 203 ।।
niścalā satatan dīptā jvālā vahnes tu jāṭharī ।

The static and ever-blazing flame of the stomach fire [located] behind that (plexus) however is 1 *āḍhaka* (a measure of grain) thick and is elevated up [to a height of] half-finger too.

parāṇusūkṣmāvaraṇā dhamanī tatparisthitā ।। 204 ।।
vāyunā pūritā vṛttā drutaṁ sañcaratā 'niśam ।

A circular artery with an extremely minute subtle surface, situated around that (the stomach fire), is filled by the air passing constantly [through it].

PRĀṆĀDĪNĀM PAÑCĀNĀṼ VĀYŪNĀṀ
STHĀNASTHITYĀDIKAM

[Aspects such as] Location, Situation of the Vital Airs Starting with Respirational Air

prāṇodānāpānasamā hṛtkaṇṭhagudanābhiṣu ।। 205 ।।
catvāras saṁsthitā dehe vyānas sarvāṅgasaṁśritaḥ ।

In the body, the four [vital airs] — the respirational air (*prāṇa*), the expirational air (*udāna*), the excretional air (*apāna*) and the digestional air (*sama*) are situated in the heart (*hṛt*), the throat (*kaṇṭha*), the rectum (*guda*)[91] and the navel (*nābhi*) [respectively while] the flatuous air (*vyāna*) is situated in all the organs.

---

[90] The word *dhamanī* is generally translated as artery. However, the translation may not be appropriate for this context since the subtle aspects of the *nāḍī*s are possibly being referred to here.

[91] The term *guda* might refer to the perineum as the excretional air involves not only anal excretion but also genital excretions and urination.

TEṢĀṀ STHŪLASŪKṢMARŪPACEṢṬĀVIŚEṢAḤ

Speciality of Their Gross and Subtle Activities

ete pañcāṁśakās tatra sthitvaivāṁśais tribhis tribhiḥ ।। 206 ।।
dvābhyān dvābhyāṁ śarīre 'smin svasvaceṣṭām prakurvate ।

In this body, these very five parts [of the vital air], situated in three and two respective portions, conduct their own operations.[92]

samas suṣīracakrasthas taundam barhiṣam āvati ।। 207 ।।

The digestional air residing in the porous energy centre (*suṣīracakra*) protects[93] the stomach fire.

nāḍīlatāśrito 'pānaś śikyamūle trikopari ।
vibhajyoccāraśamalau puraḥ paścāt kṣipaty adhaḥ ।। 208 ।।

Abiding in the creeper-like astral tube (*nāḍī*) [and] situated at the root of *śikya* (spine?) [and] above the sacrum (*trika*), the excretional air throws down the urine (*uccāra*)[94] and the faeces (*śamala*) on the front and the back [respectively] after separating [them].

sarvanāḍīs samāśritya vyānas sarvatra sañcaran ।
sadā vitanute sarvan namanonnamanādikam ।। 209 ।।

Residing in all channels (*nāḍī*), traversing everywhere, the flatuous air carries out all [activities] such as bending, lifting up etc.

---

92 *sthitvaivāṁśais tribhis tribhiḥ* ।। *dvābhyān dvābhyāṁ* . . . — this part is vague in my understanding. Further explanation is required clarifying why these five vital airs are put in groups of three and two.

93 *Avati* is generally translated as "protects". I have translated *āvati* — the same verb with an *ā* prefix as "protects" as I am unable to locate the precise meaning of the verb *āvati.*

94 In the dictionaries (Monier-Williams and Apte), the term *uccāra* is translated as "excrement"/ "discharge". In *Amarakośa, Nṛvarga* 67 (Oka 1913: 102), Amarasiṁha lists this word in between the words for urine, i.e. *mūtra, prasrāva* and faeces, i.e. *avaskara, śamala,* etc. From the context I gather that *uccāra* may refer to urine because it is clear from the text that it is distinct from *śamala,* i.e. faeces.

udāno galagartastho vyānadattaṁ rasādikam ।
ā jihvāmūlam utplutya gr̥hītvā 'ntaḥ kṣipaty adhaḥ ॥ 210 ॥

Abiding in the hole of the throat, the expirational air after rising up till the root of the tongue throws down the fluids, etc. that are given by the flatuous air, after taking them inwards.

hr̥tpadmakośapr̥ṣṭhasthe nāḍīnālanirantare ।
sthitvā sthāne balī prāṇo hrāsair vikasanair api ॥ 211 ॥

yathākramaṁ svayan datte bhuktimuktyos sr̥tim parām ।

Furthermore, the respirational air located at the back of the pericardium (*hr̥tpadmakośa*) close to the tubular pipe, strengthened by the decrease and increase, itself provides the final way of *bhukti* (enjoyment) and *mukti* (liberation) respectively.

prāṇādīnām imāś ceṣṭās sthūlās sūkṣmā tu kathyate ॥ 212 ॥

These are the gross activities of the respirational and the other vital airs. The subtle one is being elucidated:

prāṇo hr̥disthasvāṁśena kaṇṭhasthodānam aṁśataḥ ।
antar ākarṣati bahis tadaṁśo 'syāṁśakaṅ kramāt ॥ 213 ॥

The respirational air through its own portion located at the heart pulls the expirational air that is located at the throat, partially inwards and a part of it (respirational air) [pulls] its part (expirational air) respectively outwards.

ubhābhyāṁ śvāsarūpābhyām aṁśābhyān dhāryate vapuḥ ।

The body is being sustained through the portions: both the forms of breathing.

vivakṣuṇā "tmanā nunnam mano rudhvā galānilam ॥ 214 ॥
saha tena patitvā 'gnau jāṭhare tatsamutthayā ।

jvālayā bhedayaty āśu samānāvaraṇan tataḥ ॥ 215 ॥

Having obstructed the gular air (expirational air), the mind, pushed by the self wishing to speak, quickly breaks the surface of the digestional air by the flame that has risen up from the stomach fire after falling into it (the stomach fire) along with that (the gular air). Then:

bhinnāvṛtau same kaṇṭhavāyunā manasā saha ।
kaṇṭhoromadhyadeśasthe prāṇo 'ṁśaṁ svan niyacchati ॥216॥

After the surface of the digestional air is broken, the respirational air, with [the help of] the gular air and the mind, puts its own portion at the place located between the throat and the chest.

śrutyādiprakṛtiḫ kāryo nityāc chabdo 'tra jāyate ।

Here the producible sound, which is the origin of [the forms] that begin with *śruti*, is produced from the eternal [sound].

sthānaṁ kaṇṭhorasomadhyaṁ karaṇan tu samo 'nilaḥ ॥217॥
manaḫprayogo yatno 'sya syāc chabdotpattir īdṛśī ।

The origin of sound should be like this — its place is between the throat and the chest, the instrument is the digestional air, the effort is the application of the mind.

ittham uccāryamāṇeṣu śabdeṣu śvāsarodhiṣu ॥218॥
tadarthaṁ samam acchinnam ākṛṣyodanasaÿyute ।

manasy abhyutthite tasmin naiśceṣṭyaṁ soḍhum akṣamaḥ ॥219॥
samamadhye punaḫ prāṇas svāṁśenaiva pataty asau ।

While the sounds are being pronounced in such a way [that] the breath is confined, therefore the mind is raised up along with the expirational air pulling the imperforated digestional air [and] that very respirational air, unable to bear the motionlessness, falls amidst the digestional air again through its own portion.

tasmād vicchidyate tatra prāṇasaṅghaṭṭanāt samaḥ ॥220॥
chinnadhāro bhavaty āśu svasthānāntargataś ca saḥ ।

Therefore, the digestional air being situated at its own place gets separated there due to the collision with the respirational air and its edge is speedily rent.

sadyas tattvak tirodhatte prāṇodānau tu pūrvavat ॥221॥
viceṣṭete tadā tābhyām mahāñ chvāsaḫ prajāyate ।

Immediately that surface disappears. The respirational and the expirational airs become active as before. At that time, a heavy breath is produced by them.

bhūyo manaḫprayogena śabdas sampadyate tathā॥222॥

Thus the sound is brought forth through the application of the mind anew.

DHVANIBHEDĀḤ

Types of Speech Sound

kaṇṭhākāśagataḫ kāryaś śabda eva dhvanis smr̥taḥ।

The producible sound itself that appears in the space of the glottis (*kaṇṭha*) is termed as speech sound.

nādaś śvāso hakāraś cety evan tredhā dhvanir bhavet॥223॥

Thus the speech sound should be of three varieties, viz. voice (*nāda*), breath (*śvāsa*) and aspiration (*hakāra*).

kaṇṭhe tu sav̄vr̥te nādaś śvāsas syād vivr̥te sati।

There should be voice if the glottis is tense (*sav̄vr̥ta*) whereas [it should be] breath if it is lax (*vivr̥ta*).

madhyasthe tu hakāras syād varṇaprakr̥tayaś ca tāḥ॥224॥

There should be aspiration if [it] is in middle position. Those are the materials of phones (*varṇaprakr̥ti*).

TAJJĀTAVARṆĀḤ

Phones Originated from Them

nādajās svaraghoṣās syur hacaturthā hakārajāḥ।

The vowels and the voiced [consonants] are born out of voice. *H* and the fourths are born out of aspiration.

aghoṣāś śvāsajās tatra śvāso dvedhā 'lpako mahān॥225॥

The voiceless [consonants] are born from breath. In it, the breath is of two kinds — slight breath and hard breath.

prathamāś ca tadanye ca varṇā alpamahadbhavāḥ ।

The firsts and the phones other than [the firsts] originate from the slight and the hard [breaths respectively].

VARṆĀNĀṀ STHĀNAKARAṆAVIVEKAḤ

Discussion on the Places of Articulation and Articulators of the Phones

acāṁ sthānam upaśleṣo yatrānyāṅgasya tanyate ॥ 226 ॥

[That] is the place of articulation of the vowels where the approximation of another organ is rendered.

tad aṅgaṅ karaṇaṁ sthānasamīpe nīyate ca yat ।

And that organ which is brought close to the place of articulation is the articulator.

yad aṅgaṁ spr̥śyate 'ṅgena halāṁ sthānan tad iṣyate ॥ 227 ॥

The organ which is touched by another organ [i.e. the articulator] is regarded as the place of articulation of the consonants.

aṅgena spr̥śyate sthānay̐ yena tat karaṇaṁ halām ।

The organ by which the place of articulation is touched is the articulator of the consonants.

saṁhitāyām aco nityay̐ yatrāvyañjanapūrvakāḥ ॥ 228 ॥
bhavanti teṣāṁ sthānoktau pūrvaṅ kaṇṭheti sav̐vadet ।

Where the vowels do not precede a consonant in the continuous reading one should first utter *kaṇṭha* during the utterance of their place of articulation.

akāroccāraṇe cauṣṭhau hanū nātyupasaṁhr̥tau ॥ 229 ॥
kāryau tu dīrghaplutayor na cātivivr̥tā ime ।

The lips and the jaws (*hanu*) should not be too nearly approximated in the articulation of *a*, whereas in long and protracted [*a*] they [should not be] separated too widely.

upaśleṣyam ivarṇoktau jihvāmadhyan tu tāluni ॥ 230 ॥

However, during the pronunciation of the phone *i* the middle of the tongue should be brought close to the palate.

oṣṭhāv uvarṇe dīrghau sta upaśleṣayutau tathā ।

During the [articulation of] the phone *u* the lips are long (protruded) and are also brought close to [each other].

pr̥thag oṣṭhopasaṁhāro nārdhamātrāntare bhavet ॥ 231 ॥
ekamātrāntaratvasya syāt tu sarvatra sambhave ।[95]

Separate contiguity of the lips should not be there during the gap of half of a mora. However, it should always be there during the occurrence of a monomoraic gap.

r̥varṇe l̥ti ca syātām oṣṭhau nātyupasṁhr̥tau ॥ 232 ॥
hanū atyupasaṁhārye jihvāgram barsvake bhavet ।

During [the articulation of] *r̥* and *l̥* the lips should not be too nearly approximated. The jaws should be very nearly approximated. The tip of the tongue should be in the alveolar ridge.

ekāre 'vyañjane jihvāprāntāv īṣadyutoṣṭhakau ॥ 233 ॥
karaṇan tālu tu sthānam atiśliṣṭahanūrdhvayuk ।

In the [articulation of] *e* that is not [associated] with a consonant[96] the articulator is both sides of the tongue with the lips slightly brought close together, whereas the place of articulation is the palate connected to the upper jaws (*hanūrdhva*) which are in turn approximated very closely.

savyañjane 'smin karaṇam īṣacchliṣṭoṣṭhayug bhavet ॥ 234 ॥
jihvāmadhyaṁ sthānam atiśleṣavad dhanutālukam ।

If it (*e*) is associated with a consonant,[97] the articulator should be the middle of the tongue with the lips slightly approximated [and]

---

95 This verse is quoted in *Vaidikābharaṇa* (Sastri and Rangacarya 1906: 81) as well as in *Yājuṣabhūṣaṇa* commentary on *Pāriśikṣā* (Chandra 1981: 333).

96 Not preceded by a consonant.

97 Preceded by a consonant.

the place of articulation should be the palate connected to the jaws that are approximated very closely.

hanū anativiśleṣe oṣṭhau cātyupasaṁhṛtau ।।235।।
dīrghau ca bhavatas tatra tv okāroccāraṇe sati ।

However, during the articulation of *o* the jaws are not too widely separated and the lips become long (protrude) and are closely approximated.

aṇus tv ādāv ad edotor antye sa tryaṇukas tv id ut ।।236।।

In *e* and *o,* there is a minute (one-fourth of a mora) *a* in the beginning, whereas at the end *i* and *u* comprise of three minute [morae respectively].

aikāraukārayor ādāv akāras tv ardhamātrikaḥ ।
ivarṇovarṇayoś śeṣau syātām adhyardhamātrikau ।।237।।

However, in *ai* and *au, a* in the beginning is semi-moraic. The remainders of the phones *i* and *u* [respectively] should both be of one-and-half of a mora.

aikāraukārāvayaveṣv adidutsu yathākramam ।
adidutsthānakaraṇaprayatnā eva nānyathā ।।238।।

Those very places of articulation, the articulators and the manners of articulation of *a, i* and *u* should respectively be in *a, i* and *u* which are the components of the phones *ai* and *au* [and] not otherwise.

edotor adidut svalpo 'py atra na śrūyate pṛthak ।

Here in *e* and *o,* even a tiny *a, i* and *u* are not separately audible.

nāto 'sti teṣān dharmo 'sya kintv etvan tv otvam eva hi ।।239।।

They do not have the quality of this *a* as there are, however, the qualities of *e* and *o* only.

aidautor ādyakārasya karaṇībhavadoṣṭhakaḥ ।
saṽvṛtākhya iti prāhur varṇakramavicakṣaṇāḥ ।।240।।

The persons [who are] well-versed in phonic sequences call the lips, which are the articulators of the initial *a* phone of *ai* and *au,* with the term "tense" (*saṽvr̥ta*).

uccāraṇe kavargasya hanūmūlaṁ[98] *spr̥śed budhaḥ* ।
jihvāmūlena cor uktau jihvāmadhyena tālu ca ॥ 241 ॥

During the articulation of *ka*-series a knowledgeable person should touch the root of the [upper] jaws with the root of the tongue and in the enunciation of *ca*-series [he/she should touch] the palate with the middle of the tongue.

jihvāgreṇa ṭavarge tu prativeṣṭya śiras spr̥śet ।

In the *ṭa*-series one should, however, touch the roof of the oral cavity (*śiras*)[99] with the tip of the tongue rolling it back.

jihvāgratas tavarge ca dantamūleṣv adhas tathā ॥ 242 ॥

And in that manner in the *ta*-series [one should touch] below the root of the teeth.

adhareṇottaroṣṭhan tu pavargoccāraṇe spr̥śet ।

In the articulation of *pa*-series, one should, however, touch the upper lip with the lower lip.

jihvāmadhyasya parśvābhyān tālu yoccāraṇe spr̥śet ॥ 243 ॥

In the articulation of *y* one should touch the palate with the sides of the root of the tongue.

jihvāñcalasya madhyena dantamūlopari kramāt ।
āsannam atyāsannañ ca pradeśaṁ ralayos spr̥śet ॥ 244 ॥

In [the articulation of] *r* and *l* one should respectively touch the

[98] *Hanūmūla,* the word which is also used in *TP* 2.35, is an irregular form of *hanumūla.*

[99] The literal rendering of the word *śiras* or its synonym *mūrdhan* is head. Commenting on *TP* 2.37, *Vaidikābharaṇa* (Sastri and Rangacarya 1906: 86) gives the alternative term for *śiras* as *mūrdhan* — *mūrdhā śiraḥ. Tribāṣyaratna* (Sastri and Rangacarya 1906: 86) explicates the connotation of the term *mūrdhan* saying that it refers to the upper part of the oral cavity — *mūrdhaśabdena vaktravivaroparibhāgo vivakṣyate.*

place[s] that are close and very close to the root of the teeth with the middle of the blade of the tongue.

adharoṣṭhāgrabhāgena bāhyenordhvadatas spṛśet ।
oṣṭhyasvarāntarasthe ve tadbhinne tv āntareṇa cet ॥ 245 ॥

During [articulation of] *v*, if [*v*] occurs in between the labial vowels, one should touch the upper teeth with the outer edge of the lower lip whereas in other cases [one should touch the upper teeth] with the inner [edge of the lower lip].

jihvāmūlīyapūrvāṇāṁ habhinnānān tathoṣmaṇām ।
kavargādiṣu yat sthānan tad eva syur[100] *yathākramam* ॥ 246 ॥

karaṇānān tu yat teṣām madhyan tu vivṛtam bhavet ।

Similarly, those very places of articulation of the series that begin with *ka* should respectively be those of the fricatives that start with *ẖ* except *h*. The middle of their articulators should, however, be lax.

visargasya ca hasya syāt sthānañ ca karaṇaṅ galaḥ ॥ 247 ॥

The place of articulation and the articulator of *ḥ* and *h* should be the glottis.

uro hasyottamāntassthāparatve syāt tu taddvayam ।

Both of them (the place of articulation and the articulator) of *h* should be the chest[101] when followed by a last or a semi-vowel.

vargāntyā nāsikāmātrasthānakā hat pare 'pare ॥ 248 ॥
mukhāvayavanāsikyā nāsikā nasvikāsataḥ ।

[If] there are final [phones] of the series after *h*, [the nose-sound] has exclusively the nose as [its] place of articulation. [If they] (final phones of the series) do not occur after *h* (i.e. they occur after the non-nasal stops) the nose sounds have the mouth [also as their] place of articulation [along with the nose. They are] nasal because

---

100 There is an inconsistency here with regard to the agreement of number. The reading should be *syāt*.

101 As the chest is the place of articulation and the articulator of *h*, that *h* is a pulmonic sound in this case.

of the opening of the nose.

or[102]

The nose-sounds that occur after *h* and which exclusively have the nose as their place of articulation [and when they] do not occur after *h,* have the mouth [also] as their place of articulation, are [just like the] final [phones] of the series, nasal because of the opening of the nose.

VARṆĀNĀM PRAYATNABHEDĀḤ

Various Manners of Articulation of the Phones

prayatnāḫ pañcadhā jñeyā varṇānāṁ saṽvṛtādayaḥ ।। 249 ।।
saṽvṛto vivṛtas spṛṣṭa īṣatspṛṣṭo 'tipūrvakaḥ ।

The manners of articulation of the phones that begin with closed are known to be of five types — closed (*saṽvṛta*), open (*vivṛta*), touched (*spṛṣṭa*), partially touched (*īṣatspṛṣṭa*) and excessively touched (*atispṛṣṭa*).

saṽvṛto 'kāramātrasya prayatnaḫ parikīrtitaḥ ।। 250 ।।

Closed (*saṽvṛta*) manner of articulation is proclaimed to be exclusively of *a*.

prayatno vivṛto 'nyeṣāṁ svarāṇām ūṣmaṇām api ।

The manner of articulation of other vowels and also of the fricatives is open.

sparśeṣu spṛṣṭatā 'ntassthāsv īṣatspṛṣṭatvam īritam ।। 251 ।।

Touched and partially touched are said to be in the stops and in the semi-vowels [respectively].

dvitīyāś ca caturthāś cāpy atispṛṣṭaprayatnajāḥ ।

The seconds and the fourths are born through the excessively touched manner of articulation.

atispṛṣṭe caturthānān nyūnatvaṅ kiñcid iṣyate ।। 252 ।।

---

102 The verse can be interpreted in either way.

Some [amount of] slightness is required in the excessively touched [manner of articulation] of the fourths.

DEVATĀLAKṢAṆAM

Definition of Deities

devatā vedavarṇānāṽ vāyvagnikṣmendubhānavaḥ ।

The deities of the Vedic phones are the wind, the fire, the earth, the moon and the sun.

yaṣakārāv edavarṇau prathamā vāyudevakāḥ ॥253॥

Y, ṣ, e, a and the firsts belong to the god of wind.

āgneyā aidivarṇau ca dvitīyāś ca rasāv api ।

Ai, i, the seconds and also *r* and *s* belong to the fire.

uvarṇa ot tr̥tīyāś ca halau syur bhūmidevakāḥ ॥254॥

U, o, h, l and the thirds should belong to the goddess of earth.

r̥varṇa auc caturthāś ca vaḷau cāndramasās smr̥tāḥ ।

R̥, au, v, ḷ and the fourths are proclaimed to be [associated with] the moon.

l̥kārottamaśās sauryā netareṣān tu devatāḥ ॥255॥

L̥, ś and the lasts belong to the sun. However, others do not have deities.

JĀTILAKṢAṆAM

Definition of Class

vargaprathamavarṇāś ca svarās syur brahmajātayaḥ ।

The first phones of the series and the vowels should belong to the class brāhmaṇa.

kṣātrā dvitriturīyās syur viśo 'ntassthottamā api ॥256॥

The seconds, the thirds and the fourths should be kṣatriya. The semi-vowels [and] also the lasts are vaiśya.

śūdrā ūṣmavisargānusvārās syur iti niścitāḥ ।

The fricatives, *ḥ* and *ṁ* should be asserted as śūdra.

VARṆASAṀJÑĀ

Designations of the Phones

acas svarā vyañjanāni sparśāntassthoṣmaṇo halaḥ ।। 257 ।।

aghoṣaghoṣavadvargaprathamādyuttamādayaḥ ।
hrasvadīrghaplutā bhaktikamparaṅgaplutā yamaḥ ।। 258 ।।

visargajihvāmūlīyopadhmānīyādayas tathā ।
anusvārādayaś caite varṇasaṁjñā iti smṛtāḥ ।। 259 ।।

The designations of the phones are termed as *svaras*, i.e. the vowels, *vyañjanas*, i.e. the consonants, *sparśa* (stop), *antassthā* (semi-vowel), *ūṣman* (fricative), *aghoṣa* (voiceless), *ghoṣavat* (voiced), *prathama* (first), *uttama* (last), etc. of the series, *hrasva* (short vowel), *dīrgha* (long vowel), *pluta* (protracted vowel), *bhakti* (anaptyxis), *raṅgapluta* (nasally modified protracted *a*-vowel), *yama* (twin phone), *visarga* (*ḥ*), *jihvāmūlīya* (*ẖ*), *upadhmānīya* (*ḫ*) and *anusvāra* (*ṁ*).

UDĀTTĀDĪNĀN DEVATĀNIYAMAḤ

Precept Regarding the Deities of [the Accents] Beginning with the Acute

sūryāgnicandravasudhāś catvāraś ca kramād iha ।
dhṛtānudāttasvāroccasvarāṇān devatās smṛhāḥ ।। 260 ।।

The sun, the fire, the moon and the earth — these four are proclaimed as the deities of the accents — the accumulated, the grave, the circumflex and the grave, respectively.

JĀTIḤ

Class

uccanīcasvāradhṛtās svarāś catvāra eva ca ।
brahmakṣatriyaviṭśūdrā āsañ jātyā kramād iha ।। 261 ।।

Indeed, the four accents — the acute, the grave, the circumflex and the accumulated — were respectively the brāhmaṇa, the kṣatriya, the vaiśya and the śūdra by class herein.

GUṆALAKṢAṆAM

Qualities

sāttvikas syād guṇenoccas svarito rājasas smṛtaḥ ।
dvau tāmasaguṇau syātām anudāttadhṛtāv api ॥ 262 ॥

The acute should have *sattva* as its quality, the circumflex is proclaimed to have *rajas,* [and] also both the grave and the accumulated should have *tamas* as their quality.

HASTASVARAVINYĀSALAKṢAṆAM

Feature of Manual Demonstration of Accents

yas svaranyāsakṛd vidvān sa āsīnas tv atandritaḥ ।
kṛtvā gokarṇavad dhastan dakṣiṇan dakṣajānuni ॥ 263 ॥

kramāt svareṣu haste ca mano dṛṣṭin niveśya ca ।
yathāśāstraṁ svaranyāsam aṅguṣṭhāgreṇa vinyaset ॥ 264 ॥

Having fixed the mind and the gaze respectively on the accents and on the hand, the scholar who is a demonstrator of the accents should exhibit the accentual demonstration with the tip of the thumb in accordance with the theoretical system while being seated unwearied, having positioned the right hand like a cow's ear on the right knee.

tadā yady āgataḥ pūjyo gurur vā devatā 'pi vā ।
praṇamyātha nyaset tiṣṭhaṅ kṛtvā nābhisamaṅ karam ॥ 265 ॥

If an honourable one, either a *guru* or a god has come at that time, one should continue the demonstration, sitting [and] positioning the hand like the navel after bowing to [him/her].

yadi tair abhyanujñātas so 'bhyāsakaraṇe sati ।
āsīna eva kurvīta svaranyāsaỹ yathāvidhi ॥ 266 ॥

If he who is practising the [demonstration] is allowed by them, he should perform the accentual demonstration methodically only while sitting.

udāttan nirdiśen nyāse tarjanīmadhyaparvaṇi ।

nīcaṅ kaniṣṭhikādau ca madhyamāmadhyame dhr̥tam ॥ 267 ॥

svārañ cānāmikāntye tu sarvatraivaṽ vinirdiśet ।

During the demonstration, however, one should indicate the acute on the middle knot of the index finger, the grave on the first knot of the little finger, the accumulated on the middle knot of the middle finger and the circumflex on last knot of the ring finger. One should show [the indications] in this manner in every case.

yas svaras syāt pr̥thagbhaktes svarekhāsthānam āpnuyāt ॥ 268 ॥

The vowel which would belong to the discrete anaptyxis (*pr̥thagbhakti* or *svatantrā svarabhakti*) should attain its own place in the [interphalangeal] lines.

syād yatrocca iva svāras syāt tadūrdhvasthitaś ca yaḥ ।
kramād anāmikāyās tau vinyasen madhyamāntyayoḥ ॥ 269 ॥

Where a circumflex would be like an acute and [the accent] which would be situated after that, those should be demonstrated respectively on the middle and the last [interphalangeal line] of the ring finger.

ādyantyāṁśau svārakampe yau syātāṁ svāranīcakau ।
anāmikāntyādimayos tau nyased dvāv api kramāt ॥ 270 ॥

One should demonstrate both the circumflex and the grave, which would be the former and the latter portions in a circumflex tremulous, respectively, on the last and the first [interphalangeal lines] of the ring finger.

tataś codāttakampe tu yāv uccanihatau ca tau ।
madhyādyayoẖ pradeśinyāẖ kramāt sannirdiśed api ॥ 271 ॥

Furthermore, one should, however, demonstrate the acute and the grave also, which are there in the acute tremulous, respectively on the middle and the first [interphalangeal lines] of the index finger.

virāme vyañjanaỹ yat tad uccāraṇavaśāt kvacit ।
svarāntaraśrutiṁ samyak svatantram iva cāpnuyāt ॥ 272 ॥

tathā 'pi tasya vinyāse pr̥thak sthānan na nirdiśet ।

Though a consonant which, due to its articulation at a pause, would somewhere attain a tone exactly like that of another vowel [as if] it occurs separately (i.e. not as an adjunct of any other vowel) one should not indicate its separate place during the demonstration.

SVARAVINYĀSAPHALAM

Fruit of Accentual Demonstration

ya evaṁ svaravarṇārthāñ chāstradr̥ṣṭyā 'nucintayan ॥273॥

svaranyāsakrameṇaiva saha vedam imam paṭhet ।
sa pūtas sarvavedaiś ca param brahmābhigacchati ॥274॥

He, who would read this Veda in this manner along with the very sequences of the accentual demonstration contemplating on the accents, the phones and [their] significance with a vision of the theoretical system, is pure by all the Vedas and attains the Ultimate *Brahman*.

AṄGĀDYAVASTHĀ

Conditions of Organs, etc.

gātradairghyan dhvaner dārḍhyaṅ kaṇṭhākāśāṇutā tathā ।
tisro 'vasthā imāś śabdam uccaiḫ kurvanti tatra tu ॥275॥

These three conditions — the tension of the organs, the hardness of the speech sound as well as the minuteness of the space in the glottis — make a high sound therein.

hrasvatā yā ca dehasya mr̥dutā ca dhveś ca yā ।
mahattā kaṇṭhakhasyaitā nīcaiḫ kurvanti śabdakam ॥276॥

The relaxation which is of the organ, the softness which is of the speech sound and the wideness of the space in the glottis make a low sound.

ṢAḌJĀDISVARANIRŪPAṆAM

Determination of the Notes Beginning from Ṣaḍja

nīcāt ṣaḍjarṣabhau jātāv uccād gāndhāramadhyamau ।
niṣādaḥ pañcamaś caiva dhaivataś ca trayas svarāḥ ॥ 277 ॥

svaritaprabhavās teṣām punas tatkāraṇakramaḥ ।

Ṣaḍja (sa) and *ṛṣabha* (ri) are born from the grave, and *gāndhāra* (ga) and the *madhyama* (ma) are from the acute. The three notes — *niṣāda* (ni), *pañcama* (pa) and *dhaivata* (dha) — originate from the circumflex. Furthermore, their sequence of origin is:

nityābhinihatakṣaipra niṣādasvarahetavaḥ ॥ 278 ॥

The innate, the absorbed and the hastened [circumflexes] are the causes of the note ni.

hataśliṣṭāv ubhau syātām pañcamasvarahetukau ।

Both the obstructive and the coalesced should be the causes of the note pa.

tairovyañjanavṛttābhyāñ jāyate dhaivatasvaraḥ ॥ 279 ॥

The note dha is born from the consonant-interventional and the same-word hiatal [circumflexes].

dīrghahrasvānudāttābhyāñ jātau ṣaḍjarṣabhāv ubhau ।

Both sa and ri are born from the long and the short graves [respectively].

udāttapracayābhyān tu gāndhāro madhyamas tathā ॥ 280 ॥

Thus, ga and ma, however, are from the acute and the accumulated [circumflexes respectively].

rauti kvaṇaty ajā krauñco gāndhāram madhyamaṅ kramāt ।

A she-goat bleats ga [and] a crane whoops ma, respectively.

kekārutasamaṣ ṣaḍja ukṣā rauty ṛṣabhasvaram ॥ 281 ॥

Sa resembles the cry of a peacock. An ox bellows the note ri.

niṣādam bṛṁhate kumbhī pikaḫ kūjati pañcamam ।

An elephant trumpets [the note] ni. A cuckoo coos pa.

hayaheṣātulyarūpaṁ sav̄vidyād dhaivatasvaram ॥ 282 ॥

One should consider the note dha similar to the neigh of a horse.

UDĀTTĀDISVAROTPATTISTHĀNAM

Place of Origin of the Accents Beginning with the Acute

anudātto hṛdi jñeyo mūrdhny udātta udāhṛtaḥ ।

The grave is known to be in the heart. The acute is mentioned as [originating] in the head.

svaritaḫ karṇamūlīyas sarvāṅge pracayas smṛtaḥ ॥ 283 ॥[103]

The circumflex belongs to the root of the ears. The accumulated is proclaimed to be in the entire body.

VEDĀDHYAYANAPHALAM

Fruit of Vedic Studies

aṅgamātrādayo dharmāḫ pūrvam eveditāś ca ye ।
tān sarvān varṇasāre 'smin tatra tatra prayojayet ॥ 284 ॥

In this [phonic sequence of] phonic attributes, one should apply all those attributes such as adjunct and mora, which are already stated before, in their due place.

evaṁ salakṣaṇav̄ vedaȳ yo 'dhīte 'dhyāpayaty api ।
na tat kalpasahasraiś ca gadituṁ śakyate phalam ॥ 285 ॥[104]

That fruit cannot be verbalized even in thousands of aeons even if a

---

103 This verse is quoted in *Tribhāṣyaratna* (Sastri and Rangacarya 1906: 517) as well as in *Vaidikābharaṇa* (Sastri and Rangacarya 1906: 43). It is also found in *Śambhuśikṣā* (Chandra 1981: 534).

104 *Tribhāṣyaratna* (Sastri and Rangacarya 1906: 529) quotes another verse of two lines in which the first line differs but the second line is similar to verse 285 with a slight change (*sahasraiś ca* is read as *sahasreṇa*). *Tribhāṣyaratna* (ibid.) ascribes the concerned verse to *Brahma-Purāṇa*.

person learns and also teaches the Veda along with [its] definitional texts in this manner.

VEDAMAHIMĀ

Magnificence of the Veda

veda eva paro dharmo veda eva paran tapaḥ ।
veda eva param brahma sarvaṽ vedamayañ jagat ॥ 286 ॥

Veda is only the ultimate *dharma*. Veda is only the ultimate *tapas*. Veda is the ultimate *Brahman*. The whole world is permeated by the Veda.

tasmāc chreyaḫ param prāptuṽ vidhinaiva guror mukhāt ।

Therefore, it is of course better to attain the Ultimate in accordance with the precept from *guru*'s lips.

adhyetavyo 'khilair viprair eṣa dharmas sanātanaḥ ॥ 287 ॥

[The Veda] should be studied by all brāhmaṇas. This is the perpetual *dharma*.

dharmeṇa ya imām brāhmīṽ vidyāṁ śiṣyāya bodhayet ।
nandanti devatās sarve taṽ vipran nāviśed bhayam ॥ 288 ॥

All gods are delighted and fear cannot affect the brāhmaṇa who would teach this Brahmic knowledge to the disciples in accordance with the *dharma*.

ADHYAYANARAHITADOṢAḤ

Harm Done for not Studying [the Veda]

yo hitvā brāhmaṇo vedān anyagranthe pravartate ।
brahmatyāgī sa vijñeyaẖ karmaśūdra iti smṛtaḥ ॥ 289 ॥

The brāhmaṇa, who gets engaged in other treatises leaving the Vedas, is to be known as "Brahman-relinquisher" and is proclaimed as "śūdra by activity"/ "śūdra in actions".[105]

---

[105] Two interpretations of the compound word *karmaśūdra* are possible.

vedahīnasya viprasya sarvaśāstrapragalbhatā ।
vastrahīnasya dehasya sarvabhūṣaṇatā yathā ॥ 290 ॥

Without [the knowledge] of the Veda, the boastfulness of a brāhmaṇa with regard to all [other] theoretical systems is like an entire ornamentation of a body that is devoid of cloth.

yo nirākṛtinā vipras sa jagdhiṅ kurute yadā ।
sa vipras tu tadā "pnoti surāpānaphalan dhruvam ॥ 291 ॥

However, when he, who is a brāhmaṇa lacking in the knowledge of the Veda, consumes [something] he certainly obtains the fruit of drinking wine.

tadā 'nirākṛtis so 'yaĩ labhate pāvanam param ।

Therefore, he who has studied the Vedas obtains the sacred Ultimate.

tasmān nirākṛteḫ pāpan na kuryāt paṅktibhojanam ॥ 292 ॥[106]

Hence, one should not attend the sinful social feast of the brāhmaṇa who has not duly studied the Veda.

vedāṁś ca śrotriyam brahma ye ke dūṣyanti mānavāḥ ।
te ghoran narakam prāpya jāyante bhuvi sūkarāḥ ॥ 293 ॥

Those human beings who spoil the Vedas, the brāhmaṇa well-versed in the Vedas and the brāhmaṇa, take birth as hogs on the earth having attained the awful hell.

SĀṄGAVEDĀDHYAYANAPHALAM

Fruit of the Comprehensive Study of the Veda

vedarūpavilasat parāt paraỹ
ye paṭhanti vidhinā dvijottamāḥ ।

te trivargam iha cānubhūya tac
chāśvatam padam avāpnuyuḫ param ॥ 294 ॥

---

106 Both the manuscripts provide the meaning of the word *nirākṛti* as "a person who is devoid of study": *nirākṛtir adhyayanarahita ity arthaḥ.*

Those, the superiors amongst the twice-borns, who methodically read the shining form of the Veda that is beyond the supreme, would attain the ultimate eternal abode after experiencing the three categories [of possible human pursuits, i.e. *dharma, artha* and *kāma*] in this [world].

ity ātreyaśīkṣāmūlaṁ sampūrṇam ||

Thus the original [text] of the *Ātreyaśīkṣā* is completed.

Appendix 1

Index of Half-Verses

अकारेण व्यवेतः... ४७
अकारोच्चारणे चौष्ठौ... २२९
अखण्डवेष्टनं... ३७
अखण्डवेष्टनेङ्ग्या... ४२
अखण्डे स्वरयो०... ५८
अघोषघोषवद्वर्ग०... २५८
अघोषाः स्युश्च... ८
अघोषाः श्वासजा०... २२५
अघोषादूष्मणः... ६१
अङ्गं तु सप्तमः... १८४
अङ्गमात्रादयो धर्माः... २८४
अङ्गवर्णो तु तत्... १७६
अङ्गवर्णो हला०... १६२
अङ्गेन स्पृश्यते... २२८
अचः स्वरा इति... २
अचः स्वरा व्यञ्जनानि... २५७
अचां धर्माष्टके०... १८५
अचां संज्ञां च... १६२
अचां स्थानमुप०... २२६
अचामच्संज्ञकेत्युक्त्वा... १७३
अच्पूर्वं व्यञ्जनोर्ध्वं... ५३
अणुस्वादावदेदोतोरन्त्ये... २३६
अणवर्धैकद्वित्रिमात्रान्... १५१
अतिस्पृष्टे चतुर्थानां... २५२
अत्र सैव विवृत्तिस्तु... ८४
अत्वमित्वं तथोत्वं... ७९
अथ मध्यमभागे... १०३
अथातः संहिता०... १४८
अथात्र सर्ववर्णानां... १९८
अथान्त्यभागे नासिक्य... १०४
अधरेणोत्तरोष्टं... २४३
अधरोष्ठाग्रभागेन... २४५
अध्यायान्तेऽनुवाकान्ते... १२२
अध्येतव्यः सवि०... १५
अध्येतव्योऽखिलै०... २८७
अनध्ययनमानेन... २२
अनामिकान्त्यादिमयो०... २७०
अनास्यं हृदयोत्पन्नं... १०२
अनुत्तमे त्वर्ध०... १५७
अनुदात्तो हृदि ज्ञेयो... २८३
अनुस्वारस्य भक्ती०... १९१
अनुस्वारस्य वर्णो०... १९२
अनुस्वारादयश्चैते... २५९
अनुस्वारे च... ४८
अन्तराकर्षति... २१३
अन्त्यभागे तु निहतः... ११२
अन्यूना स्वरत०... १६
अन्वपात्यपिसू०... २९
अप्यनुस्वारभक्त्यंशे... १९२
अवग्रहेऽत्र... ३०

अवसाने विशेषो०...	१५९
असौ वर्णक्रमश्चेति...	१८०
आग्नेया ऐदिवर्णौ...	२५४
आजिह्वामूलमुत्प्लुत्य...	२१०
आदन्तं यदु०...	३९
अदिदुत्स्थानकरण०...	२३८
आदौ तु तस्य...	१११
आदौ प्रारम्भकोङ्कारे...	१२१
आद्यन्तौ तेषु...	७५
आद्यन्त्यांशौ स्वारकम्पे...	२७०
आधारं सर्व०...	२०३
आप्लुतो रलयो०...	७३
आम्नाया यस्य...	१
आरम्भे यजुषः...	११
आवृत्यावृत्य...	२४
आसन्नमत्यासन्नं...	२४४
आसीन एव कुर्वीत...	२६६
इङ्ग्यते हि पदस्यार्थ...	२७
इत्थमुच्चार्यमाणेषु...	२१८
इत्यन्तानि स्युरेतानि...	२९
इत्येते याजुषा...	५
इत्येवमष्ट संज्ञाः...	८६
इत्येवमिङ्ग्य०...	२८
इन्द्रियाविषयो...	१५२
इयं तूभयदीर्घौ...	९९
इवर्णोतोर्यवत्वे...	१३३
इवर्णोवर्णयोः...	२३७
उक्त्वा ततोऽङ्गशब्दं...	१७२
उच्चनीचस्वारधृताः...	२६१
उच्चपूर्वेऽप्यपूर्वे...	१४५
उच्चारणप्रसिद्ध्यर्थं...	१९८
उच्चारणे कवर्गस्य...	२४१
उच्चे नानापदस्थेऽपि...	१३५
उच्चैरुदात्तो नीचैस्तु...	१२७
उत्सवार्थं तु देवेशे...	२०
उदात्तं निर्दिशेन्न्यासे...	२६७
उदात्तपूर्वे तस्मिन्...	१३८
उदात्तप्रचयाभ्यां...	२८०
उदात्तश्च तथैवादौ...	११२
उदात्तादिस्वरेभ्यो०...	१४९
उदात्तादींस्ततो...	१७३
उदानो गलगर्तस्थो...	२१०
उदाह्रियन्ते वत्सानु...	९५
उपध्मानीयवर्णौ...	४८
उपनाभ्युदये सूक्ष्म...	२०२
उपरिस्थायिना...	१६४
उपश्लेष्यमिवर्णोक्तौ...	२३०
उभाभ्यां श्वास०...	२१४
उरो ह्रस्योत्तमा०...	२४८
उवर्ण ओत्...	२५४
ऋलृस्वरार्धावादेशौ...	७४
ऋवर्ण औच्चतुर्थाश्च...	२५५
ऋवर्णो लृति...	२३२
लृकारोत्तमशाः...	२५५
एकमात्रस्तुरीयांशः...	१०४
एकमात्रान्तरत्वस्य...	२३२
एकमात्रो भवेद्ध्रस्वो...	१५३
एकस्योच्चादियुक्तस्या०...	१८१
एकारेऽव्यञ्जने...	२३३
एकारौकारयो०...	२३८
एतत् सर्वं विदित्वैव...	१४७
एते क्रमात् प्रजायन्ते...	२०१
एते धर्माः क्रमेणैव...	१८५
एतेन विधिना...	५३

एते पञ्चांशकास्तत्र...	२०६
एते रङ्गप्लुता...	१०१
एदैदोदौदिति...	३
एवं तत्र क्रमात्...	७७
एवं पाठक्रमो यः...	१५०
एवं पाठक्रमो यस्तु...	४२
एवं सलक्षणां...	२८५
एवं स्वरितभेदानां...	१४६
एवमुच्चार्यते...	३४
एदोतोरदिदुत्स्वल्पो...	२३९
ऐकारौकारावयवे०...	२३८
ऐदौतोराद्यकारस्य...	२४०
ओष्ठावुवर्णे दीर्घौ...	२३१
ओष्ठ्यस्वरान्तरस्थे...	२४५
ककारः षपरो यत्र...	११८
कखौ गघौ...	३
कण्ठाकाशगतः कार्यः...	२२३
कण्ठे तु संवृते...	२२४
कण्ठोरोमध्यदेशस्थे...	२१६
कम्पे तद्धेतुकस्वार०...	१९३
करणं तालु तु...	२३४
करणानां तु यत्...	२४७
कवर्गादिषु यत् स्थानं...	२४६
कांस्यघण्टानादसमः...	१०३
काण्डप्रश्नानुवाकाद्यैः...	११
कारशब्दोत्तरो वर्णो...	९
कार्यौ तु दीर्घप्लुतयोर्न...	२३०
कुर्यात् सन्ध्यां स...	२१
कृत्वा गोकर्णवद्धस्तं...	२६३
केकारुतसमः...	२८१
केवलः स्वरसंयुक्तो...	१३
केवलस्वरमात्राङ्गवर्णेषु...	१८९
क्रमवत् पूर्वमुच्चार्य...	४१
क्रमात् स जिह्वा०...	११७
क्रमात् स्वरेषु...	२६४
क्रमादनामिकायास्तौ...	२६९
क्रमादिकं पठेद्...	२०
क्रमेण पञ्च पञ्च...	६
क्रमेण स्युर्यमास्तत्र...	६५
क्रमेणैवं सुविज्ञेयाः...	८३
क्रमे तावत्...	३५
क्षात्रा द्वित्रितुरीयाः...	२५६
क्षैप्रः प्राथमिकः...	१३०
क्षैप्रे नित्ये प्रयत्नः...	१४४
गात्रदैर्घ्यं ध्वनेर्दार्ढ्यं...	२७५
चतुर्थं च पठेत्...	३३
चतुर्भिरणुभिर्मात्रा०...	१५२
चतुर्भिरिव सा श्लिष्टा...	७४
चत्वारः संस्थिता देहे...	२०६
छिन्नधारो भवत्याशु...	२२१
जटाध्याये शतं प्रोक्तं...	१७
जटायां लक्षणेरुक्ता०...	४६
जटा वर्णक्रमाश्चैव...	१३
जिह्वाञ्चलस्य मध्येन...	२४४
जिह्वाग्रतस्तवर्गे...	२४२
जिह्वाग्रेण टवर्गे...	२४२
जिह्वामध्यं स्थानमति०...	२३५
जिह्वामध्यस्य पार्श्वाभ्यां...	२४३
जिह्वामूलीयपूर्वाणां...	२४६
जिह्वामूलेन चोरुक्तौ...	२४१
ज्वालया भेदयत्याशु...	२१५
तं च वर्णक्रमाध्याये...	६८
तं तु व्याघ्ररुतान्ते...	१५४
तक्राँ इत्युच्चरेदुच्चैस्तथा...	१०५

ततः षड्गादिहेतुः... १८८
ततश्चोदात्तकम्पे... २७१
ततस्तत्र द्वितीया०... ४४
ततस्त्वादिपदं... ३२
ततो रेखादर्शनं... १८७
तत्तत्कालान् विदित्वैवं... १६१
तत्परस्य योगादेर्न... १२०
तत् प्रणम्य... १
तत्प्रत्यगाढकस्थूला०... २०३
तत्र तत्र च ते सर्वे... १४९
तत्र तत्र तथा सर्वं... ४३
तत्र तावदुदात्ताद्याः... १२६
तत्र पूर्वस्वराङ्गं... १६७
तत्र रङ्गप्लुतो... १५४
तत्रादौ देवता ज्ञेया... १८७
तत्राभिनिहतश्चैक... १३१
तत्रोदात्तानुदात्तौ... १२४
तत्संज्ञा च ततश्चैतान्... १८८
तथाऽपि तस्य विन्यासे... २७३
तथाऽपि न वदेत्... १५६
तथा सवर्णदीर्घौ... ८६
तथैव सप्त... १२४
तथोपसर्गपूर्वाश्चागमं... ५९
तदङ्गं करणं... २२७
तदन्त्यांशस्य नीचस्य... १९४
तदर्धं सममच्छिन्न०... २१९
तदाऽनिराकृतिः... २९२
तदा यद्यागतः... २६५
तधोत्तरे ङतोऽनन्त्या०... ६४
तमेव वर्णपाठेषु... ५२
तयोर्नानुक्रमेत्... ३६
तस्माच्छ्रेयः परं प्राप्तुं... २८७
तस्मादयं वर्णसारभूत०... १८१
तस्मादुत्पन्नकम्पस्य... १९३
तस्माद् विच्छिद्यते... २२०
तस्माद् व्यक्तः... २००
तस्मान्निराकृतेः... २९२
तस्मिन्नकारलोपश्चेत्... १३७
तस्य धूर्षदमित्यादौ... ८२
तस्याः सवर्णदीर्घास्तु... ९४
तस्यान्ते चानुदात्तः... ११३
तस्योर्ध्वेन त्रिक्रमः... ३९
तान् सदीर्घविसर्गांश्च... ५०
तान् सर्वानङ्ग०... १७८
तान् सर्वान् कार०... ४७
तान् सर्वान् वर्ण०... २८४
तिरस्तिर्यगिति... १४१
तिस्रोऽवस्था इमाः... २७५
तुल्यं पदद्वयं... ४४
तृतीयं च चतुर्थेन... ७६
तृतीयः करणं विद्यात्... १८३
तृतीयः स्यात् प्रातिहत... १३१
ते घोरं नरकं... २९३
ते त्रिवर्गमिह... २९४
तेन व्यवेतो... १४१
तैत्तिरीये शपूर्वस्य... ६१
तैरोव्यञ्जनवृत्ताभ्यां... २७९
तैरोव्यञ्जनसंज्ञो... १३२
तैर्भूतो भूतशब्देन... १७९
त्यजेद् यदि तदा... २३
त्रयमेतदनुद्यार्य... ७९
त्रिक्रमे त्रिपदस्यापि... ४३
त्रिगुणं तत्पदे तस्मात्... १७
त्रिपादाधिकमात्रस्य... १९४

त्रिमात्रिकः प्लुतो ज्ञेयो...	१५३
थदौ धनौ पफबभा...	४
दशैतांस्तत्र तत्रैव...	१२५
दीर्घह्रस्वानुदात्ताभ्यां...	२८०
दीर्घात् परोऽन्तगो...	७२
दीर्घात् प्लुताद्य...	१५९
दीर्घौ च भवतस्तत्र...	२३६
देवता पञ्चमो ज्ञेयः...	१८४
देवता वेदवर्णानां...	२५३
देवाँ उ ताँ इम्यमृवाँ...	१०६
द्वाभ्यां द्वाभ्यां...	२०७
द्वितीयं तत्र पदवद०...	३२
द्वितीयाश्च चतुर्था०...	२५२
द्वित्वं पूर्वागमश्चैव...	६९
द्विमात्रो मात्रिकस्त्वन्यः...	१६१
द्विरूपं नाप्नुयादूष्मा...	७०
द्वौ तामसगुणौ...	२६२
धर्माः षड्विंशतिः...	१८२
धर्मान् यथावद्...	१९१
धर्मेण य इमां...	२८८
धृतप्रचयशब्दौ...	१२९
धृतानुदात्तस्वारोद्य०...	२६०
धृते ह्युकारे...	१६९
ध्वनिः प्राथमिको...	१८३
ध्वनिस्थानादयो...	१७९
न तत् कल्पसहस्रैश्च...	२८५
न तत्राभिनिधानोक्तिः...	६३
न ध्वन्यादीन् यमे...	१९७
नन्दन्ति देवताः...	२८८
न पठेत् तु जटां...	४५
न शक्यं केवलं...	१६५
नाडीलताश्रितोऽपानः...	२०८
नातोऽस्ति तेषां...	२३९
नादः श्वासो...	२२३
नादजाः स्वरघोषाः...	२२५
नानापदे ह्युद्यपूर्वं...	१३६
नासिक्यत्वमुरस्यत्वं...	११५
नासिक्यो व्यक्तिमध्ये...	१००
नित्यः कार्य इति...	१९९
नित्याभिनिहतक्षैप्र०...	१०८
नित्याभिनिहतक्षैप्रा...	२७८
नित्योऽव्यक्तो विभुः...	१९९
निश्चला सततं...	२०४
निषादं बृंहते...	२८२
निषादः पञ्चमश्चैव...	२७७
निष्फलं स्याद् यथा...	५१
नीचं कनिष्ठिकादौ...	२६७
नीचं पूर्वस्वरस्यान्ते...	१०९
नीचपूर्वेऽभिनिहते...	१४४
नीचात् षड्जर्षभौ...	२७७
नीचापूर्वस्तथोद्योर्ध्वौ...	६३
नैव तत्र यमा०...	६६
पञ्चमस्योत्तमः प्रोक्तो...	७
पठित्वा वेष्टनं...	३५
पठेत् ततस्तद्...	३३
पदत्रयमनुक्रम्य हित्वा...	४०
पदाध्याये पदान्ते...	२५
पदे तु यद्...	३८
पदे स्थितेऽप्यपूर्वे...	१३४
पराङ्गमसवर्णौ...	१७०
पराङ्गे चोष्मणि परे...	१७०
पराणुसूक्ष्मावरणा...	२०४
परायुक्तमनुस्वारो...	१६७
परिविन्याभ्युप०...	८

परेषामनुदात्तानां... १२८
परोऽपि ह्रस्वदीर्घाभ्यां... ७३
पर्यादीनि दशात्रोक्ता०... २८
पाथएषोऽतिधामातिभूते... ५९
पादं द्वितीयं पादेन... ७६
पादोनमात्रिका तत्र... ९१
पारायणे प्रयोगार्थे... २४
पिपीलिका तु ते एनं... ९८
पिपीलिकेति विज्ञेया... ९३
पुनरुच्चार्यते द्वेधा... २६
पुनश्च तत्र तौ कम्पौ... १११
पूर्वं पूर्वं पदं... ३४
पूर्वं वर्णक्रमोक्तेस्तु... ५०
पूर्वत्वेन परत्वेन... १६३
पूर्वभागो हकारे... ७८
पूर्ववाक्यान्तगं··· ३६
पूर्वस्थितो विसर्गः... ११८
पूर्वागमः क्रमात्... ५७
पूर्वाङ्गं न भवेत्... १६८
पूर्वेऽनुनासिकं... १५८
पूर्वे यत्रोत्तरे... ९०
पृथगोष्ठोपसंहारो... २३१
पौर्वापर्यक्रमात्... १७५
पौर्वापर्यक्रमेणैव... १७१
प्रग्रहानिङ्ग्युक्तं... ३७
प्रणम्याथ न्यसेत्... २६५
प्रथमस्योष्मणि परे... ६०
प्रथमाश्च तदन्ये च... २२६
प्रथमोऽभिनिधानः... ६२
प्रयत्नाः पञ्चधा ज्ञेया... २४९
प्रयत्नाश्च क्रमेणैव... १२७
प्रयत्नो विवृतोऽन्येषां... २५१
प्रयुतं त्वङ्गवर्णो... १८
प्रवदेद् यदि नाम्नाऽसौ... १२५
प्रश्लिष्टः पञ्चमः षष्ठो... १३२
प्रश्लिष्टप्रातिहतयोः... १४५
प्रश्लिष्टाख्यः स सूद्गाता... १३८
प्राग् यद्यघोषवर्णाभ्यां... ११७
प्राणादीनामिमाश्चेष्टाः... २१२
प्राणोदानापानसमा... २०५
प्राणो हृदिस्थस्त्वांशेन... २१३
प्राप्ते पूर्वागमद्वित्व०... ६९
प्राप्ते महाप्रदोषेऽपि... २२
प्रायश्चित्तविधौ कृच्छ्रे... १९
बर्हिः करेणुसंज्ञा... ८०
बोधनार्थं तु... २५
ब्रह्मक्षत्रियविट्शूद्रा... २६१
ब्रह्मत्यागी स विज्ञेयः... २८९
ब्राह्मणी नकुलश्चाषो... २५१
भक्तिरुत्तरभागा... ७८
भवन्ति तेषां... २२९
भवन्ति नादप्रमुखा... २०२
भवन्ति यद्यद्वर्णानां... १४८
भवेत् परस्वरस्याङ्गं... १६६
भिन्नावृतौ समे... २१६
भूयो मनःप्रयोगेन... २२२
मः स्पर्शयवलोर्ध्वश्चेत्... ७२
मनःप्रयोगो यत्नोऽस्य... २१८
मनस्यभ्युत्थिते... २१९
मध्यमान्तिममुच्चार्य... ४०
मध्यमा या... ९८
मध्यमालक्षणे... ९२
मध्यस्थे तु हकारः... २२४
मध्याद्ययोः प्रदेशिन्याः... २७१

मध्ये पदस्य या...	१४०	येनावसीयते वाक्यं...	५२
महत्ता कण्ठखस्यैता...	२७६	ये ये धर्माश्च...	१८९
मात्राकालश्च वक्तव्यो...	१८६	योगात् पूर्वमनुस्वारो...	५६
मात्राणां कालनियमा...	१५०	योगाद्यसंयुतो...	१६८
मात्राश्च मात्रिकावर्णो...	१७७	योगो यत्रोभयाङ्ग...	१७५
मिथोऽपृथक्त्वमेतेषां...	२०१	यो धर्मः पञ्चम०...	१९०
मुखावयवनासिक्या...	२४९	यो निराकृतिना...	२९१
मूर्धजस्त्वर्धमात्रः...	१०७	योऽनुस्वारः केव०...	१२०
य एवं स्वरवर्णार्था०...	२७३	योऽनुस्वारो यजुष्यत्र...	५५
यः समानपदे...	१४३	योऽपदान्ते पदान्ते...	६७
यः स्वरः स्यात्...	२६८	यो हित्वा ब्राह्मणो...	२८९
यः स्वरन्यासकृद्...	२६३	रङ्गदीर्घा इति...	१०६
यत् पदं वेष्टनोपेतं...	२६	रङ्गप्लुते त्ववर्णोद्युप्लुता०...	१९५
यत्र यस्माद्...	६६	रङ्गप्लुते द्विमात्रं...	१०२
यथाक्रमं स्वयं...	२१२	रस्य त्वेफस्त्वयाणां...	४९
यथाशास्त्रं स्वर०...	२६४	राजतेऽसौ स्वयं...	१६४
यथा सौराष्ट्रिका...	१०५	रौति क्वणात्यजा...	२८१
यदङ्गं स्पृश्यतेऽङ्गेन...	२२७	लकार ऊष्मणि स्पर्शे...	७१
यदि तैरभ्यनुज्ञातः...	२६६	लक्षणैः प्रग्रहा ये...	३१
यदि मध्ये विसर्गः...	८९	लक्षणैः शब्द एवात्र...	१८२
यद् यदुक्तं शुद्ध०...	१७६	लक्ष्यानुसारसंज्ञो...	५८
यद्यात्माधः सरूर्ध्वे...	५५	लोपालोपादयो ये च...	४५
यरो लवौ चतस्रो०...	४	वकारश्च परे...	७०
यशो ममोपहूताँ...	१०१	वत्सानुसारिणी प्रोक्ता...	९६
यषकारावेदवर्णौ...	२५३	वत्सानुसारिणी सेय०...	८८
यस्तस्याः परतः...	१३९	वत्सानुसृतिराख्याता...	८५
यस्तु पारायणं...	२१	वत्सानुसृतिसंज्ञा...	९६
यस्तु संहितया...	५१	वदेद् धर्मान् वर्णसारे...	१९६
यस्याः सवर्णदीर्घौ...	९१	वर्गप्रथमवर्णाश्च...	२५६
या त्वखण्डपदे...	१३९	वर्गान्त्या नासिका०...	२४८
यास्ततोऽन्या...	१२	वर्गेषु तेषु संज्ञाः...	६
ये अत्र सांहिता...	४६	वर्गोत्तरस्तु वर्गाख्या...	१०

वर्णक्रमप्रपाठेषु... १२२
वर्णक्रमस्याध्ययने... ११९
वर्णसंज्ञामपि... १९७
वर्णस्य स्वरहीनस्य... ११९
वर्णानामङ्गवर्णोऽस्मिन्... १६३
वर्षं हंसपदा... ८१
वस्त्रहीनस्य देहस्य... २९०
वाक्यान्तगं द्वयोरादि... ३०
वाचस्तु वृत्तयस्तिस्रो... २३
वायुना पूरिता वृत्ता... २०५
विचेष्टेते तदा... २२२
विभज्योच्चारशमलौ... २०८
विभागवत्पदस्यार्थो... २७
विरामश्चैकमात्रः... ११६
विरामस्थेषूत्तमेषु... १५८
विरामे व्यञ्जनं यत्... २७२
विवक्षया लक्षणानि... १४७
विवक्षुणाऽऽत्मना... २१४
विवृत्तिमध्ये यत्र... ११६
विसर्गजिह्वामूलीयो०... २५९
विसर्गस्तत्र च स्वारः... ९२
विसर्गस्तत्र नो चेत्... ९५
विसर्गस्य च हस्य... २४७
वेद एव परो धर्मो... २८६
वेद एव परं ब्रह्म... २८६
वेदरूपविलसत्परात्... २९४
वेदहीनस्य विप्रस्य... २९०
वेदांश्च श्रोत्रियं ब्रह्म... २९३
वेदेष्वक्षरमेकैकमेकैकं... १५
वैकृतत्वं प्राकृतत्वं... ११४
वैशेषिका पाकवती... ८५
वैशेषिका स्यात् ता... ९७
व्यक्तेरभावे भावेऽपि... १३६
व्यक्तेराद्यन्तयोर्यस्या... ८९
व्यक्तेश्च साणुमात्रत्वं... १००
व्यञ्जनं यन्निमित्तेन... ५७
व्यञ्जनानामकारः... ९
व्यञ्जनानामुदात्तादीन्... १२६
व्यञ्जनानि च सर्वाणि... १६६
व्यञ्जनेन व्यवहितः... १४२
शषसेष्वच्परेष्वत्र... ११४
शसौ यत्रागमौ... ६२
शुद्धवर्णक्रमे... १२३
शुद्धवर्णो यथा तत्र... १९५
शूद्रा ऊष्मविसर्गा०... २५७
शोत्तरे हरिणी... ८१
श्रुतेर्नादस्ततो नाली... २००
श्रुत्यादिप्रकृतिः कार्यो... २१७
षडूष्माणो विसर्गो०... ५
षणत्वटत्वविधिना... ३८
स एव द्वित्वमाप्नोति... ५६
स एव पादवृत्तः... १४०
संयुक्तं वाऽप्यसंयुक्तं... १५५
संयोगो यत्र पूर्वाङ्गं... १७४
संवृताख्य इति प्राहु०... २४०
संवृतोऽकारमात्रस्य... २५०
संवृतो विवृतः... २५०
संहिताग्रन्थमात्रस्य... १२
संहितापठनं... १९
संहितायां तु तन्मात्रः... १६०
संहितायां तु प्रचय... १२९
संहितायामचो नित्यं... २२८
संहितावत् पठेत्... ३१
सकृत् पारायणे... १६

सकृदेव वदेत् तत्र...	१७४
स च कम्पोऽत्र...	११०
स च त्वैप्राभिधः...	१३३
स तथोक्तश्च वर्णानां...	१८०
स तैरोव्यञ्जने पादवृत्ते...	१४६
स तैरोव्यञ्जनो ज्ञेय...	१४३
स त्रिपादद्विमात्रः...	१२१
सदा वितनुते...	२०९
सद्यस्तत्त्वक् तिरोधत्ते...	२२१
स द्वितीयमवाप्नोति...	६७
सन्धितश्च पुनः...	४१
सन्धौ तत्र प्रकम्पन्ते...	१०८
सपरे यत्र...	८२
स पूतः सर्ववेदैश्च...	२७४
स प्रातिहत एव...	१३५
समः सुषीरचक्रस्थ०...	२०७
सममध्ये पुनः...	२२०
समे वर्णद्वयं...	६०
सम्मेलने द्विमात्रः...	११३
सर्वत्राभिनिधानाख्यो...	१९६
सर्वथा नाधिगन्तव्यो...	१४
सर्वनाडीः समाश्रित्य...	२०९
सर्वेषामेव वर्णानां...	१७८
सवर्गीयानुत्तमोर्ध्वे...	७१
सवर्णादीर्घी संयत्ता...	९९
सवर्णादीर्घो यद्यादावन्ते...	९३
सवर्णादीर्घ्येकमात्रा...	९४
स विप्रस्तु तदा०...	२९१
सव्यञ्जनेऽस्मिन्...	२३४
सह तेन पतित्वाऽग्नौ...	२१५
साङ्गश्च वर्णसारश्च...	१४
सा तु पाकवती...	९७
सा तु वैशेषिकाख्या...	९०
सात्त्विकः स्याद् गुणो०...	२६२
सा पराङ्ग भवत्येव...	१६९
सापेक्षं व्यञ्जनं नित्यं...	१६५
सा मल्हा...	८०
सा वत्सानुसृतिः...	८७
सिद्धेऽप्यर्धाणुमात्रत्वे...	१५६
सूर्याग्निचन्द्रवसुधाश्च०...	२६०
स्थानं कण्ठोरसो०...	२१७
स्थित्वा स्थाने बली...	२११
स्पर्शश्च लवपूर्वो...	५४
स्पर्शेषु स्पृष्टता०...	२५१
स्पर्शो यद्यूष्मविकृतिर्न...	६५
स्याद् यत्रानुत्तमात्...	६४
स्याद् यत्रोद्य...	२६९
स्थितो मध्ये...	७५
स्वरकालं वदेत् तत्र...	१५५
स्वरन्यासक्रमेणैव...	२७४
स्वरभक्त्यंशभूतानामचां...	१९०
स्वरयोरुभयोः...	८४
स्वरवर्णोऽयुतं...	१८
स्वरवर्णो स्वरा...	१७७
स्वराणां निहतादीनां...	१८६
स्वरात् कारपरादर्वाङ्...	४९
स्वरान्तरश्रुतिं...	२७२
स्वरितः कर्णमूलीयः...	२८३
स्वरितः स्यात् समा०...	१२८
स्वरितो यः स एव...	१४२
स्वरितप्रभवास्तेषां...	२७८
स्वर्यते यत्र नित्यः...	१३४
स्वारं चानामिकान्त्ये...	२६८
स्वारकम्पः संहिताया०...	११०

स्वारोऽभिनिहतो ज्ञेयः... १३७
स्वाराः सप्तविधा... १३०
हकारान्नणमा... ११५
हतश्लिष्टावुभौ स्यातां... २७९
हनू अत्युपसंहार्ये... २३३
हनू अनतिविश्लेषे... २३५
हयहेषातुल्यरूपं... २८२
हरिप्रणवमध्येऽपि... १२३
हलन्ता स्यात् पूर्व०... ७७
हलस्त्ववसिता... १५७
हलां तु पूर्वशब्दं... १७१
हल्संज्ञकेति... १७२
हान्योष्मा प्रथमाश्चैव... ७
हारिता लशयोर्योगे... ८३
हृज्ञातो मात्रिक०... १०७
हृत्पद्मकोशपृष्ठस्थे... २११
ह्रस्वता या च देहस्य... २७६
ह्रस्वदीर्घप्लुप्ता भक्ति०... २५८
ह्रस्वदीर्घप्लुप्तावर्णोवर्णो०... २
ह्रस्वपूर्वा च या व्यक्ति... ८७
ह्रस्वपूर्वो पदान्तस्थौ... ५४
ह्रस्वमप्यत्र कम्पे०... १०९
ह्रस्वात् परस्तु यो... ६८
ह्रस्वात् परोऽवसानस्थः... १६०
ह्रस्वात् पूर्वे विवृत्तिः... ८८
ह्रस्वोऽदिदुदृकारश्च... १०

Appendix II

Index I: References Used in This Book

Aindra School 31

Amarakośa 153

Amarasiṁha 153

Amoghanandinī Śikṣā 4

Anantabhaṭṭa 7

Anukramaṇī 5

Āpastamba 30

Āpiśaliśikṣā/Āpiśalīyaśikṣā 3, 10, 16, 40, 106, 142

Āraṇyaśikṣā 3, 10

Arjuna 29

Atharvaveda 4, 8

Atharvaveda Prātiśākhya 8

Ātreya 27-38

Ātreyabhāṣya 33

Ātreyaśikṣā 1, 3, 5-6, 12-13, 15-16, 29, 37-39, 66

Ātreyaśīkṣākārika (AK) 19-20, 45, 59, 60-65

Ātreyaśīkṣāmūla (AS) 2, 12, 14-16, 19-20, 24-27, 29, 31-32, 35, 38-42, 45-46, 53-55, 59, 61-65, 68, 133, 142

second variety of (*AS* 2) 13-16, 19, 38-39

Ātreyasūtra 13

Ātreyī Śākhā 28, 38

Atri 27

Atrisūtra 13

Audavraji 8

Baiṭh 5

Baudhāyana Dharmasūtra 30

Baudhāyana Gṛhyasūtra 30

Bhāradvājaśikṣā 3, 5, 10

Bodhāyana 28, 30

Brahma-Purāṇa 169

Cārāyaṇīya School 3

Cārāyaṇīyaśikṣā 3, 10

Chandas 5, 8

Classical Sanskrit 6

Devarājayajvan 28

Dharmaśāstra 35

Dharmasūtra 30

Galadṛkśikṣā 4

Gārgya Gopāla Yajvan 35

Gautamī Śikṣā 4, 10

Gṛhyasūtra 28, 30

Hiraṇyakeśi-Gṛhyasūtra 28
Hiraṇyakeśin 28

Indo-Aryan language 6

Jaiminisūtra 27
Janamejaya 29-30
Jyotiṣa 5

Kaiyyaṭa 34
Kālanirṇaya 34-35
Kālanirṇayaśikṣā 3, 10, 34-35
Kalpasūtra 30
Kaṇva Bodhāyana 30
Kāṇva School 4
Kāṭhaka 26, 129
Kāṭhaka Āraṇyaka 26, 129
Kāṭhaka recension 129
Kāṭhaka School 118
Kātyāyana 8, 35
Kātyāyanī Śikṣā 4
Kauhalīyaśikṣā/Kauhaliśikṣā 3, 10, 28-29
Kauṇḍinya 30
Kauṇḍinyaśikṣā 3, 10
Kauśikī Śikṣā 4
Kauthuma branch 8
Kautsa 8
Keśavī Śikṣā 4
Kramakārikā-Śikṣā 3
Kramasandhānaśikṣā 3
Kuru 30
Kṛṣṇa-Yajurveda 1, 3, 7, 20, 25-27, 131

Laghumādhyandinī Śikṣā 3
lakṣaṇa 5, 12, 15
Lakṣaṇacandrikā 16-18
Lakṣaṇagrantha 5
Lakṣmīkāntaśikṣā 3, 10
Lomaśī Śikṣā 4

Mādhava 35
Madhusūdana Sarasvatī 6
Mādhyandina branch 8
Mādhyandina School 3
Mādhyandinī Śikṣā 3
Mahābhārata 29
Mahābhāṣya 34
Mahādeva Rāmacandra Gadre 16
Māhiṣeya 33, 35
Maitrāyaṇī branch 7
Maitrāyaṇīya Prātiśākhya 7-8, 28
Manassvāraśikṣā 4
Mañcibhaṭṭa 36
Māṇḍavī Śikṣā 4
Māṇḍukī Śikṣā 4, 10, 16

Nāradaśikṣā 4, 10
Nirukta 28

Padakārikāratnamālā Śikṣā 4
Padakramasadana 35
Paiṅgi Yāska/Paliṅgi/Phaliṅgu 29

Pāṇinian grammar 31
Pāṇinian School 31-32
Pāṇinian system 31
Pāṇinīyaśikṣā 2-4, 10, 16
Pārāśarī Śikṣā 3
Parīkṣit 30
Pāriśikṣā 3, 10, 13, 20, 25-26, 40-41, 59, 106, 108, 158
Pārṣadavṛtti 33
Phullasūtra 8
Pradīpa 34
Prasthānabheda 4, 6
Prātiśākhya 1, 4-5, 7-9, 11, 29-32, 133
Prātiśākhyakāra 9
Prātiśākhyapradīpaśikṣā 4
Pratyāhārasūtra 31
Purāṇa 27
Puṣpa 8
Puṣpasūtra 8

Rājā Ghanapāṭhin 37
Rāṇāyanīya branch 8
Ṛgveda 2
Ṛgveda Prātiśākhya 7-8, 30, 40, 44, 130
Ṛgveda Saṁhitā 27
Ṛktantra 8

Śabdabrahmavilāsa 32
Śaiśirīya School 3
Śaiśirīyaśikṣā 3, 16
Śākala branch 7
Śākaṭāyana 8
Śamānaśikṣā 2, 5
Sāmatantra 8
Sāmaveda 4, 8
Śambhuśikṣā 3, 10, 40-41, 133, 140, 169
Saṁhitāprakārā Ekādaśa 37
Sāṁhitī Upaniṣad 11
Saṅgītaratnākara 150-51
Saptalakṣaṇa 5
Sarvalakṣaṇamañjarī 9, 37, 109
Sarvasammataśikṣā 3, 9-10, 26, 32, 36, 42, 129
Śaunaka 7, 9
Śaunaka branch 8
Śaunakaśikṣā 3, 10
Śaunakīyā Caturadhyāyikā 8
Sāyaṇa 34-35
Siddhāntakaumudī 56
Siddhāntaśikṣā 3, 13, 37-38
Śikṣā 1-4, 6-11, 20, 25-26, 29, 32, 36-39
Śīkṣā 11, 25, 106
Śīkṣā Vallī 6, 11, 25
Śikṣādivedāṅgasūcī 35
Śikṣākāra 5, 35, 37-38
Śikṣāsaṅgraha 10
Skanda Purāṇa 109
Skandamaheśvara 28
Somayārya 32, 33-35
Śrīnivāsa Makhin 37
Śrīnivāsādhvarīndra 38
Śukla-Yajurveda 3, 8, 10

Sūryanārāyaṇa Surāvadhānin 16
Svarāṅkuśaśikṣā 2
Svarasampat 36
Svaravyañjanaśikṣā 2

Taittirīya Āraṇyaka (TA) 6, 9, 11, 25-26, 117, 126, 128-29
Taittirīya Brāhmaṇa (TB) 123-24, 126-28, 138, 148
Taittirīya branch/*śākhā* 7, 38
Taittirīya Kāṇḍānukrama 27, 29, 38
Taittirīya Prātiśākhya (TP) 1-2, 7-8, 15-18, 20, 25, 28-35, 40, 44, 68, 106, 129, 133, 160
Taittirīya recension 129
Taittirīya Saṁhitā (TS) 12-13, 27-29, 32, 119, 124, 126-28, 136-38
Taittirīya School 1, 3, 10-12, 19-20, 25-27, 29-30, 36-39, 44, 118, 133
Taittirīya tradition 27, 32
Taittirīya Upaniṣad 6, 11, 25
Tittiri 29
Traisvaryaśikṣā 4
Tribhāṣyaratna 5, 14, 32-35, 40-41, 129, 133, 160, 169

Ukha 29
Upaśikṣā 36
Uvaṭa 8

Vaidikābharaṇa 5, 14, 29, 35, 39-42, 56, 106, 129, 141-42, 158, 160, 169
Vaiśampāyana 27, 29-30
Vājasaneyi-Prātiśākhya 7-8
Vararuci 8, 33, 35
Vararuciśikṣā 3
Varṇaratnadīpikā Śikṣā 4
Vārttika 56
Vārttikakāra 35
Vasiṣṭhaśikṣā 3, 10
Vāsiṣṭhī Śikṣā 4
Veda 2, 4-6, 24, 105-06, 109, 167, 170-72
Vedalakṣaṇa 4-5, 9, 11, 14, 35-36, 43
Vedalakṣaṇānukramaṇikā 5, 37
Vedāṅga 2, 5, 9
Vedataijasa 16, 18
Vedic Sanskrit 6
Vīrarāghavakavi 32
Viṣṇumitra 33
Vyākaraṇa 5, 8, 32
Vyāsa 29
Vyāsaśikṣā 3, 10, 16, 26, 35, 40

Yājñavalkyaśikṣā 3, 9-10, 16
Yajurveda 26, 107-08, 117, 150
Yajurvidhānaśikṣā 4
Yājuṣabhūṣaṇa 10, 38, 158
Yudhiṣṭhira 29, 30

Index II: Important Terms Occurring in Ātreyaśīkṣāmūla

(Verse nos. are indicated)

aṁśa 190-94, 206, 213-14, 216, 220, 270

a-kāra 9, 47, 121, 137, 229, 237, 240, 250

akṣara 15, 134

akhaṇḍaveṣṭana 37, 42

agni 215, 253-54, 260

aghoṣa 7-8, 61, 117, 225, 258

aṅga (adjunct) 162-63, 166-72, 174-75, 184, 196, 284

aṅga (organ) 187, 206, 226-28, 283

aṅgaśabda 172

aṅgavarṇa/sāṅga 14, 18, 162-63, 176, 178, 189

aṅgāvasthā 187

aṅguli 203

aṅguṣṭhāgra 264

ac 2, 53-54, 70, 73-74, 114, 162, 173, 181, 185, 190-91, 223, 228, 257

acsaṁjñā 173

ajā 281

aṇu/-mātrā/aṇumātrika 100, 151-52, 156, 236

aṇutā 275

at 10, 236, 238-39

atandrita 263

ati 29, 59

atidṛḍha 144

ativivṛta 230

atiśliṣṭa 234

atiśleṣa 235

atispṛṣṭa 250, 252

atyāsanna 244

atyupasaṁhārya 233

atyupasaṁhṛta 229, 232, 235

atva 79

adhara 243, 245

adhi 8

adhyāya 17, 25, 34, 68, 122, 148, 160

anadhyayana 22

anativeśleṣa 235

ananta 18

anantya 64, 67

anāmikā 268-70

anāmikāntya 268, 270

anāsya 102

aniṅgya 37

anila 214, 217

anu 29

anuttama 64, 71, 157

anudātta 113, 124, 127-28, 260, 262, 280, 283

anunāsika 72, 158, 160

anuvāka 11, 36, 122

anusvāra 5, 48, 55-56, 120, 167, 191-92, 257, 259

antassthā 4, 65, 170, 248, 251, 256-57

antya (*parvan*) 268-70
apa 29
apāna 205, 208
api 29
abhi 8
abhinidhāna 62-63, 196
abhinihata 108, 131, 137, 144, 278
abhihata 131
abhyāsa 24, 266
amṛvā́ áva 106
ayuta 18
artha 27-28, 179, 273
alopa 45
alpa 225-226
alpatara 146
ava 8, 30
avagraha 28, 30
avaca 200
avayava 238, 249
a-varṇa 2, 195, 253
avasāna 32, 159, 160, 167
avasita 157
avasthā 187, 275
avyakta 199
aṣṭan 17, 185
asavarṇa 89, 170

ā 8, 39
ākāśa 223, 275
āgama 57-59, 62-65, 69, 176
āgneya 254
āḍhaka 203
āt 39
āti 59
ātman 214
ādi/-ma (*parvan*) 267, 270-71
ādeśa 60, 74
ā́paḥ 143
āmnāya 1
āraṇyaka 110
āvaraṇa 204, 215
āvṛti 216
āsanna 244
āsīna 263, 266

iṅgya 26-28, 35, 42
it 10, 236, 238-39
iti/-śabda/ityanta 25, 29-31, 38
itva 79
indu 253
indriya 152, 203
i-varṇa 2, 133, 230, 237, 254

īt 71
īṣacchliṣṭa 234
īṣatspṛṣṭa 250-51

u-kāra 121
ukti 47, 50, 63, 126, 178, 229-30, 241
ukṣan 281
ucca 91, 108, 110, 133, 135-36, 143, 145, 181, 200, 260-62, 269, 271, 277
uccā 63
uccāra 208
uccāraṇa 198, 201-02, 229, 236, 241, 243, 272
uccais 275

ut 10, 133, 236, 238-39
ut (*upasarga*) 29
uttama 7, 64, 71, 157-58, 248, 255-56, 258
uttaroṣṭha 243
utpatti 188, 198, 218
utpattisthāna 188
utva 79
utsava 20
udātta 39, 112, 124, 126-27, 129, 138, 142, 149, 173, 267, 280, 283
udāttakampa 271
udāttaśruti 129
udāna 205, 210, 213, 219, 221
unnamana 209
upa 8
upadhmānīya 48, 117, 259
upanābhi 202
upaniṣad 20
upaśleṣa 226, 231
upaśleṣya 230
upasaṁhāra 231
upasarga 8, 28, 39, 59
upahūtā̃ 101
upāyávaḥ 143
ubhayadīrghī 86, 95, 99
uras 216, 217, 248
urasyatva 115
u-varṇa 2, 231, 237, 254

ū-bhāva 138
ūrdhvadat 245
ūṣman 5, 7, 60-61, 65-66, 70-71, 73, 168, 170, 246, 251, 257

ṛ 2, 10, 74, 168-69, 232, 255
ṛ-kāra 10, 169
ṛ-varṇa 232, 255
ṛṣabha 277, 280-81

ṝ 2

ḷ 2, 74, 232, 255
ḷ-kāra 10, 255
ḷt 232

eka 5, 15, 29, 56, 88, 90, 94, 103-04, 116, 131, 151, 153, 159, 175, 181, 232,
e-kāra 233
ekonaviṁśati 29
ekonāṣṣaṣṭi 5
et 3, 236, 239, 253
etva 239
epha 49
eṣaḥ 59

ai-kāra 237-38
ait 3, 71, 240, 254

o-kāra 236
oṅkāra 121
ot 3, 236, 239, 254
otva 239
oṣṭha 229, 231-35, 240, 243, 245

au-kāra 237-38
aut 3, 240, 255

ka 3, 6, 64, 117, 182, 241, 246
ka-kāra 118
kakṣīvā̃ auśijaḥ 97
kaṇṭha 205, 213, 216-17, 223-24, 229, 275-76
kaṇṭhavāyu 216
kaṇṭhākāśa 223
kaniṣṭhikādi 267
kampa 103, 109-11, 193, 258, 270-71
kara 265
karaṇa 183, 217, 227, 228, 234, 238, 240, 247
kareṇu 80
karṇamūla 283
karmaśūdra 289
karviṇī 80
kalpa 285
ka-varga 117, 241, 246
kākalika 104
kāṭhaka 61, 106
kāṇḍa 11
kāra/-śabda 9, 47-49, 122, 172
-*kāra* 9-10, 47, 55, 63, 70-71, 78, 80, 115, 118, 121-22, 137, 169, 223-25, 229, 233, 236-38, 240, 250, 253, 255
kāraṇa 278
kārya/-śabda 199-200, 217, 223
kāla 87, 148, 150-51, 155-58, 160-61
kuhvā̀ 134
kumbhin 282
kekāruta 281
kevala (*anusvāra*) 120
kevala (*varṇakrama*) 13, 189
kevalāgama 63
krama/-pāṭha/ kramādhyāya 12, 17, 20, 34-35, 38-43, 45
krauñca 281

kṣatriya 261
kṣātra 256
kṣaipra 108, 130, 133, 144, 278
kṣamā 253

kha 3
kha (*ākāśa*) 276
khi 59

ga 3, 55, 64
gakāra 55
garbhageha 20
gala 210, 214, 247
galagarta 210
galānila 214
gātra 275
gāndhāra 277, 280-81
guṇa 187, 262
guda 205
guru 15, 265, 287
gokarṇavat 263
grantha 12, 289
gha 3
ghaṇṭānāda 103, 154
ghuṭibandhana 202
ghoṣa/-vat 7, 8, 225, 258

ṅa 3, 54, 64, 168

ca 3
cakṣus 1
catur 4, 6, 189, 206, 252, 260-61
caturtha 57, 225, 252, 255
candra 260
cāndramasa 255
cāṣa 151
citravilekhana 51
cu 241
ceṣṭā 207, 212
cha 3, 59

ja 3
jagat 286
jagdhi 291
jaṭā 13, 17, 42-43, 45-46
jāṭhara 204, 215
jāti 184, 187, 256, 261
jānu 263
jihvāgra 233, 242
jihvāñcala 244
jihvāprānta 233
jihvāmadhya 230, 235, 241, 243
jihvāmūla 210, 241
jihvāmūlīya/jihvāmūlya 48, 117, 246, 259
jyotis 1
jvālā 204, 215
jha 3

ña 3, 61

ṭa 3, 242
ṭa-varga 242
ṭha 3

ḍa 3
ḍha 3

ṇa 3, 115
ṇatva 38, 45

ta 3, 64, 242
ta enam bhi 96
takrā̃ 105
tapas 286
tarjanīmadhyaparvan 267
ta-varga 242
tasya dhūrṣadam 82
tā̃́ imi 106
tā eva 97
tāmasa 262
tālu 230, 234-35, 241, 243
turīya 256
tṛtīya 254
te enam 98
tè 'bruvan 137
taittirīya 61
tairovyañjana 132, 141-43, 146, 279
taunda 207
tri/traya/tredhā 30, 40, 43, 49, 79, 106, 111-12, 121, 124, 151, 153, 187, 194, 206, 223, 236, 256, 277
tri (*tṛtīya*) 256
trika 208
trikrama 39, 40, 43
trivarga 294

tryàmbaka 133
tvac 221

tha 4

da 4
da-kāra 63
dakṣa 263
dakṣajānu 263
dakṣiṇa 263
dantamūla 242, 244
darśaḥ 81
daśan 28, 125, 186, 188,
dārḍhya 275
dīrgha 231, 236
dīrgha (*svara*) 2, 50, 72-73, 87-89, 91, 93, 106, 109, 111, 153, 159, 230, 258, 280
dṛḍha 145
dṛḍhatara 144
dṛṣṭi 264, 273
deva/-tā 184, 186-87, 253-55, 260, 265, 288
devā́ ú 106
deveśa 20, 22
deha 206, 276, 290
dairghya 275
druta 23, 24
drvànnaḥ 133
dvi/dvedhā/dvaya 26, 30-31, 41, 44, 60, 63, 68, 70, 72, 77, 102, 104, 110-11, 113, 115, 121, 131, 151, 153, 158, 161, 199, 207, 225, 248, 256, 262, 270,
dvija 15, 294
dvijottama 294
dvi/-tīya 7, 57, 60, 67, 252, 254, 256
dvitva 53-54, 56-58, 66, 69, 73, 120, 176
dvirūpa 68, 70
dha 4, 64
dhamanī 202, 204
dharma 179, 182-83, 185-86, 188-94, 196-97, 239, 286-88
dhātu 203
dhāma 59
dhūrṣadam 82
dhṛta 129, 169, 260-62, 267
dhaivata 277, 279, 282
dhvani 102, 178-79, 182-83, 191, 197, 223, 275-76

na 4, 54, 61, 115, 168
nakula 151
namana 209
naraka 293
nas 249
nāḍī 208-09, 211
nāḍīnāla 211
nāḍīlatā 208
nāda 68, 103, 154, 200, 202, 223-25
nābhi 202, 205, 265
nāman 15, 100, 119, 124-26, 131, 162, 172-73
nālī 200
nāsika 249
nāsikā 107, 248
nāsikya 48, 100, 249

nāsikyatva 115
nāsikyarandhra 104
nāsya 5
ni 8
nitya (*śabda*) 199, 217
nitya (*svarita*) 108, 130, 134, 144, 278
niyuta 18
nirākṛti 291-92
niśśvāsa 1
niṣāda 277-78, 282
niṣkarmin 21
nihata 30, 112, 127, 186, 271
niḥ 29
nīca 91, 109, 134, 136, 144, 194, 261, 267, 270, 277
nīcā 63
nīcais 276
naiśceṣṭya 219
nyàñcam 134
nyāsa 263-64, 266-67, 273
nyūna 16, 252

pa 4, 117, 243
paṅktibhojana 292
pañcan 5, 6, 14, 206, 249,
pañcama 277, 279, 282
pañcaviṁśati 4
pada (abode) 294
pada (word) 27-29, 31-33, 35, 37, 39-41, 43-44, 54, 58, 60, 67, 134-37, 139-40, 142-43
pada/padādhyāya 12, 17, 19, 25, 31, 38, 160
padānta 25, 54, 67
parama 59
paraśabda 171
parā 29
parāṅga 169, 170
parāṇu 204
parāyukta 167
pari 8, 28
parśu 81
pa-varga 117, 243
pākavatī 85, 91, 97
pāṭha 14, 41-42, 49, 52, 122, 150
pātakin 21
pātha 59
pādavṛtta 132, 139-40, 146
pāpa 292
pārāyaṇa 16, 21-22, 24
pika 282
pipīlikā 85, 93, 98
pūjya 265
pūrvaśabda 171
pūrvāgama 57, 69
pūrvāṅga 168, 174
pṛthagbhakti 268
pra 8
práügam 97, 140
prakṛti 217, 224
pragalbhatā 290
pragraha 31, 37
pracaya 124, 129, 169, 280, 283
pradeśinī 271
praṇava 123
prati 8
prathama 6, 7, 10, 60, 62-63, 67, 70, 226, 253, 256, 258

prayatna 124, 127, 130, 144-46, 183, 186, 238, 249-52
prayuta 18
praśna 11
praśliṣṭa 108, 132, 138, 145
prākṛtatva 114
prāṇa 205, 211-13, 216, 220-21
prātihata 131, 135-36, 145
prāyaścitta 19
prārambhakoṅkāra 121
pluta 2, 88, 101-02, 123, 153-54, 159, 195, 230, 258
pha 4
phala 16, 51, 285, 291

ba 4
barsam 82
barsvaka 233
barhis 207
barhiḥ 80
brahman/-jāti 256, 261
brahman 19, 199, 274, 286, 289, 293
brahmatyāgin 289
brahmayajña 19
brahmahatyā 23
brāhmaṇa 289
brāhmaṇī 151
brāhmī 288
bha 4
bhakti 74, 77-79, 83, 167, 169, 190-92, 258, 268
bhaya 288
bhānu 253
bhitti 51
bhukti 212
bhuja 59
bhū 293
bhūtaśabda 172, 179
bhūte 59
bhūmi 254
bhūṣaṇa 290

ma 4, 72, 115, 121-22
madhya/-ma (*parvan*) 267, 269, 271
madhyama (*svara*) 277, 280-81
madhyamā (*aṅguli*) 267
madhya/madhyamā (*vāgvṛtti*) 23-24
madhyamā (*svarabhakti*) 85, 92, 98
madhyastha 224
manas 214, 216, 218-19, 222, 264
manaḥprayoga 218, 222
mandra 102
malhā 80
mahat 225, 226
mahattā 276
mahāpradoṣa 22
-*mātra/mātrikā/mātrā/-kāla* 56, 87-88, 90-95, 102-04, 106-07, 111-13, 116, 121-22, 139, 150-54, 156-62, 173, 177, 186, 192, 194, 231-32, 237, 284
mātrikāsahita/mātrikāyuta/mātrikāvarṇa/mātrā 13, 18, 150, 161, 177, 189
mānava 293
mukti 212
mukha 107, 249

mūrdhan 103, 107, 283
mr̥dutara 145
mr̥dutā 276
moha 23

ya 4, 72-73, 133-34, 253
yajus 11, 12, 55
yatna 15, 218
yad ghrā̃₃ 101
yama 65-66, 170, 176, 197
yaśo mamā̃₃ 101
yā āviviśuḥ 98
yājuṣa 5, 198
yoga 56, 80-81, 83, 120, 168, 174-75
yogādi 120, 168

ra 4, 49, 73, 80-81, 244, 254
raṅga 101-02, 105-06, 154, 195, 258
raṅgadīrgha 106
raṅgapluta 101-02, 154, 195, 258
rasa 210
rājasa 262
ruta 102, 154, 281
rekhādarśana 187
rekhāsthāna 268
repha 54, 70, 81-82, 168-69

la 4, 54, 72-73, 80, 83, 244, 254
la-kāra 71
lakṣaṇa 31, 46, 58, 69, 92, 94, 147-48, 177, 182, 285
lakṣyānusāra 58
likhitapāṭha 14
lopa 45, 137

va 4, 54, 72, 133-34, 245, 255
va-kāra 70
vatsānusāriṇī 85, 88, 96
vatsānusr̥ti 85, 87, 95-96
vapus 214
varga 6, 10, 71, 117, 241-43, 246, 248, 256, 258
vargāntya 248
vargottara 10
varṇa 2, 5, 9, 16, 44, 46, 48-49, 52, 60, 117, 119, 133, 148, 163, 178, 180, 184, 195-98, 202, 224, 226, 230-32, 237, 249, 253-56, 259, 273
varṇakrama 13, 14, 47, 50-51, 53, 68, 119, 122, 147, 156, 180-81, 240
varṇapāṭha/-ka 49, 52
varṇaprakr̥ti 224
varṇasaṁjñā 184, 196-97, 259
varṇa/-sāra/-ka 14, 18, 181, 190-92, 196, 284
varṇasārabhūta-varṇakrama 181
varṇokti 126
varṇottara 49
varṣam 81
vasudhā 260
vastra 290
vahni 204
vā āpasta 99
vā āraṇyam 98
vā iyam 96

vākya 30, 32, 36-37, 52
vāc 23
vā́cam 143
vāyasa 151
vāyu 205, 216, 253
vi 8
vikasana 211
vikṛti 12-13, 15, 65, 168
vigraha 180
vidyā 288
vidhi 19, 38, 43, 46, 53, 116, 120, 127, 130, 149, 163, 194, 266, 287, 294
vinyāsa 273
vipra 287-88, 290-91
vibhu 199
virāma 116, 157-58, 272
vilambita 23, 25
vivakṣu 214
vivṛta 78, 224, 247, 250-51
vivṛtti 84, 86, 88, 116
viś 256, 261
viśeṣa 12, 159, 198
visarga 5, 7, 48, 50, 70, 89, 92-93, 95, 114, 116-18, 167, 247, 257, 259
vṛ 72
vṛtta 279
vṛtti 23-25
veda 14-15, 253, 274, 285-86, 289-90, 293-94
vedyā ādan yat 98
veṣṭana/-pada 26, 35, 37, 42
vaikṛtatva 114
vaiśeṣikā 85, 90, 97
vya 72
vyakta 200
vyakti 84, 87, 89, 93, 95, 100, 136, 139, 140,
vyaṅgya 164, 192,
vyañjana 2, 9, 53, 57, 74-75, 126, 141-42, 155, 164-66, 175, 181, 228, 233-34, 257, 272
vyāghraruta 102, 154
vyāna 206, 209-10
vra 72

śa 4, 9, 61-62, 67, 78, 81, 83, 114, 255
śata 17
śatavalśa 83
śabda 182, 198-201, 217-18, 222-23, 275-76
-śabda 9, 25, 28, 47-48, 129, 171-72, 179
śabdārtha 28
śamala 208
śarīra 207
śākhā 11, 12
śāśvata 294
śāstra 46, 147, 264, 273, 290
śikyamūla 208
śikhin 151
śiras 242
śīkṣā 1
śuddhavarṇa/-krama 17, 123, 176, 195
śūdra 257, 261, 289
śruti 200, 217, 272
śrotriya 293

śliṣṭa 114, 135
śliṣṭa (*svarita*) 279
śvāsa 214, 218, 222-25

ṣa 4, 9, 67, 78, 81, 114, 118, 253
ṣa-kāra 253
ṣaḍja 188, 277, 280-81
ṣaḍjādihetu 188
ṣaḍviṁśati 282
ṣa-ṇa-tva-ṭa-tva-vidhi 38
ṣatva 38, 45
ṣaṣ 5,

sa 4, 9, 62, 67, 78, 82, 114, 254
sa āyurā 96
sa ij jane 97
sá idhānáḥ 135
saṁjña/saṁjñā 6, 58, 80, 86, 96, 116, 119, 130, 132, 141, 162, 172-73, 184, 188, 196-97, 259
saṁhitā 11-12, 16, 19, 31, 46, 50-52, 110, 129, 148, 160-61, 228
saṅghaṭṭa 220
sátejasam 135
sandhi 41, 49, 84, 92, 94, 108, 118, 123
sandhyā 21
saptan 83, 124,
sam 29
sama 205, 207, 216-17, 219-20
samāna 215
samānāvaraṇa 215
sammelana 113
saỹyattā āsan 99
saỹyoga 80, 174
sarvāṅga 206, 283
savargīya 71
savarṇa 71, 89, 91, 93, 170
savarṇadīrgha 91, 93
savarṇadīrghī 86, 94, 99
saṽvṛta 77, 224, 240, 249-50
sahasraka 17
sāttvika 262
sāra 178
su 29
sumaṅgalā̃$_3$ 101
surāpāna 291
suślokā̃$_3$ 101
suṣīracakra 207
sūkara 293
sūkṣma 202, 204, 212
sūdgātā 138
sūnnīyam 138
sūrya 260

sṛti 212
sed agne astu 96
sò 'bravīt 137
saurāṣṭrikā 105
saurya 255
sthāna 62, 179, 183, 188, 197, 211, 217, 221, 226-29, 234-35, 238, 246-48, 273
sthitisandhi 118
sthūla 203, 212
sparśa 4, 6, 54, 61, 64-65, 70-72, 168, 170, 251, 257
spṛṣṭa 250-51

svatantra 272

svatantrā 82

svara 2, 3, 10, 16, 44, 49, 52, 58, 74-75, 78-79, 84, 109, 119, 122, 124-26, 149, 155-56, 162, 164-67, 173, 177, 186, 200, 225, 245, 251, 256-57, 260-61, 263-64, 266, 268, 272-74, 278-79, 281-82

svaranyāsa 263-64, 266, 274

svaranyāsakṛt 263

svarabhakti 74, 77, 79, 83, 190

svarabhaktitā 74

svarasaẏyukta 13

svara/-varṇa/-krama 13, 18, 125, 147, 149, 177

svarita 94, 108, 124, 128, 132, 140, 142, 146, 262, 278, 283

svā̃ ahá 106

svāra 92, 110-11, 128, 130, 133, 137, 139, 141, 143-44, 193-94, 260-61, 268-70

svārakampa 110, 270

ha 4, 7, 73, 80, 115, 225, 246-48, 254

haṁsapadā 81

ha-kāra 78, 115, 223-25

hata 279

hanu 229, 233-35, 241

hanumūla 241

hanūrdhva 234

hari 15, 123

hariṇī 81

hal 2, 8, 47, 69, 71, 141, 156-57, 162, 171-72, 185, 191, 227-28, 257

halsaṁjñaka 172

hasta 263-64

hastinī 82

hayaheṣā 282

hāritā 83

hṛt 205, 211, 213, 283

hṛtpadmakośapṛṣṭha 211

hrasva 2, 10, 49, 54, 56, 68, 73 87, 88, 90, 109, 111, 153, 158, 160, 258, 280

hrasvatā 276

hrāsa 211

ẖka 4

ḫpa 4

ḷa 5, 255

Appendix 3

English Equivalents of Some Important Sanskrit Terms Used in Ātreyaśīkṣāmūla

Absorbed circumflex (*abhinihata/abhihata svarita/svāra*)

Accent (*svara*)

Accentual demonstration (*svaranyāsa*)

Accentual phonic sequence (*svaravarṇakrama*)

Accumulated (*pracaya/dhṛta*)

Activity (*ceṣṭā*)

Acute (*udātta*)

Acute tremulous (*udāttakampa*)

Adjacent imposition (*abhinidhāna*)

Adjunct (*aṅga*)

Adjunct of predecessor (*pūrvāṅga*)

Adjunct of successor (*parāṅga*)

Adjunction (*aṅga*)

Adjunctive phonic sequence (*aṅgavarṇakrama/sāṅgavarṇakrama*)

Aeon (*kalpa*)

Alteration (*vikṛti*)

Alveolar ridge (*barsvaka*)

Anaptyxis (*svarabhakti*)

Antecedence (*pūrvatva*)

Appellation (*nāman/saṁjñā*)

Application (*prayoga*)

Approximation (*upaśleṣa/upasaṁhāra*)

Artery (*dhamanī*)

Articulation (*uccāraṇa*)

Articulator (*karaṇa*)

Artificial reading (*vikṛti*)

Aspiration (*hakāra*)

Astral tube (*nāḍī*)

Attribute (*dharma*)

Base (*ādhāra*)

Bending (*namana*)

Bimoraic (*dvimātra/dvimātrika*)

Blade of the tongue (*jihvāñcala*)

Blazing (*dīpta*)

Blowing sound/*ḫ* (*upadhmānīya*)

Body (*śarīra/vapus/deha*)

Brahman-relinquisher (*brahmatyāgin*)

Breath/breathing (*śvāsa*)

Cause (*hetu*)

Channel (*nāḍī*)

Chapter (*adhyāya*)

Chest (*uras*)

Circumflex (*svarita/svāra*)

Circumflex tremulous (*svārakampa*)

Class (*jāti*)

Closed (*saṽvṛta*)

Coalesced circumflex (*praśliṣṭa svarita/svāra*)

Collision (*saṅghaṭṭa*)

Component (*avayava*)

Condition (*avasthā*)

Conjunct (*yoga/saỹyoga*)

Connected (*śliṣṭa*)

Consonant (*vyañjana*)

Consonantal (*vyañjanātmaka*)

Consonant-interventional circumflex (*tairovyañjana svarita/svāra*)

Constituents of the body (*dhātu*)

Contiguity (*upasaṁhāra*)

Continuous reading (*saṁhitā*)

Crane (*krauñca*)

Cry of a peacock (*kekāruta*)

Cuckoo (*pika*)

Decrease (*hrāsa*)

Definable-according (*lakṣyānusāra*)

Definitional texts (*lakṣaṇa*)

Deity (*devatā*)

Demonstrator of accents (*svaranyāsakṛt*)

Dependent (*sāpekṣa*)

Designation (*saṁjñā*)

Dha (*dhaivata*)

Digestional air (*sama/samāna*)

Discrete anaptyxis (*svatantrā svarabhakti/pṛthagbhakti*)

Duplication (*dvitva*)

Earth (*kṣmā/bhūmi/vasudhā*)

Effort (*yatna*)

Elephant (*kumbhin*)

Elevated (*samucchrita*)

Elision (*lopa*)

Energy centre (*cakra*)

Enjoyment (*bhukti*)

Entwining word (*veṣṭana/veṣṭanapada*)

Enunciation (*ukti*)

Eternal (*nitya*)

Etymology (*nirvacana*)

Euphonic change (*sandhi*)

Excessively touched (*atispṛṣṭa*)

Excretional air (*apāna*)

Expirational air (*udāna*)

Explanatory rules (*paribhāṣā*)

Faeces (*śamala*)

Fast mode of speech (*drutavṛtti*)

Feebler (*alpatara*)

Final detachable vowel (*pragraha*)

Final nasal stop (*nāda*)

Finger (*aṅguli*)

Fire (*agni*)

Firm (*dṛḍha*)

Firmer (*dṛḍhatara*)

First (*prathama*)

Flame (*jvālā*)

Flatuous air (*vyāna*)

Fluid (*rasa*)

Fourth (*caturtha*)

Fricative (*ūṣman*)

Ga (*gāndhāra*)

Gap (*antara*)

Gentler (*mṛdutara*)

Glottis (*kaṇṭha/gala*)

Grave (*anudātta/nihata*)

Gross (*sthūla*)

Gular air (*galānila/kaṇṭhavāyu*)

H̱ (*jihvāmūlīya*)

Ḫ (*upadhmānīya*)

Ḥ (*visarga*)

Hard breath (*mahāñchvāsa*)

Hardness (*dārḍhya*)

Harm (*doṣa*)

Hastened circumflex (*kṣaipra svarita/svāra*)

Heart (*hṛt*)

Held (*dhṛta*)

Heterogeneous phone (*asavarṇa*)

Hiatus (*vivṛtti/vyakti*)

High (*ucca*)

Hole of throat (*galagarta*)

Homogeneous phone (*savarṇa*)

Horse (*haya*)

Humming sound (*kākalika*)

Imperforated (*acchinna*)

Increase (*vikasana*)

Increment (*āgama*)

Independent (*nirapekṣa*)

Index finger (*tarjanī/pradeśinī*)

Indication of the accents through the interphalangeal lines

(*rekhādarśana*)
Ingredient (*sāra*)
Innate circumflex (*nitya svarita/svāra*)
Inseparability (*apṛthaktvam*)
Inseparable word (*aniṅgya*)
Insertion (*kevalāgama*)
Intermediate mode of speech (*madhya/madhyamavṛtti*)
Jaw (*hanu*)
Junctional ritual (*sandhyā*)
Juncture (*sandhi*)
Juxtaposition (*sandhi*)
Knot (*parvan*)
Labial (*oṣṭhya*)
Last (*uttama*)
Lax (*vivṛta*)
Liberation (*mukti*)
Lip (*oṣṭha*)
Little finger (*kaniṣṭhikā*)
Long / long vowel (*dīrgha*)
Long tremulous (*dīrghakampa*)
Low (*avaca*)
Lower lip (*adhara*)
Ṁ (*anusvāra/kevalānusvāra*)
Ma (*madhyama*)
Manner of articulation (*prayatna*)
Manual demonstration of accents (*hastasvaravinyāsa*)
Material of phones (*varṇaprakṛti*)
Middle finger (*madhyamā*)
Middle of the tongue (*jihvāmadhya*)
Mind (*manas*)
Minute (*aṇu*)
Minuteness (*aṇutā*)
Modes of speech (*vāgvṛtti*)
Modification (*vaikṛta*)
Monomoraic (*ekamātra/ekamātrika*)
Moon (*indu/candramas*)
Mora (*mātrā*)
Moraic phonic sequence (*mātrāvarṇakrama*)
Moraic time duration (*mātrākāla*)
Motionlessness (*naiśceṣṭya*)
Musical note (*svara*)
Nasal (*nāsikya/anunāsika/nāsika*)
Nasalization (*nāsikyatva*)
Nasalized (*anunāsika*)
Nasally modified *a*-vowel (*raṅga*)
Nasally modified long *a*-vowel (*raṅgadīrgha*)

Nasally modified protracted *a*-vowel (*raṅgapluta*)

Navel (*nābhi*)

Neigh (*heṣā*)

Ni (*niṣāda*)

Non-elision (*alopa*)

Nose-sound (*nāsikya*)

Note (*svara*)

Obstructive circumflex (*prātihata svarita/svāra*)

Om (*praṇava*)

Omnipresent (*vibhu*)

Open (*vivṛta*)

Organ (*aṅga/gātra/deha*)

Origin (*utpatti*)

Originality (*prākṛta*)

Ox (*ukṣan*)

Oxytone (*udāttānta*)

Pa (*pañcama*)

Palate (*tālu*)

Partially touched (*īṣatspṛṣṭa*)

Pause (*virāma*)

Pericardium (*hṛtpadmakośa*)

Phone (*varṇa*)

Phonic sequence (*varṇakrama*)

Phonic sequence of the phonic attributes (*varṇasāra/varṇasārabhūta-varṇakrama*)

Physical condition (*aṅgāvasthā*)

Place close to navel (*upanābhi*)

Place of articulation (*sthāna*)

Place of origin (*utpattisthāna*)

Plexus (*ghuṭibandhana*)

Porous (*suṣīra*)

Prefix (*upasarga*)

Producible (*kārya*)

Protracted/protracted vowel (*pluta*)

Pulmonic-ness (*urasyatva*)

Pure *ṁ* (*kevalānusvāra*)

Quality (*guṇa/dharma*)

Re (*ṛṣabha*)

Reading of phonic sequence (*varṇakramapāṭha/varṇakramokti*)

Recitation (*pārāyaṇa*)

Rectum (*guda*)

Relaxation (*hrasvatā*)

Remainder (*śeṣa*)

Resonance (*nāda*)

Respirational air (*prāṇa*)

Ring finger (*anāmikā*)

Roof of the oral cavity (*śiras*)

Root of the jaws (*hanumūla*)

Root of the teeth (*dantamūla*)

Root of the tongue (*jihvāmūla*)

Sa (*ṣaḍja*)

Sacrum (*trika*)

Same-word hiatal circumflex (*pādavr̥tta svarita/svāra*)

Ṣa-substitution (*ṣa-tva*)

Science of proper pronunciation (*śikṣā*)

Second (*dvitīya*)

Semi-moraic (*ardhamātra/ardhamātrika*)

Semi-moraic quality (*ardhamātratva*)

Semi-vowel (*antassthā*)

Sense-organ (*indriya*)

Sentence (*vākya*)

Separable word (*iṅgya*)

Separative word (*avagraha*)

Sequence of antecedence (*pūrvāṅgakrama*)

Sequence of antecedence and succession (*paurvāparyakrama*)

Sequence of succession (*parāṅgakrama*)

Sequential reading (*krama/kramapāṭha/kramādhyāya*)

Series (*varga*)

She-goat (*ajā*)

Short/short vowel (*hrasva*)

Short tremulous (*hrasvakampa*)

Sibilant (*ś* or *ṣ* or *s*)

Sides of the tongue (*jihvāprānta*)

Simple phonic sequence (*kevala/śuddha-varṇakrama*)

Slight breath (*alpaśvāsa*)

Slow mode of speech (*vilambitavr̥tti*)

Softness (*mr̥dutā*)

Sound (*śabda*)

Sound produced by the root of the tongue) (*jihvāmūlīya*)

Space (*ākāśa/kha*)

Speech sound (*dhvani*)

Stability in juncture (*sthitisandhi*)

Static (*niścala*)

Stomach fire (*jāṭharāgni / brhis taunda*)

Stop (*sparśa*)

Subtle (*sūkṣma*)

Succession (*paratva*)

Śūdra by activity (*karmaśūdra*)

Sun (*bhānu/sūrya*)

Surface (*āvaraṇa / āvr̥tti / tvac*)

Syllable (*akṣara*)

Synonym (*paryāya*)

Tangled reading (*jaṭā/jaṭāpāṭha*)

Ṭa-substitution (*ṭa-tva*)

Tense (*saṽvṛta*)

Tension of the organs (*gātradairghya*)

Termination (*avasāna*)

Tetramoraic (*caturmātra/caturmātrika*)

Thick (*sthūla*)

Third (*tṛtīya*)

Three categories of possible human pursuits (*trivarga*)

Throat (*kaṇṭha/gala*)

Thumb (*aṅguṣṭha*)

Time duration (*kāla*)

Tip of the tongue (*jihvāgra*)

Tongue (*jihvā*)

Touched (*spṛṣṭa*)

Tremulous (*kampa*)

Trimoraic (*trimātra/trimātrika*)

Tri-sequence (*trikrama*)

Tubular pipe (*nāḍīnāla*)

Tune (*svara*)

Twin Phone (*yama*)

Ultimate (*para*)

Undivided entwining word (*akhaṇḍaveṣṭana*)

Unmanifested (*avyakta*)

Uplifting (*unnamana*)

Upper jaw (*hanūrdhva*)

Upper lip (*uttaroṣṭha*)

Utterance (*ukti*)

Very firm (*atidṛḍha*)

Vessel (*nāḍī*)

Vital airs (*vāyu*)

Vocalic (*svarātmaka*)

Vocalic *l* (*ḷ-varṇa*)

Vocalic *r* (*ṛ-varṇa*)

Voice (*nāda*)

Voiced (*ghoṣavat/ghoṣa*)

Voiceless (*aghoṣa*)

Vowel (*svara*)

Vowel-fragmentation (*svarabhaktitā*)

Way (*sṛti*)

Wideness (*mahattā*)

Wind (*vāyu*)

Word (*pada*)

Word-reading (*pada/padapāṭha/padādhyāya*)

Appendix 4

The Text in Grantha Script with the Spellings Found in the MSS

||ஞூ௭ெயஶீக்ஷாகாரிகா||

காரிகாம் ஸம்ப்ரவக்ஷ்யாமி ப்ரயதம் பாரிஹாஷிகம் |
ஸம்ஹிதாவிஷயம் வெதவாராயணவழஜுதஃ ||க||
பாராயணகூஉலெதெவ பாஶூத்திஃ பஉவஹஷணம் |
கூஉஸ்யாய ஜடாயாஸ்ய ஶாஉவணாகூஉஸ்ய ச ||உ||
ஶக்ஷணஞ கூஉாதுகு யள ச ஶிகாமஉள ஷ்யூதள |
தயொரஹிநியாநஸ்ய கெவஶாவ்யாமஉஸ்ய ச ||ந||
யஉாநாஞஹிஷெயாநாந்[1]காமஉநிஷெயயொஃ |
ஶக்ஷணம் ஷ்வாரஶக்தீநாம் ஸொாஉாஹரணஸஂஜ்ஞகாஃ ||ச||
விவ்ருத்தெஹூ[2]க்ஷணஜஸ்யாம் ஸஂஜ்ஞொாஉாஹரணாநி ச |
வ்யக்திஉஶ்யஷுநாஸிக்யொ ரஂமாவ்யஷ்மதஶீஷயொஃ ||ரு||
ஶக்ஷணம் ஷ்வரிதொாஉாத்தகம்பாநாஞ விஶெஷதஃ |
ஸ்யாஸெகூதவ்ராகூதயொஞூா[3]ஸிக்யூஎரஸ்யயொரவி ||சு||
வியிஸ்ய ஜிஹ்வாஉுலீயொ[4]வஹ்மாநீயாவ்யயொரவி |
ஷ்ரிதிஸஙிவியிலெதெவ தயா ப்ரணவஶக்ஷணம் ||எ||
ஷ்வரவணாகூஉஷ்தொாஉாத்தாஉீநாஹிரபெணம் |
உஉாஹரணஸஂயுக்தஸஷ்வரிதஶக்ஷணம் ||அ||

---

[1] T நாம் ஶி

[2] H ஶூ

[3] T யொஃ நா

[4] T யொ்யா

தத்ரு[5] யத்நவ்ரு ஹெஊாஶ ஊாசூாவணூகூஊேஹூயா |
ஊாசூாஊாநநிரூவெஞ ஊாசூாகூாவொக்திவிஸ்ரூவி ||கூ||
கூ௦ஶவணூகூஊேஹூசு வாரவாூவபூா௦ஶயக்ஷண௦ |
கூ௦ஶவணூகூஜொக்ஷெஶ ஸாஹூஷ௦ யக்ஷணஜதஃ ||ய||
நிவபூவநு௦ வணூஸாரஜூதவணூகூஊஸு தா|
ஸ௦வ்ரா வ வணூயஜூாணாஜ[6] ஊாக்ஷெராநாவாூவிபூகா||யக||
ஜக்ஷூநாஹூாரகூ௦வாநா௦ ர௦ஶஸூாவ்யுக்தியக்ஷண௦|
ஶஜொாத்ரு[7] த்திவ்ருகூாரஶ தசு ஹூநிநிரூவெண௦||யஉ||
ஶரீராஜஶூதஜ[8]சு ஸவூவ்ராவாரயக்ஷண௦|
ஜாலாரா ஹிஹூதிஃ வஞவாயூநா௦ ஹூாநவெஹிகாஃ||யங||
ஹூநிஹெஊாஹூசு ஜாதவணூாநாஞ விநிஶயஃ|
தெஷாஜ[9] ஹூாநகூரணவிவெகூஹூத்ரு[10]காரகூஃ||யச||
வ்ருயத்நஹெஊா வணூாநாநெவதாஜாதிஸ௦ஜ்ஞகாஃ|
உஊாத்தாஹிஹூராணாஞ ஜெவதா ஜாதயொ ஶுணாஃ||யரு||
ததொ ஹஹூஹூரநூாஸயக்ஷணஜஸூ தத்ரூய௦|
கூ௦ஶாஊூவஹூா ஷஜ்ஞாஹிஸவ்ரூஹூரநிரூவெண௦||யசு||
உஊாத்தாஹிஹூரொாத்ரு[11] த்திவெபூஊஸூ ஊஹிஊா ததஃ|
விகூூத்யூஷகூஸ௦யூக்ஷவெஊஸூாஹூயநெ வாய௦||யஎ||
ஐத்யெவஊாநாவாூவெபூண ஶீக்ஷா ஸ௦வ்ரொாவூதெயாநா||
ஐத்ராசெயஶீக்ஷாகாரிகா ஸஊாத்வா||

---

[5] H க்வ்ரு

[6] T ணா௦ த

[7] H க்வ

[8] H த௦ த

[9] T ஷா௦ தா

[10] H க்வ்ரு

[11] H க்வ

||ஶ்ரூதெயஶீக்ஷாஜீவலூ||

வாரிஹாஷா

ஶ்ரூஹ்நாயா யஸ்ய நிஸ்ஷாஸாஸஙந்ரஸ்யூள[12] ச சக்ஷூஷீ|
தக் ஷ்ர[13]ணஜ்ய வாஶஜ்ஞாதிஸ்ஷீக்ஷாம் வக்ஷ்யாஶி நிஜூஷாம்||க||
கூச ஷ்யா ஐதி ஷ்ராக்தா வூஜநாநி ஹஶ ஷூ்தாஃ|
ஹுஷ்ஷீஷயூஷ்மதாவணெயவணெயாவணயா ஜ ஜு ள ச||உ||
ணஷெஷொஜஉஷீதி ஜேூயாஷ்ஷா[14]ஷஶெஹாஷித ஷ்யாஃ|
கூவள மவள ஐசசஜா ஈலக்ஷள டூலஷா ணதள||ந||
யஜள யநள வஷபஹா உ ஷ்ஶயாஃ வஞ்விம்ஶதிஃ|
யாள வவள சதஸ்யாஜ்ஷாஸஙஃகூஶஷஸஃவஹாஃ||ச||
ஷஷஷ்ஷாணொ விஸஷெயாநூஷ்யாரொ ஜொ நாஸ்யவஞகூம்|
ஐதெ்தெ யாஜூஷா வணயா ணகொநாஷ்ஷாரீரிதாஃ||ரு||
ஶ்ரூஜெண வஞ வஞ ஸ்யூ ஷ்ஶயாநாம் வஶயஸம்ஜ்ஞகாஃ|
வஷெயஷூ தெஷூ ஸம்ஜ்ஞா ஸ்யூஸஙதூணயாம் ஷ்ரயஜாஉயஃ||கூ||
வஞஉஸ்யாத்தஉஃ ஷ்ராக்தா வொஷாவொஷள தூ தெஷூ வெ|
ஹாநெ்யாஷ்ஷா ஷ்ரயஜாவெஷவ விஸஶயஸங ஶிதீயகாஃ||எ||
கூவொஷா ஸ்யூஸங தெஷ்யாநெ்ய வொஷவஞொ ஹஶ ஷூ்தாஃ|
வாரிவிநாஹ்யூவஷ்ராவஷ்ரத்யயீத்யூவஸஶயகாஃ||அ||
காஶஶஷ்யாத்தரொ வணெயா வணயாவ்யா ஷ்ரதிவாஉ்யதெ|
வூஜநாநாஉகாஶ ஸ்யாத்து[15]ஷஷெத்யாஶிஸம்ஹ்ஹாக்||கூ||
ஹுஷ்ஷாஶிஉூஉ்யகாஶஸங தயஜ்ஞாஶ ஷ்ரெஷூ வெ|
வஷெயாத்தஶஸ்ஷூ வஶயாவ்யா ஷ்ரயஜொ ஹவதீத்யவி||ய||
ஐத்யாதெயஶீக்ஷாவாரிஹாஷா ஸஜாஷ்தா||

---

[12] H யூள

[13] T த்ரீ

[14] T யாஃ ஷெொ

[15] T ஜ்ஜ

ஸம்ஹிதாவிஷய

ஞூரம்ஹெ யஜுஷஸ்ரூாவா யா ஸ்யாக் ஸா[16] ஸம்ஹிதா ஷ்ரூதா|
காணூவ்ரூஸ்ரூாநுவாகாஜெஜ்யூ: வ்ரூவிஹக்தாஞராஞரா||௧||
யாஷ்தொந்யா யஜுஸ்ரூாவா ந தாஸாம் விக்ரூதீ: வடெக்|
ஸம்ஹிதாஹ்ரூஞூஊாகுஸ்ய ஸவிஶெஷள வஉக்ரூஊள||௨||
ஜடா வணாக்ரூஊாவெவ க்ரூஊாதிக்ரூதய ஷ்ரூதா:|
கெவஶ ஷ்ரஸம்யுக்தா ஊாதிகாஸஹிதஷ்யா||௩||
ஸாம்ஹஞ வணாஸாரஞ வஞ வணாக்ரூஊாந் விஉ:|

வெஉவாராயணவஶ

ஸவாயா நாயிஹஞவ்யா வெஉா ஶிவிதவாஂக:||௪||
சுவொதவ்யஷ்விக்ரூதிதிமெஜயாத்தாக் ஹுரொஜரூவாக்|
வெஉஷ்க்ஷரஉகெகஉகெக்கம் ஹரிநாஉகம்||௫||
சுந்யூநா ஷ்ரதவெவ வணாதொ யா உ ஸம்ஹிதா|
ஸக்ரூக் வாராயணெ தஸ்யா யாவக் வஶஉிஹொசூதெ||௬||
திஹுணஞக் வ[17]உஉ தஷ்யாக் க்ரூஉ கூஷஹுணம் ஹவெக்|
ஜடாயூாயெ ஶதம் வ்ரொக்தம் ஶுஉவணெ ஸஹஸ்ரகம்||௭||
ஷ்ரவணெயுதம் விஉ்யாஷி[18]யுதஜாதிகாயுதெ|
வ்ரயுதகூம்ஹவணெ ஸ்யாஉ[19]நஜம் வணாஸாரகெ||௮||

வாராயணக்ரூஉ:

வ்ராயஶித்தவியள க்ரூஜெ[20] ஞ்ரூஹயஜ்ஞெ க்ரியாவியள|
ஸம்ஹிதாவாஂநம் கூயாஷி[21]யஉாஞ வஉாஉிகாந்||௯||
உத்ஷ[22]வாகூஞு ஜவெஶ நிஹாதெ ஹஹாமெஹத:|

---

[16] T ஷ்ரூா

[17] T த்ஷ

[18] T க் நி

[19] T க் சு

[20] H & T ஜெ

[21] T க் நி

[22] H க்ஸ

க்ரூஶாஜிகம் வமெஜூசா தயொாவநிஷஜம் வமெக்||உய||

கநஜ்யநவ்ரகாரண॰

யஷ்ட்ு வாராயணம் ஹிகூா காஶாதிக்ரஶம்கயா|
கூயூா[23]க் ஸஙூாம்[24] ஸ நிக்ஷஜீூ விஜ்ஞெயஷ்டு வாதகீ||உக||
வ்ராவை ஶஹாவ்ரஷொஷெவி தஜா ஜெவெஶஸளியள|
கநஜ்யநஶாநெந ந ச வாராயணஜூெக்||உஉ||
தூஜெஜூஜி தஜா ஜொஹாக் ஙூஹுஹதூாம் ஸஶாவிஶெக்|

வாஃூத்திஃ

வாசஷ்டு வூத்தயஷ்டிஸெ்ரா ஓூதஶஜ்யவிளம்விதாஃ||உந||
க்ருவூதூாவூதூ சாஹூாஸெ ஓூதவூத்தூா வமெசிஜஃ|
வாராயணெ வ்ரயொாமாகூெ ஶஜ்யஶாம் வூத்திஶாசஶெக்||உச||
ளொயநாகூஙு ஶிஷூாணாம் வூத்திம் கூயூாசிளம்விதாம்|

வஜயக்ஷண॰

வஜாஜ்யாயெ வஜாஞெ யஜி[25]திஶஷ்பம் வ்ரயாஜூ ச||உரு||
வாநாஞ்சாயூதெ ஜெயா தஜெஷநவஜம் ஷூதம்|
யக் வ[26]ஜம் வெஷநொாவெதஜஜிம்ஹூஜிதி ககூதெ||உகூ||
ஐம்ஹூதெ ஹி வஜஸூாகூ ஐதூஷாஜிம்ஹூஜூசூதெ|
விஹாமவக்வஜஸூாகூா[27] விஹாமெந விசாஞூதெ||உஎ||
ஐதூெவஜிம்ஹூஶஷ்பாகூஷ்டஸூ வாவகூஸவஹூஹஃ|
வயூாஜீநி ஜஶாகூாஞாநூவஸமூவஜாநி ச||உஅ||
கஙவாதூவிஸூஃஷ்ஷு[28]ஞிஃவாரா நவ வஜாநி ச|
ஐதூஜாநி ஸூஶெதாநி வஜாநெூகொநவிம்ஶதிஃ||உகூ||

---

[23] H யூா
[24] T ஷ்ஷும்யூா
[25] T க் ஐ
[26] T த்ஸ
[27] T கூஃ
[28] H க்ஸ

வாக்யாஙமந்[29]யொராஉி நிஹதஜ்ரிஷு உ்யுஉ|
சுவஹுஹெகு நெகூஙு யத்தக் ஸ்யா[30]உஜ்லராவ ச||ங்ய||
ஞக்ஷணெ: ஷாஹூஹா யெ ஸ்யுமி[31]தூஙாஷெ்ஸ ஷஜெ ஸதி|

கூஉ்ஞக்ஷண

ஸஂஹிதாவக் வ[32]ஂெக் வு[33]வடி[34]நுகூஉ்ய வஉசயஂ||ங்க||
ஷிதீய[35]ஜகு வஉவஉவஸாநெ ஸஉாவயெக்|
ததஸ்ஜாஉிவஉஂ ஹிக்ஜா ஷிதீய[36]ஞ தூதீய[37]கஂ||ங்உ||
வஂெத்தஸ்தஷிதீயஂ[38] வஉஂ ஹிக்ஜா தூதீய[39]கஂ|
உது கூஊங வஂெக் வ[40]ஷாக் கூஉாஉெவஂ வஂெக் வு[41]ந:||ங்ங||
வுவடஂ வுவடஂ வஉஜுக்ஜா ஸஂயுஜ்ஜாதூஉ்துஂ|
ணவஉுஜ்ஞாயடிதெ யஸ்தூ கூஉாஷாயஸ்ஸ உஜ்யெ||ங்ச||
கூஉெ தாவத்தயொஜ்ஞாயெடி யஉீஂஹுஂ வுவிடகஂ வஉஂ|
வரிக்ஜா வெஷநஜஸ்ய வஂெக் வ[42]ஷாஉ்யாகூஉஂ||ங்ரு||
வுவடவாக்யாஙஂஂ யஜ்ஜு வாவாக்யாஉிகஜயா|
தயொளடாநுகூஉெத்தஉஜஉாஉ்யநுவாகயொ:||ங்சு||

---

[29] H மஂ ஷ

[30] T ஸ்ஸா

[31] T ஸ்யு: ஐ

[32] T த்த

[33] T த்வு

[34] T வடஂ சு

[35] T யு

[36] T யு

[37] T யு

[38] T யுஂ

[39] T யு

[40] T த்த

[41] T த்வு

[42] T த்த

ஷூஹூஹாநிம்ஹுயுுக்ஷுவு யதி ஸூாதாதிஃம் வதம்|
சுவணுவெஷுநஜஸூ வாகூாஜெ யதநிம்ஹுகம்||ந௭||
வஜெ த யஜூஜிதூஜஜளெதூஜம் வஃெக் கூஜெ|
ஷணசுடசுவியிநா ஸஹ நிதூஉநுகூஜெக்||ந௮||
கூஉஜம் யதுதாத்தாஜம் வுவூம் யஜூொவஸமூதஃ|
தஸூொஜ்லூந திகூஉ ஸூாஜஃ[43]வாம் ஷுவாஜயஃ||நகூ||
வதகுயஉநுகூஜூ ஹிகூா வாஜிவதம் வுநஃ|
உஜூஉாதிஉஜுதூாயூ திகூஜெ கூஉஸொ வஜெக்||சம||

ஜடாலக்ஷணஂ

கூஉவக் வுவூஜுதூாயூ ஷுதிஹொஉம் வஃெது தக்|
ஸஙிதஷு வுநஃ கூயூா[44]க் கூஉவாஂம் வதவயம்||சக||
ஹவம் வாஂகூஜொ யஜு ஸா ஜடெதி ஷுகீத்திூதா|
சுவணுவெஷுநெம்ஹூாஜி யஜூஜுக்ஷம் கூஜெ யஸா||சஉ||
தகு தகு தயா ஸவூஜ[45]டாயாஞு வஃெக் ஙயஃ|
திகூஜெ திவதஸூாவி ஜடாஜுக்கூா யஸாவியி||சந||
ததஹூகு ஜிதீயா[46]ஜிவதாநாம் வுவூவக் வ[47]ஃெக்|
துஜூம் வதவயம் யகு ஹூாஜொ வணூதொவி வா||சச||
ந வஃெது ஜடாஜகு கூஉாகும் வஃெக் ஸதா|
ஸொவாஸொவாதயொ யெ வ ஷசுணசுாதயஷு யெ||சரு||
ஜடாயாம் லக்ஷணெஜுக்தாஹூாஙு வஃெது யஸாவியி|

கெவலவணூகூஉலக்ஷணஂ

யெ சுகு ஸாம்ஹிதா வணூாஹூஉாநுதாஂஷு ஶாஹூதஃ||சகூ||
தாஙு ஸவூாஙு கூாஶஷூாஜாங[48]ஜெவணூகூஜொக்திஷு|

---

[43] T ஸூாக் நஃ

[44] H யூா

[45] T வூம் ஜ

[46] T யூா

[47] T தீ

[48] T ஙு வ

சுகாரெண வுவெத ஸ்யாக் காரஶஸ்யோ ஹனாஜிஹ||சஎ||
சுநுஷ்யாரெ ச நாஸிகெ்யு ஜிஹ்வாஉஶ்யுவிஸஜநயொ:|
உவஞ்மாநீய[49]வணெர ச காரஶஸ்வதூ் நெஷ்யுதெ||சஅ||
ரஸ்யு கெவஷதயாணாஞ ஹுஷ்யோ வணெராத்தரொ ஹவெக்|
ஷ்ராக் காரவாராஉவநாஜ்[50] ந ஸஙிவநணநவாஂகெ||சகூ||
தாநு ஸஂஉவநவிஸஜநாஂஷ[51] வஜெஉூக்திஸஉாவநெ|
வஶவநஂ வணநகூஜொகெதஷூ் தத்தாவக் ஸஂ[52]ஹிதாஂ வடெக்||ருய||
யஷூ் ஸஂஹிதயா ஹீநாஞூ[53]ஷ்காஙணநகூஉாநு வஜெக்|
நிஷ்தயஂ ஸ்யாஉ்யா ஹித்திஹீநஞிசுவிஜெவநஂ||ருக||
யெநாவஷீயதெ வாகூஂ வணெநாவி ஷ்ரெண ச|
தஜெவ வணநவாஂஷெ் வுவஜெஞ ச ஸாஂஹிதஂ||ருஉ||
ணதெந வியிநா விதாநு கூஉாசணநகூஉாங[54]ஜெக்|

ஶிக்ஷவுகரணஂ

சுஷூ[55]வநஂ வுஜநொஷூநஂ யஶு[56]ஜநந்[57]கூஉாநூ்யாக்||ருங||
ஷ்ஶநஷ மவவஶவெூ யொ யதூ் ரெவாக் வாஞ தக்|
ஹுஷ்வஶவநள வஉாஷஷ்ள ஜநள ஶிகூஂ வரெவுஶி||ருச||
யொநூஷ்யாரொ யஜூஷ்யுகு ஸ ஸ்யாஉஉநகாரயுக் |
யஉ்யாதூாயஷ்ஶஶ்லூ ச ஶாஜிஷ்ராஷ்லூ ந ஜெ ஹவெக்||ருரு||
யொஜாக் வஶ[58]வநஉநூஷ்யாரொ ஹுஷ்யாஉ்யஷ வாரஷூிதஃ|

[49] T யு

[50] T க்

[51] T நு ச

[52] T க்ஷஂ

[53] T நு ஶ்

[54] T நு வ

[55] T ஶ்வஶ

[56] T க் வு

[57] T நஂ ஶி

[58] T தூ

ஸ ஷவ ஶிக்ஷாஷ்ேைாதி தஸ்ய ஸ்யாஜெகஶாகுதா||௫௯||

க்ஶுரஃ

வ்ஜநம் யஜிஶித்ேந ஶிக்ஷாஷ்ேைாதி தெந ெவெ|

வ௶ப்ரஃ க்ஶாத்து ஸ்யாஶிதீய[59] வதுகூய்யொஃ||௬௦||

கவணெ ஷ்யொஜயெ்யா யஶி ஶிக்ஷரஶா வஜெ|

ஷக்ஷ்யாநூஸாஸஂஜ்ஞா தள ஷவெதாஂ ஷக்ஷணெஃ வ்யகீ||௬௧||

வாய ஷஷொதியாஶாதிஷ்௶ெவாஶவ௶விபுகாஃ|

தயொவஸமவ௶வாஶுதாஶஶுவிஷூஜா ஐயூஃ||௬௨||

வ்யஶஷொஷணி வஶெ ஶிதீயாஜெஶகஃ வஜெ|

ஷஶெ வணபுயஂ ஷிளெ.....................................||௬௩||

தெத்திரீயெ ஶவ௶வஸ்ய நஸ்ய ஆ ஸ்யாஜ காஂகெ|

கஷிநியாநீ

கவொஷாஉ௶ஷண ஷ்யூபவாராசு வாஷ்திஃ||௬௪||

வ்யொஷிநியாந ஸ்யாத்தஸ்ய ஸ்ஷாந ஷவ ச|

ஶஸள யகுாஶஶ ஸ்யாதாஂ வ்யஶஃ வாஶொ யஶி||௬௫||

ந தகுாஷிநியாநொக்திஃ வ்யஶ்விபுஜெகீ ஶூ[60]யஃ|

கெவஷாஶஃ

நீசாவ௶வஷ்யொஷ்யொஷ்டா உகாரஃ கெவஷாஶஃ||௬௬||

தயொத்ஶெ ஐதொநஞ்யாஉா[61]ஶஶ ஷ்ஃ கஶள க்ஶாகீ|

யஶாஃ

ஸ்யாஉசுாநூத்தூஶாகீ ஷ்[62]ஶ்ஶாஉா[63]த்தஃ வாஶொ யஶி||௬௭||

க்ஶெண ஸ்யூயபு[64]ஶாஷ்து நாஜஷ்யா வாஶொ யஶி|

---

[59] T ய்ய

[60] T த்பூ

[61] T கீ க்ஶூ

[62] T த்ஷ்

[63] T கீ உ

[64] H யபு

யஜநிஷெயஃ

ஷூஸெ௷ா யஊ௺ஷவிகூதிஊ தகு ஸூாஊஜாமஜஃ||சுரு||
யகு யஷூாஊஜஹூாஷிஷூகூஷா வத்தூதெ யஜி|
நெைவ தகு யஜாவாஷூிரவஹுஷா ஷிகூஜாஹூ஽யாக||சுசு||
யொவஊாஞெ வஊாஞெ வா ஹுயஊ ஸூாக ஸ[65]ஷொாத்தரெ|
ஸ ஷிதீய[66]ஜவாஹுாதி ஸொஷூநஞூஸூ ஷெத்தயா||சுஎ||

நாஊஃ

ஹூஷூாக வ[67]ரஷூ஽ யொ நாஜொ ஶவதூகு ஷிர௺வவக|
தஞ வணூகூஜாஊாயெ ஸகூஜவ வஜக ஷ஽[68]யஃ||சுஅ||

ஷிகூாமஜநிஷெயஃ

ஹுாஷூ வ௺வூமஜஷிகூஞக்ஷணெ யஸூ வெ ஹஷஃ|
ஷிகூஂ வ௺வூமஜஷெஷவ நிவதூத தஊ஽ஞூதெ||சுகூ||
ஷிர௺வஊாஹூ஽யாஊ௺ஷா ஹுயஜொஷூஷூரெவி வா|
வகாரஷ வரெ ஷூஸெ௷ விஸமெ௷ா ரெவ ஷவ உ||எம||
ஷகார ஊஷணி ஷூஸெ௷ வர ஈஜெஊயஷ யஃ|
ஸவமீூயாநூ஽த்தஜொஷூ ஸவணெூாஷூ உ ஹஜ் த[69]யா||எக||
ஜ ஷூஶூயவஷொஷூஷெதூஷாஜதூநா஽நாஸிகஂ|
ஊஷஷாக வ[70]ரொஞமொ வொஷூ ந ஷிஊூா ந ஷூ ஷூ ஞூ உ||எஉ||
வரொவி ஹூஷூஊஷூாஹுாஊ[71] உ ஷிகூஂ யஹொாத்தரெ|

ஷூரஶக்திவிஷெய

கூஹூ஽தொ ரஷயொயஷூஷூாஊ௺ஷூ ஸதூஷூரொஷணி||எங||

---

[65] T ஞீ

[66] T யூ

[67] T ஷீ

[68] T ஷீ஽

[69] T ஷூ

[70] T ஷீ

[71] T ஹுாஂ ந

ஜ்ஊஷ்லாராஊாவாஜெஶள தஷ்லாக் ஷ்யா[72]க் ஷ்லாரஹக்ஷிதா|
உதூஷிாெரவ ஷா ஶ்ரிஷ்டா வாஜெரஜ்ஞநாதகா||எச||
க்ருஷ்யுஷள தெஷூ வாஜெஷூ வாஉள ஷ்யாதாம் ஷ்லாராதகள|
ஷ்திதள ஊஜெ்யு தூ யள வாஉள தள ஜ்ஞேயள வ்யுஜநாதகள||எரு||
வாஉந்தி[73]தீயம் வாஜெந வ்யுயஉெஜெநெவ யொஜயெக்|
த்ருதீய[74]ஞ உதூகெஊந வாஉம் வாஜெந யொஜயெக்||எசு||
ஊவஞகு க்ருஜாக் வாஉள உள உள தூ விஹஜெக் வ்யுயக்|
ஹஜஞா ஷ்யாக் வூ[75]வூஹாமஷ்லாரஹக்ஷிஷ்தூ ஷம்வ்ருதா||எள||
ஹக்ஷிரூத்தரஹாமா ஷ்யாஜி[76]வ்ருதா உ ஷ்லொாஉயா|
வூவூஹாமொ ஹகாரெ ஷ்யாஜ்ஜ[77]ஷஷெஷூத்தரஷ்தயா||எஅ||
சுகூஉிகூஞயொகூஞ ஹகெதரூஜ்லூஷ்லாரஷ்யு உ|
குயஜெதஉநூஜ்ஜாயூ ஷ்லாரஹக்ஷிம் ஷஜூஜ்ஜுரெக்||எகூ||

ஷ்லாரஹக்ஷீநாம் ஷொஉாஹாரணஷம்ஜ்ஞாஃ

பஹிூஃ கரெணூஷம்ஜ்ஞா ஷ்யாஜெ்யா[78]மெ தூ ரஹயொயூஜி|
ஷா ஜஹ்ணா கவிூணீ ஜ்ஞேயா ஷம்யொமெ ஞஹகாரயொஃ||அய||
வஷூம் ஹம்ஷவஉா ஜ்ஞேயா யொமெ தூ ரஷயொரவி|
ஶொத்தரெ ஹரிணீ ரெஷொ உஶூஃ வஶூரூஉாஹ்ருதஃ||அக||
ஷவரெ யகு ரெஷஃ ஷ்யாஊ[79]ஷ்திநீ பஷூஜிதுவி|
தஷ்யு யூஷூஉஜித்யாஉள ஷா ஷ்லதஞா வ்யுஉக்ஷதெ||அஉ||
ஹாரிதா ஞஶயொயூயாமெ ஶதவஜ்ஜூஉாஹ்ருதம்|

---

[72] T ஷ்யா
[73] T உம் ஜி
[74] T யு
[75] T ஜூ
[76] T க் வி
[77] T க் ஶ
[78] T க் யொ
[79] T க் ஹ

க்ஷெணைவம் ஸாவிஜ்ஞேயாஸ்ஸ[80]த்வைதா ஷ்ஷாஜஹசயஃ||அந||

விவ்ருத்தியக்ஷணஜஸ்யாஸ்ஸஂஜ்ஞாபஞ

ஷ்ஷாரயொரூஹயொஸ்ஸஙிவிபுவ்ருத்திரிதி கக்ஷ்யு[81]தெ|

சுகு ஸெவ விவ்ருத்திஷ்ஷா வுக்திரிதுவி ஜொபுதெ||அச||

வத்ஸா[82]நுஸ்ருதிராவ்யாதா தயா வத்ஸா[83]நுஸாரிணீ|

வெஸெஷிகா வாகவதீ ஜஷ்யுஜா ச விவீஷிகா||அரு||

தயா ஸவணபுஉீவீபு ஜொஹயஉீவீபு தயா ஷ்ரூதா|

ஐத்யுவஉஷ ஸஂஜ்ஞா ஸ்யூவிபு[84]வ்ருத்தீநாஜு ஹெஉதஃ||அசு||

ஹுஷ்ஷஉவபுா ச யா வ்யக்திஷ்ஷ[85]யெவொத்தரஉீவிபுகா|

ஸா வத்ஸா[86]நுஸ்ருதிஃ ஜ்ரொக்தா ஸஉாகுாகாஜதஷ்ஷயா||அஎ||

ஹுஷ்ஷாகல் உஉவெபு விவ்ருத்தி ஸ்யாகல் ஷ்ஷாதாஉீ உீவபுாகல் உ[87]ரா ச யா|

வத்ஸா[88]நுஸாரிணீ ஜெயஜெகஉாசெண ஸஂயூதா||அஅ||

வுக்ஷராஉுஜயொயபுஸ்யா உீவபுள யஉுஸவணபுகள|

யஉி ஜஷ்யு விஸஹபு ஸ்யாத்த[89]உஹாவொய வா யஉி||அகூ||

ஸா தூ வெஸெஷிகாவ்யா ஸ்யாஜெகஉாகுா ச தகு வெ|

உஉவெபு யசொத்தரெ வெசவ ஹுஷ்ஷொ யஉி ஹவெத்தஉா||கூய||

வாஜொநஉாதிகா தகு ஸா ச வாகவதீ ஷ்ரூதா|

யஸ்யாஸ்ஸவணபுஉீவபுள ஷ்ஷ உஹயசொஜுநீசகள||கூக||

விஸஹபுஷ்ஷகு ச ஷ்ஷாரஸ்ஸஙள ஜாகுா ச ஜஷ்யுஜா|

---

80 T யாஃ ஸ

81 T யு

82 H கஸா

83 H கஸா

84 T ஸ்யூஃ வி

85 T க்திஃ த

86 H கஸா

87 T தீ

88 H கஸா

89 T கதி

உ௰ூஉஊயக்ஷணெ தகு விஸமெூா ந ஹவெஉூ௰||கூஉ||
விவீ௯ிகெதி விஜ்ஞேயா ஸா வூக்ஷிஃ வாஉஊசிகா|
ஸவண௱ூ௲வூள யஉூாஉாவஞெ ஹிளெ விஸமூகஃ||கூந||
ஸவண௱ூ௲வெூகஊசா ந ஸஙள ஷூாஙிதொ ய௰|
தஸூாஷ்ஸவண௱ூ௲வூூாஷ்ஷ ஸ௨ூணெூ யக்ஷணெ ஸதி||கூச||
விஸமூஷ்கு நொ வெக ஸா[90] ஸஊசொஹயீவூூய|

விவூத்தூஉாஹாரண

உஉாஹிூயஞெ வஷ்ஷா[91]நூஸூதூா௰வூக்ஷயஃ கூஊக||கூரு||
வஷ்ஷா[92]நூஸூதிஸஂஜ்ஞா ஸூாத்த ஶநஂ ஹி ஸ கூயூரா|
வஷ்ஷா[93]நூஸாரிணீ வூாக்ஷா வெஉஷெ கூஷ்ஷ வா ஐயஂ||கூசு||
வெஶெஷிகா ஸூாத்தா ஶவ ககூ௲வாஂ ஒளஶிஜஷ்ஷயா|
ஸா தூ வாகவதீ ஜ்ஞேயா வூஉமஞு ஸ ஐஜ்ஜநெ||கூள||
உ௰ூஉா யா கூவிவிஶூவெூஉூா கூஉநு ய௰தூவி|
விவீ௯ிகா தூ தெ ஶநஂ வா கூரணூஉாஹூதஂ||கூஅ||
ஸவண௱ூ௲வீூ ஸஂயத்தா கூஸளிதூா௰உஶூநாக|
ஐயஞூஹயீவீூ ஸூாசா[94] கூவஷ்ஷ தயெதூவி||கூகூ||

வூக்ஷிஉ௰ூஷ்ஷநாஸிகூஃ

நாஸிகெூா வூக்ஷிஉ௰ெூ யஷ்ஷ ஹவெக ஸா[95]ணூஊசிகஃ|
வூக்ஷெஶஷ ஸாணூஊசுகூளா[96]உ வூவெூாக்ஷஉவ ஹி||ா||

ஶஂமஷ்டூதாஃ

யஶா உஉொவஹூதா உ ஸூஷ்டூாகா உ ஸூஉஂமயா|

---

[90] T ஷ்ஷா
[91] H கஸா
[92] H கஸா
[93] H கஸா
[94] T க வா
[95] T ஷ்ஷா
[96] T கூஂ நா

ணதெ ஈஂஒஞ்ஷூதா ஜெஷயாஷ்யா யஞ்ஷா்ஂ[97] ஐதீதூவி||ஈக||
ஈஂஒஞ்ஷூதெ ஷிஊகுஂ ஷூாஊா[98]ஊள வூாஷூஈஷொவஊஂ|
சுநாஷூஂ ஹூஊயொத்து[99]ஞஜ[100]நுஷூநியூதஂ ஹவெகு||ஈஉ||
சுயூ ஊஷூஊஹாமெ ஷூாத்தூதீயொ ஊஷூஷஂஹவஃ|
காஂஷூவணாநாஊஷஊஷூ[101] கஂவஷ்லுகஊஷுகஃ||ஈங||
சுயாஞூஹாமெ நாஷிகூஈஷூயவிநிஷூஈதஃ|
ணகஊஷுஷ்ஷூஷ்யாஂஶஷூ து காகஷிகொ ஹவெகு||ஈச||
யயா ஷளஈாஷூகா மொவீ ஊயூஷெண ஷூஷெண வெ|
தகூாஂ ஐதூஷூஷெஊஷெஷூஷ்யா ஈஂஒஂ ஷஊஷூஷெகு||ஈரு||

ஈஂஒஷீவயூாஃ

ஷெவா உதா ஐஷூஷூவா சுவ ஷூா சுஹ காஂகெ|
ஈஂஒஷீவயூா ஐதி வூாகஷாஷ்ஷெ ஷவாஊஷுஊஷுகாஃ||ஈசு||
ஹூஜ்ஜாதொ ஊஷுகஷ்ஷூநு ஷூாகு ஷ[102]வாஊஷுஊஷுகெ|
ஊஷூஜஷ்ஷூஷூஊகு ஷூாத்து[103]ஷ்ஷு[104]ஷொ ஊவநாஷிகாகு||ஈள||

ஷூஈிதொஊாத்துகஂவவிஷயஃ

நிதூாஹிநிஹதகெஷூவூவூஷூஷா ஷூஈிதா ஐஷெ|
ஷஙஊள தகு வூகஂவஞெ யஷொாஷூஷூஈிதொஊயாஃ||ஈஅ||
நீசஂ வஊவஷூஷூஈஷூாஞெ கூயஷூாகு ஷூா[105]கு கஂவ ணவ ஷஃ|
ஹூஷூஊவூகு கஂவெஷூநூ[106]யாஷீவயூஙஊஷூஷெகு||ஈகூ||

---

[97] T கு ஷூாஂ

[98] T கு கூ

[99] H குவ

[100] T ஞஂ ஊ

[101] T ஊஃ ஷ

[102] T ஷீ

[103] T கு த

[104] T ஷெூ

[105] T யஷூாஷ்ஷூா

[106] T நு ய

ஸ ச கஂவொசு விஜ்ஞேய[107] ஷ்ாா உச்சு ஐதி ஜியா|
ஷ்ாாகஂவஸ்ஸஂஹிதாயாஸுசுஷ்ாாணுகெ ஹவெக்||ாய||
வாநபஞ தசு ஙள கஂவள ஹுஷ்ஊீவயூாவிதி ஷ்ூதஂ|
சூஉள தூ தஸு கஂவஸு ஷ்ாாஷ்ஸ சுணுஉாசிகஃ||ாயக||
சுஞுஹாமெ தூ நிஹதஃ வாஉஉாசுஃ வுகீத்திபூதஃ|
உஉாத்தபஞ தயெவாஉள சிவாஉாயிகஉாசிகஃ||ாயஉ||
தஸுாஞெ சாநூஉாத்த ஸுாஉணுஉாசொ ஹவெத்தயா|
ஸஜெஊநெ ஜிஉாசு ஸுாத்தயொரெவஂ ஸுநிஶதிதஃ||ாயங||

வெகூதவுாகூதெ

ஶஷஸெஷ்சுரெஷ்சு விஸமெூா யசு ஊுஶுதெ|
வெகூதகஂ வுாகூதகஂ கூஉாக் ஸுாஜ்ஜிஷெ ணவ ஹி||ாயச||

நாஸிகுகொாாஸுகெ

ஹகாாாளணஉா யசு ஊுஶுஞெ வாதஷ்உா|
நாஸிகுகஉாாஸுகஂ ஹஷ்ூ தசு ஜிாசுுதெ||ாயரு||

வுக்திஉகுஷ்விஸமூஃ

விவுத்திஉகெு யசு ஸுாஜிஸமூஷ்ஸாஊூஉாசிகஃ|
விாாஉமெஞகஉாசு ஸுாத்த[108]ஸுாஸ்ஸஂஜ்ஞா யயாவியி||ாயசு||

ஜிஷ்ாாஉஶீயொவஷ்ாநீயவியிஃ

வுாமுஊுவொஷவணூாஹுாஂ விஸமூஃ கவவமூயொஃ|
கூஉாக் ஸ[109] ஜிஷ்ாாஉஶீய[110] உவஷ்ாநீய உசுுதெ||ாயள||

ஷ்ஷிதிஸஙிஃ

ககாாஷ்வரொ யசு ஹவெத்தஷ்ிஙு வ[111]ரெ ஸதி|
வஉவூஷ்ஷிதொ விஸமூ ஸுாக் ஷ்ஷிதிஸஙிரிதி ஷ்ூதஃ||ாயஅ||

---

[107] T யஃ

[108] T க் த

[109] T க் ஸ

[110] T யு

[111] T ஙீ

ஞ்லாரஷீநஸ்ய வணாஸ்ய வாசகஷாஉ

வணாஸ்ய ஞ்லாரஷீநஸ்ய நாஉ வாசகஊஞ்யதெ|
வணாக்ரூஉஸ்யாஞயநெ ந வஜெஉநூஸம்ஜீகாம்||ாயகூ||

கெவயாநுஞ்லாரஃ

யொநுஞ்லாரஃ கெவயாவுஞ்ஸ உஞுஞ்யொ வியொரஷி|
தஞ்[112]ரஸ்ய யொமாஜெஷூ ஜாதூ ஞிகூஞிஷுதெ||ாஉய||

ஞுணவஉகூஷண?

கூஉள ஞுாரம்ஹகொம்காரெ கூகாரஃ ஞாஉஊாகுகஃ|
ஸ குஞாஉஞிஊாகு ஸ்யாஉூ[113]காரொ உஞூ ஊாகுகஃ||ாஉக||
கூஞுாயாஞெநுவாகாஞெ உகாரஞூஞூஊாகுகஃ|

ஸாஙிநிஷெயஃ

வணாக்ரூஉஞுஞாஞெஷு ஞ்லாராக் காரஞாரஉயஃ||ாஉஉ||
ஹரிஞுணவஉஞுஞி ஸாஙிஷூ ஸ்யாக் ஞூதெஷு ச|

ஞ்லாரவணாக்ரூஉஞகூஷண?

ஶுஞவணாக்ரூஉெ தஞிஷு[114]ஞுஊாநெ யயாக்ரூஉம்||ாஉங||
தஞொஉாதூாநுஉாதூள ஞுசயஶு குய ஞ்லாராஃ|
தயெவ ஸஞூ ஞ்லரிதாஞ்ஸ[115]ஞுயதூாஞ்ஸநாஉகாஃ||ாஉச||
உஞெதாம்ஞூகு தஞெவ ஞ்லரெஞுஞாவூாகீ ஞுயொஜு ச|
ஞுவஜெஉூஞி நாநூாஸள ஞ்லாரவணாக்ரூஞொ ஹவெக்||ாஉரு||
வுஜநாநாஊஉாதூாஉீங[116]ணொாகதள ந வஜெக் ஞ்லாரநு|

உஉாதூாஉீநாம் ஸம்ஜூாஃ

தகு தாவஉுஉாதூாஉுா ஞ்லாராஞூஷாஉவாசகஃ||ாஉகூ||
ஞுயதூாஶு க்ரூஉெணெவ நிரூஞுஞெ யயாவியி|
உஞுரூஉாதொ நீஞெஞூ நிஹதஶுாநுஉாதூகஃ||ாஉஎ||

---

[112] H கூஞ

[113] T கூ உ

[114] T நு உ

[115] T தாஃ ஸ

[116] T நு வ

ஷ்ரித ஸ்ாக் ஸ[117]ஶாஹா௱[118] ஷ்ா௱ ஐதாவி வொசுாதெ|
வரெஷாஶநுஶாத்தாநாம் ஷ்ரிதாக் வ[119]உவத்திூநாம்||ாஉஅ||
ஸம்ஹிதாயாஞு ஞுவய உஶாத்ரு௵திரிஷ்ாதெ|
யூதஞுவயஶஷ்ள உ வயயூாயள ஷ்தஃ வா௱ஷ்ா௱ம்||ாஉகூ||

ஸஷ்ஷ்ரிதலகூஷணாநி ஸொஶாஹா௱ணாநி

ஷ்ா௱ாஷ்ஷ்வியா ஜ்ஷுயாஷ்த்ர[120]யத்நாமுசுதுவியாஃ|
கெூஞுஃ ஞுாயஶிக ஷ்ாரெ[121] ஷிதீயொ நிதாஸம்ஜ்ஞகஃ||ாநுய||
தாதீய[122] ஸ்ாக் ஞுா[123]திஹதமுசுதுகெூா நாஶதொ ஷியா|
தகுாஹிநிஹதவெவுக ஐதரொஹிஹத ஷ்ாதஃ||ாநுக||ாநுக||
ஞுஶ்ரிஷ்ஃ வஞஶஷ்ஷொ வாத்த ஸ்ாக் வா[124]உவாத்தகஃ|
தெரொவாஜநஸம்ஜ்ஜொ ய[125] ஷ்ரிதஷ்ஷ்ஶொ ஹவெக்||ாநுஉ||
ஐவணாதொயூ[126]வகெூ ஸதாுஷ்யொ ஷ்யயூாதெ உ யஃ|
ஸ உ கெூஞுாஹிய ஷ்ா௱ஷ்ாம்பகந்ள ஐதாவி||ாநுநு||
வஜெ ஷ்திதெவாவஃவெூ வா நீசுவஃவெூ யவாகூாம்|
ஷ்யயூா[127]தெ யகு நிதா ஸ்ாளு[128]ஞம் கூஹ்ா உஶாஹாதம்||ாநுச||
உஜ்ஜெ நாநாவஉஷ்ஜெவி ஶ்ரிஷ்ந ஷ்யயூாதெ உ யஃ|
ஸ ஞுாதிஹத ஊவ ஸ்ாக் ஸ ஐயாநஷ்தெஜஸம்||ாநுரு||

---

[117] T க் ஸ

[118] T ரஃ

[119] T த்தி

[120] H க்ஞு

[121] T ரஃ

[122] T யா

[123] T த்ா

[124] T த்ா

[125] T யஃ

[126] H யூ

[127] H யூ

[128] T க் நா

நாநாவஜெ ஹ்ரூச்சுவுௗவுளீ[129]உ௦ யகஃ ஷு[130]யபூதெ யஜி|
வூக்ஷொ ஹாவெ ஹாவெவி ஸ வாதிஹத ஐஷூதெ||ாகூ||
தஷிஷகாரயொவலெக ஒூயகீ ஊதவஜெ தஐா|
ஷாரொஹிநிஹதொ ஜெூயஷ்ஸாபுவீதெபுவஷவி||ாஎ||
உஜாத்தவுவெ தஷிந் ஸ்யாஉ[131]ஹாவ ஷுயபூதெ யஜி|
வஞ்ஷிஷாவூஷ்ஸ ஸூஷ்தா ஸஷீயஜிவ யஷுயா||ாஅ||
யா கூவணுவஜெ வூக்திஸா ஹவெஉஐபூஉாஜிகா|
யஷுஸ்ஸாஃ வாத ஷாஃ வாஉவூத்தஷ்ஸ ககூதெ||ாகூ||
ஐஸ்யூ வஉஸூ யா வூக்திஷுஸ்ஸாஷு ஷுரிதஶ யஃ|
ஸ ஷவ வாஉவூத்த ஸ்யாகஃ வஉமஷாநூஜிஷூதெ||ாசய||
திரஷியபூ[132]ஹிதி வொகூ௦ ஹஷூஜநஜிதி ஷுதம்|
தெந வூவெதொ ய ஷாரஷெ்யொவூஜநஸம்ஜூகஃ||ாசக||
வூஜநெந வூவஹிகஃ வஜெ தஉஜாத்தவுவபூகஃ|
ஷுரிதொ யஷ்ஸ ஷவ ஸ்யாதெ்[133]ஹொவூஜந உஷுதெ||ாசஉ||
யஷ்ஸஐாநவஜெ ஷார[134] ஷுயபூதெ ஹ்ரூச்சுவுவபூகஃ|
ஸ தெஹொவூஜநொ ஜெூய சூவொ வாஉஜுவாயவஃ||ாசங||

ஷுரிதாநா௦ வயதஹெஐாஃ

கெஷவெ நிதெ வயத்த ஸ்யாகஃ ஷாரெ ஊஐதஹொ ஹவெகஃ|
நீசவுவெபூஹிநிஹதெ வயதொதிஊஐ ஷுதஃ||ாசச||
உச்சுவுவெபூவுவுவெபூ உ வயதொ ஊஐ ஐஷூதெ|
வஞ்ஷிவாதிஹதயொஷ்ஸ வெ ஊஊதர ஷுதஃ||ாசரு||
ஸ தெஹொவூஜநெ வாஉவூதெ்த ஊஷுதர ஷுதஃ|
ஷவ௦ ஷுரிதஹெஐாநா௦ வயதாநாஷு ஹெஉதஃ||ாசகூ||

---

[129] T வபூ௦ நீ

[130] T ஷ்டீ

[131] T ஸ்யாகஃ ஊ

[132] H யபூ

[133] T கஃ தெ

[134] T ரஃ

விவக்ஷயா ஸக்ஷணாநி தேஷாஂஸ்தாநி ஶாஸ்தக꞉।
ஊதக் ஸ[135]வூ꞉ விஓிகேவ ஸ்ஸ்ரவணாகூ꞉ வக்ஷக்॥ாசஎ॥

ஊசுாவணாகூஉஸக்ஷண꞉

சுயாதஸ்ஸஂஹிதாஷாயெ ஸக்ஷணொமாநுவுவகூமு꞉।
ஹவந்தி யஓூவணூநாஂ யஓூக்காஸாஸ்ஸுநிஶ்விதா꞉॥ாசஅ॥
தசு தசு வ தெ ஸவெூ ஸ்ஸ்ரவணெூ யயாவியி।
உஓாத்தாஓிஸ்ஸரெஹ்ஹொவூாக் வுயாஜ்யெ தயா யஓி॥ாசகூ॥
ஊவஂ வாஂகூஓொ ய ஸ்யாநா[136]சிகாவணூ உஷூதெ।

ஊசுாகாஸஸக்ஷண꞉

ஊசுாணாஂ காஸநியஊா உசூஙெ ஹெதுஹி꞉ வுயக்॥ாருய॥
ஙூாஹுண நகூஸஶ்யாஷொ வாயஸஶ்ய ஶிவீ கூஊாக்।
சுணூெலூகஷிசிஊாசுாநு ஙூவதெ காஸதஸ்ஸுவஂ॥ாருக॥
ஐந்ரியாவிஷயொ யொஸாவணாரிதுூசூதெ ஙுயெ꞉।
உதுஹிூரணுஹிஜூாசுாவரிஊாணஊிதி ஷூதஂ॥ாருஉ॥
ஊகஊாசொ ஹவெஙூொ ஓீவூ ஸ்யாத்து ஷிஊாசிக꞉।
சிஊாசிக꞉ ஸ்ஹுதொ ஜ்ஞெயொ[137] ஹஸ்ஸாஙூகூஙூஊாசிகஂ॥ாருந॥
தசு ஙஂமஹ்ஹுதொ ய ஸ்யாத்து[138]துஜூாசுஸ்ஸ கூதெ।
தஞு வூாவுாதாஙெ யொ வணூநாஓொநுவத்தூதெ॥ாருச॥

ஊசுாகாஸொக்கிவிவெக꞉

ஸஂயுக்தஂ வாவுஸஂயுக்தஂ வூஜநஂ ஸஸ்ஸரஂ யஓி।
ஸ்ஸரகாஸஂ வஓெத்தசு ந வுயஹ்ஜநஸ்ய து॥ாருரு॥
ஸிஙெவூஙூாணாஊாசுகெ ஸஸ்ஸரெ வா வுயஹ்[139]ஸி।
தயாவி ந வஓெதஸ்ய காஸஂ வணூகூஓெஷு வெ॥ாருகூ॥
ஹஸஸ்ஸவஹிதா யசு தக்ஷெஷாஂ காஸ ஐஷூதெ।

---

135 T ஸ்ஃ
136 T க் ஊா
137 T ய꞉
138 T க் உா
139 H & T ஹு

சுநுதுஜெ கூஊூஉாசொ விராஉஹ்ஹு வியீயதெ||ாருள||

விராஉஹ்ஹுஷஹுதுஜெஷு கூாரூாயிகூூஂ ஹுஉஜுஞூதெ|

ஒஙவெூநுநாஸிகஂ ஹூஹ்வாஷிஉாகுஂ யதுஉுஙூதெ||ாருஅ||

ஊஉவூாகூ ஹூு[140]தாஹு தநாகுஜெ[141]கூஉாகுஉிதி ஞுுதிஃ|

சுவஸாநெ விஶெஷொயஉ[142]நெூஷாஞ ந விஉூதெ||ாருகூ||

ஸஂஹிதாயாஞு தநா[143]குஃ ஒஉகாஜெயிகொ ஹவெகூ|

ஹூஹ்வாகூ ஒ[144]ஶொவஸாநஹுஃ ஒஉாஊூாயெநுநாஸிகஃ||ாசுய||

ஷிஉாசொ உாதிகூஹுநூ[145]ஹூஂஹிதாயாஞயாவிஃ|

ததுகூகாரூாஙிஉிகெவஜாதிகாவணூஉுஹுஶெகூ||ாசுக||

சுஂமவணூகுஉெகூஷண

சுஂமவணூ ஹருாஉாஉாவஂ[146]மஂ ஸஂஜூாஞ நாஉ ஙு|

சுஙுாஂ ஸஂஜூாஞ உாகுாஞ ஹூரஞாஉ வஜெகூ குஉாகூ||ாசுஉ||

சுஂமஉகூஷண

வணூாநாஉஂமவணூஹூிநு ஸுவூகுஞாஂமஉகூஷணஂ|

ஒஙவூகெூந ஒரகெூந வியிநா வா ஸஹொஙுூதெ||ாசுந||

ராஜதெஸள ஹூயஂ யஹூாது[147]ஹூாது ஹூர உஙூதெ|

உஒரிஹூாயிநா தெந வூஂஹூஂ வூஜநஉுஙூதெ||ாசுச||

ந ஶகூஂ கெவஉஂ ஹூாதுஂ வூஜநஞு ஹூரஂ விநா|

ஸாவெகூஷஂ வூஜநஞி[148]தூஂ ஹூரஹுு நிரவெகூஷகஃ||ாசுரு||

வூஜநாநி ஙு ஸவூாணி ஹூராஂமாநி ஹவஙி ஹி|

---

140 T ஹூு

141 T ஂ ஶ

142 T ஂ சு

143 H ஹூா

144 T ஷ

145 H ஹூ

146 T உள சுஂ

147 T கூ த

148 T நஂ நி

வாாஂமவஂுவபூாஂமலக்ஷண௴

ஸவெக் வ[149]ரஜூரஸ்ாஂமஂ வ்ஜநஂ வ்ாயமொவி ஹி||ாசுசு||
தசு வஂுவபூஜூராஂமஂ ஸ்ாஊ[150]வஸாநெ ஷூிதஞ யக்|
வாாய஼க்ஷஉந஼ஜூாரொ விஸமெூா ஸக்திரெவ வ||ாசுஎ||
யொமாஜ்ஸஂய஼தொ ஜொ நொ ரெவஃ ஸ்ாஜ்வரெ ஸதி|
வஂுவபூாஂமஞ[151] ஸவெக் ஜூஶூ[152] ஊஷணொ விக்ருதியூ[153]ஓ||ாசுஅ||
ஸா வாாஂமஂ ஸவதெ்வ யா ஸக்திஃ வ்வயாக் வ[154]ரா|
யுதெ ஹ்காரெ வாரதொ ரெவஶந ஸ்க் வ[155]ராஂமஹாகீ||ாசுகூ||
வாாஂமஉஸவணூஂ ஸ்ாஊ[156]ஜூாவாரஉெவ யக்|
வாாஂமெ வொஷணி வரெ வாாஂமஂ ஜூஶூகொ யஉாஃ||ாஎம||

சுஂமவணூக்ரூஉொக்திலக்ஷண௴

வளவபூாவயூக்ரஉெணெவ விஉக்ஷாஂமஂ வ்யொஜயெக்|
ஸஶாஞ஼ வஂுவபூஶஜூஂ வா வாஶஜூஉயாவி வா||ாஎக||
உசுக்ஷா ததொஂமஶஜூஞ஼ ஸஂுதஶஜொஉ்ரஂ க்ரஉாக்|
ஹஜூஂ[157]ஜூகெதி ஸஂஜூாஞ[158] நாஉ காரொஉ்ரஂ வஉெக்||ாஎஉ||
சுவாஉஜூஂஜூகெத்஼சுக்ஷா தநா[159]குாஂஶ[160] தத ஜூராநு|

---

[149] T ஜூ

[150] T க் சு

[151] T ஂ ந

[152] T ஶூஃ

[153] H யூ

[154] T ஜூ

[155] T ஜூ

[156] T க் சு

[157] H ஸஂ

[158] T ஂ வ

[159] H ஜூா

[160] T நு வ

உஶாத்தாஃம்ஷ்த[161]தொ நாஶாந்யாந ஊ ஹவெபூண ஸம்வஜெக||ாஎந||
ஸம்யொமொ யகு ஊவபூாம்ஶம் ஸ்யாக ஸ[162]வணாூாதூகொ யஶி|
ஸகூஜெவ வஜெத்தகு ஊவபூாம்ஶாஶி வஶெத்ததஃ||ாஎச||
யொமொ யதொாஹயாம்ஶம் ஸ்யாஶ்ஜொகவ்யூநாதூகஃ|
வளவூாவயபூகூஶாத்தகு வ்யூமம்ஶம் வ்யயொஜயெக||ாஎரு||
யஶ்ஶஂதம் ஶஂஜவணொ ஷிகூாஶயஶாஶிகம்|
கும்ஶவணொ து தக ஸ[163]வபூஜகு தகு வஜெக கூஶாக||ாஎகூ||
ஷ்ராவணொ ஷ்ரா யஶ்ஷ்கூஷணொஃ வ்யதிவாஶிதாஃ|
ஶாதுாஶ ஶாதிகாவணொ யயா யகு விநிஶிதாஃ||ாஎஎ||
தாந்ஃ ஸவபூாநம்ஶவணொாக்ஷள தயா தகு வஜெக ஸ[164]யீஃ|

வணூஸாராஹதவணாகூஶ ஜதூஸ்ய நாஜ்ஜோ நிவூசந

ஸவெஷாஜெவ வணாநாம் ஸாரா ஜ்நாய ஷ்யூதாஃ||ாஎஅ||
ஜ்நிஷ்மாநாஶயொ யெ ஸ்யூஷ்தெ[165] யஜூா ஜதி கீத்திதாஃ|
தெஹூதொ ஹதஶஜ்நெந வ்யாவிதாகூ ஜஹொாவ்யூதெ||ாஎகூ||
ஸ தயொாகுஶ வணாநாம் கூஜொ வணாகூஶஷ்ட வ|
குஸள வணாகூஶஶெதி விஶஹொ விஶஃகூதஃ||ாஅம||
தஷ்ாஶயம் வணாஸாராஹதவணாகூஶ ஷ்யூதஃ|

வணாயஜாகூஃ

ஹகஸ்யாஜ்ஞாஶிய்தஸ்யாவ்யூவஷ்ஷவ்யூநஸ்ய வ||ாஅக||
யஜூாஷ்ஷிம்[166]ஶதிஃ வ்யாக்ஷாஃ கூ ஜதீகூஶாஜ்யூதஃ|
ஷகூஷணொஶ்ஶூ ஹவாகு ஜ்நிரிதூவ்யூதெ தயா||ாஅஉ||
ஜ்நிஃ வ்யாயஶிகொ யஜெூ ஷிதீய ஷ்ாநஶவ்யூதெ|
தூதீயஃ காணம் விஶ்யாக வ்யயதூ ஸ்யாத்தீயகஃ||ாஅந||

161 T நுத
162 T ஷீ
163 T ஷீ
164 T ஷீ
165 T ஸ்யூஃதெ
166 T டுவிம்

ஜெவதா வஙுஜொ ஜ்ஜேயஷ்ஷொ ஜாதிரிஹொசூதெ|
சுஂமஞு ஸவூஃ ஷுாகொ வணூஸஂஜுாஷுஜொ ஹவெக்||ாஅச||
ணதெ யஜூஃ கூஜெஷொவ வியீயஞெ ஹஊரிஹ|
சுஉாஙஜூாஷுகெவூஷீஞு[167] சூஉாநெ ஸதி கூஉாக்||ாஅரு||
உாசுாகாயஶு வக்ஷவொா உஜொ ஜெவஷுயதூயொஃ|
ஷூஈாணாளிஹதாஈநாநு[168]ஶ யஜூாஷூஈரிதாஃ||ாஅசூ||
தசுாஉள ஜெவதா ஜ்ஜேயா தஜொ ஜாதிஷூஜொ ஶுணஃ|
தஜொ ஶெவாஉஶூநஂ ஷுாஉஂ[169]ஶாவஷூாசுயஂ வுநஃ||ாஅள||
ததஷ்ஜுாஉிஹொது ஷுாஉு[170]த்[171]திஷூாநகூஷுதஃ|
தஷ்ஂஜுா உ ததஷெதாநுஶ யஜூாஙஜெக் கூஉாக்||ாஅஅ||
கெவயஷூாஉாசுாஂஶவணெூஷு உதூஷுஉிதாஃ|
யெ யெ யஜூாஶு தாநு ஸவூாநு ஷுயுஜுாஷூிநு கூஉாத்[172]ஂெக்||ாஅகூ||

சுநுஷூாஈஹக்ஷிகஂவுவிஷயெ ஈஂஶஷுதவிஷயெ உ

யொ யஜூஃ வஙுஉசெவந ஷுாஉஉாஂ வணூஸாஈகெ|
ஷூஈஹக்ஷுஂஶஹிதாநாஉ[173]உாஂ ஷுாக் ஸ[174]ஷுஜொ ஹி ஸஃ||ாகூய||
சுநுஷூாஈஷு ஹக்ஷீநாஉஂ[175]ஶஹிதாஜு[176]ஊாஉவி|
யஜூாநுயாவஷ்நுாஈங[177]ணூஸாஶெ வஜெக் ஸஉா||ாகூக||

[167] T ஙு உ
[168] T ஂ உ
[169] T க் சுஂ
[170] T க் உ
[171] H க்வ
[172] H க்வ
[173] T ஂ சு
[174] T ஷ்
[175] T ஂ சுஂ
[176] H & T ஜு
[177] T ஙு வ

சுநுாஷ்ராரஸ்ரு வணெரூஷ்ஙிளும்[178]ஶாகல் ஶுவரூஜு ஊதிகாம்|
சுவ்ருநுாஷ்ராரஹக்துஂஶெ வுஂஶுாஙஜரூாநு் க்ருஊாசவெக்ஷ||ாகூஉ||
கூஂவெ தவெதுாகூஷ்ராரயஜரூாநாஊள வமெத்தயா|
தஷ்ராஊுத்[179]ஞகூஂவஸ்ரு ய க்ருஊுஂஶாஶக தஸ்ரு து||ாகூங||
திவாஊாயிகூஊாதுஸ்ரு யஜரூாநு் ஷ்ராரஸ்ரு நொத்துரெக்ஷ|
தஊஞுாஂஶாரஸ்ரு நீசஸ்ரு ஞுாஙியாஙஜரூாநுயாவியி||ாகூச||
ஶுாஙவணெரூா யயா தது தயெவாதுாவி யொஜயெக்ஷ|
ாஂஶஷுாதெ கூவணெரூாத்துஷுாதாநாஊாநுாஶுவரூஶ||ாகூரு||
வமெஙஜரூாஙணரூஸாரெ தஊஞெ வணரூஸஂஜ்ஞகாஂ|
ஸவரூதுாஹிநியாநாவெ்ா யஷ்தஸ்ராஂஶஙயெவ ச||ாகூசு||
வணரூஸஂஜ்ஞாஊவி ஞுாஙியாஞா[180]நுயஜரூாநு் வமெக்ஷ ஸ[181]ஊா|
ந ஷ்நுாஈநு[182]ஶெ ஞுாஙியாக்ஷ ஷ்ராநாஞ நிஷிஙுதெ||ாகூஎ||

ஶஷொ த்துதிவ்ருகாரணஃ

சுயாது ஸவரூவணரூாநாஂ யாஜுாஷாணாஂ விஶெஷதஃ|
உத்துாரணவ்ருஸிஙுகூமூஂ ஶஷுஸொத்[183]திஶுாசுதெ||ாகூஅ||

தத்ருகாரஃ

நிதுஃ காயரூ ஐதி செயா ஶஷுஷ்ஸாஊாநுதொ ஹவெக்ஷ|
நிதெுாவுக்தொ விஶுஶ்ஷஶொ யொ ஞுஹஙவுவமெஶஹாகீ||ாகூகூ||
தஷ்ரீதுக்தஃ காயரூஶஷுஃ காயரூாஊுத்[184]ஊுதெ ஶுாதிஃ|
ஶுாதெஞரூாஊஷ்தொ நாஸீ நாஞுா உத்துாவசஷ்ராரஃ||உா||
ஹதெ க்ருஊாக்ஷ வ்ரு[185]ஜாயஞெ வணெரூாத்துாரணஊாதுதஃ|

---

[178] T நுு் சு
[179] H க்ஷவ
[180] T நுு் நா
[181] T ஷ்
[182] T நுு் ய
[183] H க்ஷவ
[184] H க்ஷவ
[185] T த்ரு

ஊயொஉ்யகீகூஜெதெஷாநீ[186]வதத்ரு[187]ஹயொரிவ||உாக||
ஹவதி நாஉவ்ரு ஜ வா வணெுாத்தாரணஹெதவஃ|

ஸ்ரநிநிர வணவ்ரகரணெ ஶரீதாஜமூதஜாரா நிஷ்டிதிஃ

உவநாஹ்ரூஜயெ ஸ கூஷயஉநீவ பிவந்நம்||உாஉ||
குயாரம் ஸவூயாத நாஜ[188]நி்யாணாம் ஹவதூவி|
தத்ரு[189]துமாஉகஷ்ஷ ஊாவுஉூாம்ஶ ஜ[190]ஸஜ ஷ்ரிதா||உாந||
நிஶ்யா ஸததநீவ்தா ஜ்ஞாயா வஹெஷ்ஷ ஜாரஸீ|
வாஉாண ஸ கூஷாவரணா யஉநீ தத்[191]ரிஷ்டிதா||உாச||
வாயு நா உ ரிதா வூத்தா ஊ தம் ஸஞரதாநிஶம்|

வ்ராணாஉீநாம் வஞாநாம் வாயூநாம் ஷ்டாநவூிதூாஉிகூ?

வ்ராணொஊநாவாநஸஉா ஹுக்குண ஶ ஊநாஹிஷ||உாரு||
உகூாரஸ்ஸம்ஷ்டிதா ஜெஹெ வ்யாநஸ்ஸவூாம்ஶஸம்ஸ்ரிதஃ|

தெஷாம் ஷ்ஷ ஷஸ கூஷர வசெஷ்டாவிஶெஷஃ

ணதெ வஞாம்ஶகாஷ்டகு ஷ்டிகெூவாம்ஶெஷ்டிஹிஷ்டிஹிஃ||உாகூ||
உாஹ்ராந்நாஹ்ராம் ஶரீரெஷிநு ஸ்ஸவெஷாம் வ்ரகூவூதெ|
ஸஉஸ்ஸ ஷீரஉகூஷ்ஷஸ்தளநம் பஹிூஷஉாவதி||உாஎ||
நாஉீஶதாஸ்ரிதொவாநஸ்ஷிகூஜஊெ ஸ்ரிகொவாரி|
விஹஜொஹ்தாரஶஉஶளஉ ரஃ வஶ்தாக கூஷிவதூயஃ||உாஅ||
ஸவூநாஉீஸ்ஸஉாஸ்ரிதூ வ்யாநஸ்ஸவூகு ஸஞரநு[192]|
ஸஊா விதந தெ ஸவூஞ[193]உநொளஉநாஉிகம்||உாகூ||
உஊாநொ மஉமதூஸ்ஸொ வ்யாநஊத்தம் ரஸாஉிகம்|

---

[186] T ◌ம் ஊீ

[187] H க்வ்ர

[188] T ◌ம் ஐ

[189] H க்வ்ர

[190] T ஷி

[191] H க்வ

[192] H ஞு

[193] T ◌ம் ந

க்ருஜிஹ்வாஜஉஷஜஈத்ஜ[194] த்ரு ஞுஹீகவாஙஃ கூஇவதுயஃ||உாய||

ஹுத்வ[195] ஜகொமவ்யூஷஷ்ஷொ நாஜீநாஊநிரஙரெ|

ஷ்ரிகவா ஷ்ஷாஙெ பஷீ வ்ராணொ ஹுாஷெஸவிபுகஸஙெநாரவி||உாயக||

யயாக்ருஜஂ ஷ்யநுதெ ஹுஈக்திஜஈக்ஷெதுாஷ்ஸூதிஂ வாராஂ|

வ்ராணாஉீநாஉிஜாபெதஷ்டா ஷ்ஜஉஷாஷ்ஸஉக்ஷூா தஈ ககூதெ||உாயஉ||

வ்ராணொ ஹுூஉிஷ்ஷ்வாஂபெரந கணொஷ்ஷாஉாநஜஂம தஃ|

சுஙராகஷபுதி பஹிஷ்ஹஉஂமொஸ்யாஂமகஂ க்ருஜாக்||உாயந||

உஹாஹாஂ ஷ்வாஸாஉவாஹாஜஂமாஹாஙாயபுதெ வஉாஈஃ|

விவக்ஷஈணாதூநா நஈஙஜநொ ரஈஷ்வா மஙாநியஂ||உாயச||

ஸஹ தெந வதிகவாஷ்நள ஜாமரெ தஷ்ஸ[196] ஜஈகூயா|

ஜ்வாயயா ஹெஉயதுாமஈ ஸஜாநாவரணஙதஃ||உாயரு||

ஹிஙாவூதள ஸஜெ கணவாயஈநா ஜநஸா ஸஹ|

கணொரொஜஷுஷெமஷ்ஷொ வ்ராணொஂமஂ ஷ்ஙியக்ஷுதி||உாயசு||

முஈதுாஉிவ்ருக்ருதிஃ காயெபுா நிநுாஷுஷ்ஷொக ஜாயதெ|

ஷ்ஷாநஂ கணொரஷொஜஷுஂ காணஙஈ ஸஜொநியஃ||உாயள||

ஜநஃவ்ரயொமொ யதூாஸு ஸுாஷுஷ்ஷொத்வ[197] த்ரீஜுமீ|

ஐகூஜஈஷ்ஷாயபுஜாணெஷஈ மஷ்ஷெஷஈ ஷ்வாஸரொயிஷஈ||உாயஅ||

தஉகூபுஂ ஸஜஜஷ்ஷிஙஜாக்ருஷெுாஉாநஸஂயஈதெ|

ஜநஸுஹுஈகிதெ தஷ்ஷிளெபெதஷ்டுஂ ஷொஜஈஜக்ஷஜஃ||உாயகூ||

ஸஜஜஷு வஈநஃ வ்ராண[198] ஷ்வாஂபெரநெவ வததுஸள|

தஷாஉிஷ்ஷிஉுதெ தக வ்ராணஸஂவடநாக் ஸ[199] ஜஃ||உாஉய||

உிஙயாரொ ஹவதுாமஈ ஷ்ஷ்ஷாநாஙமபுதபத ஸஃ|

---

[194] H க்ஷ்ஜ

[195] H க்வ

[196] H க்ஸ

[197] H க்வ

[198] T ணஃ

[199] T க்ஷ

ஸஊ்யஷ்த்க்ஷ[200]க்தி[201]ரொயதெ்த ப்ராணொஊாநள த்ு ப்ூவுவக்||உாஉக||
விசெஷெ்த தஊா தாஹ்யாஜ[202]ஹாஷ்ா[203]ஸஃ ப்ரஜாயதெ|
ஹூயொ ஊநஃப்ரயொமெந ஶஷ்பஷ்ஸ்ஂபஊ்யதெ தயா||உாஉஉ||

ஷ்நிஹெஊாஃ

கண்ாகாஶமதஃ காயுூஶ்ஶ்ஷ ஷப ஷ்நி ஷ்ய்தஃ|
நாஊ ஶ்வாஸொ ஹகாரஶெ்துதெ்யவஞெ்[204]யா ஷ்நிஹுவெக்||உாஉங||
கணெ்த்ு ஸஂவ்யதெ நாஊ ஶ்வாஸ ஸ்யாஜிவ்யதெ ஸதி|
ஊஷெ்ய த்ு ஹகார ஸ்யாஜணுப்ரக்யதயஶ்த தாஃ||உாஉச||

தஜ்ஜாதவணுாஃ

நாஊஜா ஷ்ரவொஷா ஸ்ு்ஹுஉத்ுகூுா ஹகாரஜாஃ|
கவொஷா ஶ்வாஸஜாஷ்து ஶ்வாஸொ செயாஷ்கொ ஊஹாந்||உாஉரு||
ப்ரயஊாஶ்த தஊநெ்ய[205] உ வணுா கஷ்ஊஹக்ஹவாஃ|

வணுாநாஂ ஷ்ாநகரணவிவெகஃ

கஉாஂ ஷ்ாநஜ்ுஷெ்ஷ்ஷொ யகுாந்யாஂ[206]மஸ்ய தந்யதெ||உாஉகு||.
தஊஂமஂ கரணஂ ஷ்ாநஸஶீவெ நீயதெ உ யக்|
யஊஂமஂ ஷ்ய்ஶ்யதெஂமெந ஹஶாஂ ஷ்ாநஜஊிஷ்யதெ||உாஉள||
கஂமெந ஷ்ய்ஶ்யதெ ஷ்ாநஂ யெந தக் கரணஂ ஹஶாஂ|
ஸஂஹிதாயாஊசொ நித்யஂ யகுாவ்ஜநவூவுகாஃ||உாஉஅ||
ஹவந்தி தெஷாஂ ஷ்ாநொகதள வூவுஂ கணெ்தி ஸஂவஊக்|
ககாரொஞ்ாரணெ சொஷ்ள ஹநூ நாதூ்யவஸஂஹ்யதள||உாஉகூ||
காயுூள த்ு ஊீவுஷ்ுதயொஷு உாதிவிவ்தா ஐஊெ|
உவஷெ்ஷ்யஊிவணெுாகதள ஜிஹ்வாஊஷ்யஙு தாஶ்நி||உாஙய||

200 T கூ

201 T க்ஷ்தி

202 T ஂஊ

203 T ந்) ஶ்வா

204 T ஂ செ

205 H ளெ்ய

206 H ஞ்யாஂ

ஒஷாவ௱வணெ௴ ஶீவ௴ள ஷு உவஸ்ஶ௷யாதள தயா|
வ௷யமொஷொவஸ௦ஹாஜொ நாஊ௴ஸாகுாஜெ ஹவெக்||உாஙக||
ணகஸாகுாஜஈகுஸ௵ ஸ௵ாத்து ஸவ௴கு ஸ௦ஹவெ|
ஜவணெ௴ ணதி வ ஸ௵ாதாஜொஷள நாதஜ௱வஸ௦ஹ௵தள||உாஙஉ||
ஹநூ குதஜ௱வஸ௦ஹாயெ௴௵ ஜிஹ்வா௶௦ பஹ்வ௴கெ ஹவெக்|
ணகாஜெவஜநெ ஜிஹ்வாஹ௵ாஜாவீஷஊ௱தொஷகள||உாஙங||
கஈணஜாஜ௱ து ஷுாநஉதிஸ்ஶிஷ ஹநூஷு௴யாகீ|
ஸவஜநெஷிஹ் கஈணீஷஷு௵ஷொஷயாஹ்[207]வெக்||உாஙச||
ஜிஹ்வாஊ௵௦ ஷுாநஉதிஸ்ஶ௷வஊந௱தாஜ௱கு௦|
ஹநூ குநதிவிஸ்ஶ௷ஷ ஒஷள வாதஜ௱வஸ௦ஹ௵தள||உாஙரு||
ஶீவ௴ள வ ஹவதஷுகு கெூாகாஜொத்துாஈணெ ஸதி|
குண௱ஷூாஊாவஉஷொதொஈஜெ௵ ஸ கூ௵ண௱குஷுிஊ௱க்||உாஙகு||
ணெகாஈளகாஈயொஈாஊாவ[208]காஈஷுஊ௴ஸாகுிகஃ|
ஜவணெ௴ாவண௴யொஸ்ஶ௷ள ஸ௵ாதாஊ௵ஊ௴ஸாகுிகள||உாஙஎ||
ணெகாஈளகாஈாவயவெஷிஊ௱ஷு௱[209] யயாகூ௵ஊ௦|
குஊிஊ௱க்ஷுாநகஈணவ௵யத்நா ணவ நாந௵யா||உாஙஅ||
ணஷொதொஈஊிஊ௱க் ஷ்ஹொவ௵கு ந ஶ௱யதெ வ௵யகீ|
நாதொஷ்தி தெஷாஙூ[210]ஜெ௴ாஸ௵ கிஸெகுகஷெூாகூஊெவ ஹி||உாஙகூ||
ணெஊளதொஈாஊ௵காஈஸ௵ கஈணீஹவஷொஷகஃ|
ஸ௦வ௵தாவ௵ ஐதி வ௵ாஹ௱வ௴ண௴கூ௵ஊவிவக்ஷணாஃ||உாசய||
உத்துாஈணெ குவம௴ஸ௵ ஹநூஊூஹ௦ ஷூ௵ஶெக் ஶ௱யஃ|
ஜிஹ்வாஊூஹெந ஞொஈ௱குள ஹிஹ்வாஊஷெ௵ந தாஜ௱ வ||உாசக||
ஜிஹ்வாஹ௵ண டவமெ௴ து வ௵திவெஷ௵ ஶிஈ ஷூ௵ஶெக்|
ஜிஹ்வாஹ௵தஷுவமெ௴ வ ஊஙூஊூஹெஷியஷுயா||உாசஉ||
குயஜெணாத்துஜொஷஙு௱ வவமெ௴ாத்துாஈணெ ஷூ௵ஶெக்|

---

[207] T கீஹ

[208] T ஊள கு

[209] H க்ஸ௱

[210] H ௦ ய

ஜிஹ்வாஉஞ்யஸ்ய வாஸ்ஹரஹ்யாஞா[211]ஶு யொஜ்வாரணெ ஸ்யஞெச||உாசங||
ஜிஹ்வாஞுயஸ்ய உஞெயந உஞஊஞொவுரி க்ருஉாசு|
க்ருஸஞஉத்யாஸஞு வ்யஜெஶ ரஶயொ ஸ்யஞெச||உாசச||
சுயொரோஷாஹ்ருஹாமெந பாஹொநொஜ்வூஉத ஸ்யஞெச|
ஒஷ்யஸ்ஹராஞரஷ்ஸெ வெ தசுஹி[212]ஞெ சுாஞரெண ஞெச||உாசரு||
ஜிஹ்வாஊஞீய[213]வுஊவுரணாம் ஹஹிளாநாஞயொஷணாம்|
சுவமூாஉிஷு யசு ஷ்டாநஞ[214]ஞெவ ஸ்யுயூயாக்ருஉம்||உாசசு||
சுரணாநாஞு யதெ்ஷாஜஞ்யஞு விவ்ருதம் ஹவெசு|
விஸமூஸ்ய ச ஹஸ்ய ஸ்யாசு ஷ்டாநஞு சுரணம் மஞ:||உாசஎ||
உரொ ஹஸெ்யாத்ரஉாஞஷ்டாவுரகெ ஸ்யாத்ரு தசுயம்|
வமூாஞ்யா நாஸிகாஉாகுஷ்டாநகா ஹாசு வ[215]ரெவுரெ||உாசஅ||
ஊவாவயவநாஸிக்யா நாஸிகா நஸ்விகாஸத:|

வணூாநாம் வ்யயத்நஹெஉா:

வ்யயத்நா: வுஞயா ஜெ்ஞயா[216] வணூாநாம் ஸம்வ்ருதாஉய:||உாசகூ||
ஸம்வ்ருதொ விவ்ருத ஷ்ஸ்ருஷ்ட ஈஷசுஷ்ஸ்ருஷ்டாதிவுஊவூக:|
ஸம்வ்ருதொகாரஉாகுஸ்ய வ்யயத்ந: வுரிகீர்த்தூத:||உாருய||
வ்யயத்நொ விவ்ருதொநெ்யஷாம் ஷ்வராணாஊஷணாஉவி|
ஷ்வெஹூஷு ஷ்ஸ்ருஷ்டதாஞஷ்டாஷ்வீஷசுஷ்ஸ்ருஷ்டசுவஈரிதம்||உாருக||
த்விதீயாஶ்ச சதுஃகூாஶ்சாவுர்திஷ்ஸ்ருஷ்டவ்யயத்நஜா:|
சுதிஷ்ஸ்ருஷ்டெ சதுஃகூாநாஞ்யூ[217]நக்ஷம் கிஞிஉிஷ்யதெ||உாருஉ||

ஜெவதாயக்ஷண?

ஜெவதா வெஉவணூாநாம் வாயுவ்நிகெ்ஷநூஹாநவ:|

---

[211] T ○ம் கா

[212] T த்தி

[213] T யூ

[214] T ○ம் த

[215] T த்

[216] H யா:

[217] T நாம் ந்யூ

யஷகாராவெஉவணூள வூ்யஊா வாயுஃஷெவகாஃ||உாருந||
சூஜெயா ஹெஊிவணூள வ ஷிதீயாமூ ஈஸாவவி|
உவணூ ஒத்துதீயாமூ ஹஉள ஸூ்ஜஊூிஷெவகாஃ||உாருச||
ஜவணூ ஒளத்துதுகூ ூாமூ வஉள வானூஉஸா ஷூதாஃ|
ணகாரொத்துஊஸாஹூஉயூா நெதரெஷாஞு ஷெவதாஃ||உாருரு||

ஜாதிலக்ஷண

வமூவூ்யஊவணூாமூ ஹூரா ஸூ்ஜூஜாதயஃ|
கூஷாகுா ஷிகு[218] தூரீயா ஸூவிூஸொஞலுொத்துஊா கூவி||உாருசு||
ஸூஊூா ஊஸூவிஸமூாநூஹூரா ஸூரிதி நிமூிகாஃ|

வணூஸஂஜ்ஞா

கூவ ஹூரா வூஜநாநி ஹூஸூாஞலுொஷணொ ஹஉஃ||உாருஎ||
கூவொஷவொஷவூமூவூ்யஊாஉூததூாஉயஃ|
ஹூஹூஉீவூஹூதா ஸகதிகஂவாரஂமஹூதா யஉஃ||உாருஅ||
விஸமூஜிஹூாஊூீயொ[219] வஹூாநீயா[220] உயஹூயா|
கூநுஹூராாஉயயெஷதெ வணூஸஂஜ்ஞா ஐதி ஹூதாஃ||உாருகூ||

உஊாத்தூஉீநாநெவதாநியஉஃ

ஸூயூாஹூிவநூவஸூயாமூகூாமூ கூஊாஊிஹ|
யூதாநூஊாத்துஹூாரொத்துஹூாணாநெவதா ஹூதாஃ||உாகூய||

ஜாதிஃ

உத்துநீவஹூாரயூதா ஹூராமூகூார ஹவ வ|
ஜூஹூகூஷகுியவிஹூூ[221] ஊூா கூஸநு ஜாதூா கூஊாஊிஹ||உாகூக||

ஹுணலக்ஷண

ஸாகூிக ஸூாகூ மூணெநொத்து ஹூரிதொ ராஜஸ ஹூதஃ|
வள தாஉஸமூணள ஸூாதாஉநூஊாத்துயூதாவவி||உாகூஉ||

---

[218] H க்ஷி
[219] T யொூ
[220] T யூா
[221] H ஹூூ T டுமூூ

ஹஹ்ஸ்வ்ஸ்ரவிந்ராஸலக்ஷண௺

ய ஷ்வரந்ரா[222]ஸக்ரூதிபாந்) ஸ க்ஷுஸீநஷ்ஸதந்ரிதஃ|
க்ஷுக்ஷா மொகணூவஷஷ்தந[223]க்ஷிணநக்ஷஜாநு௱நி||உாசுங||
க்ஷுஉாக் ஷ்வ[224]ரெஷு௱ ஹஷ்தெ வ உநொ ஊஷிஸிவெஶ வ|
யயொாஶாஷ்டும் ஷ்வரந்ராஸஉம்ஶு௱ஷ்காரெண விந்ரஷெக்||உாசுச||
தஉா யஉ்ராமதஃ வு௵ஜ்ஜ்ரா ஶு௱ரு௱வுா ஜெவதாவி வா|
வுணஉ்ராய நுஷெத்திஷ்நு) க்ஷுக்ஷா நாஹிஸஉம் கரம்||உாசுரு||
யஉ் தெொரஹுநு௱ஜ்ஞாதஷெ்ஸா[225]ஹ்ராஸகரணெ ஸதி|
க்ஷுஸீந ஊவ கு௱வீூத ஷ்வரந்ராஸம் யயொாவியி||உாசுசு||
உஉாத்தஸிஉ்ூஶெஞ்ரா[226]ஷெ தஜூநீஉஷ்ஷவவூணி|
நீசம் கநிஷ்திகாஉள வ உஷ்ராஉஷ்ஷெ யுதம்||உாசுஎ||
ஷ்வாரஞாநாஉ்காஞெ் து௱ ஸவூஶெவம் விநிஉ்ூஶெக்|
ய ஷ்வர ஸ்ராக் வுயக்ஷஹகெ ஷ்வரெவாஷ்டாநஉாஹ்ரு௱யாக்||உாசுஅ||
ஸ்ராஉ்ரெொத்து ஐவ ஷ்வார ஸ்ராத்துஉு௵ஷ்வூஷ்டிதஶ்த யஃ|
க்ஷுஉாஉநாஉ்காயாஷ்தள விந்ரஜெநுஷ்ராஞரயொஃ||உாசுகூ||
க்ஷுஉஞ்ராம்ஶள ஷ்வாரகம்வெ யள ஸ்ராதாம் ஷ்வாரநீசகள|
கநாஉ்காஞ்ராஉ்உயொஷ்தள[227] நுஷெதாவவி க்ஷுஉாக்||உாஎய||
ததஶெதாஉாத்தகம்வெ து௱ யாவு௱த்துநிஹதள வ தள|
உஷ்ராஉ்ரயொஃ வுஜெஶிஞ்ராஃ க்ஷுஉாக் ஸ[228]ஸிஉ்ூஶெஉவி||உாஎக||
விஶாஉெ வுஜநம் யத்தஉ௱[229]த்துாரணவஶாக் க்ஷுவிக்|
ஷ்வாஞாரஞு௱திம் ஸஉ்ரக் ஷ்வதஞஉ்வ வாஹ்ரு௱யாக்||உாஎஉ||

---

[222] H ஞ்ரா

[223] T ஂ உ

[224] T க்ஷ்வ

[225] T தஃ ஷொ

[226] T ந்ரா

[227] T யொஃ தள

[228] T க்ஷ

[229] T க் உ

தயாவி தஸ்ய விந்யாஸெ வ்யக் ஷ்தாநஞ[230] நிஓ்பெஸ்கூ|

ஷ்ஸவிந்யாஸவிவ்யஃ

ய ஹவம் ஷ்ஸவண்ாகூ்ாஞ்ஞா[231]ஷ்ஜ்ஷ்ஷ்ாநுவிஞயந்||௨௱௭௩||

ஷ்ஸந்யாஸக்ரஜெணைவ ஸஹ வெஜஓஂ வெஸ்|

ஸ வ்ஶதஸ்வ்வெஜெஶு வாஂ ஜ்ரஹ்ராஹிஶ்த்ஜு[232]தி||௨௱௭௪||

கூஂமாஜ்யவஷ்டா

மாகுஜெவய்ஞ்ஞு[233]நெஜ்ாஜ்ஂ கஞாகாமாணுதா தயா|

திஷ்யாவஷ்டா ஜஊாஷ்ஷ்ஜு[234]ஞ்ஷெஃ கூவ்ஞி தகு தூ||௨௱௭௫||

ஹ்ஷ்தா யா வ ஜெஹஸ்ய ஜ்ஜுதா வ ஷ்நெஶு யா|

ஊஹத்தா கஞவஷெஸ்யதா[235] நீசெஃ கூவ்ஞி மஜுகஂ||௨௱௭௬||

ஷஜ்ஜாஓஷ்ஸநிஶ்வணஊ

நீவாஸ் ஷஜ்ஷ்ஹள ஜாதாவூஞ்ாஸ் மாஙாஸஊஷ்யஊள|

நிஷாஜஃ வஞஊபெஶுவ ஹெவதஶு குய ஷ்ஸாஃ||௨௱௭௭||

ஷ்ஸிதவ்ஹவாஷெ்ஷாஂ வூநஷ்ஸ்காஸணக்ரஊஃ|

நித்யாஹிநிஹதகெஷவ்ா நிஷாஜஷ்ஸஹெதவஃ||௨௱௭௮||

ஹதஶ்ஷிஷ்ாவூஹள ஸ்யாதாஂ வஞஊஷ்ஸஹெதுகள|

தெஙொவ்ஜநவ்த்தாஹ்யாஜ்ாயதெ ஹெவதஷ்ஸஃ||௨௱௭௯||

ஊவ்ஹ்ஷ்ாநுஜாத்தாஹ்யாஜ்ா[236]தள ஷஜ்ஷஹாவூஹள|

உஜாத்தவ்வயாஹ்யாஞு மாஙாரொ ஊஷ்யஊஷ்ஷ்யா||௨௱௮௰||

ஸளதி ஷ்ணத்யஜா க்ரளஞொ மாஙாஸஜஷ்யஊஂ க்ரஊாஸ்|

கெகாஶுதஸஊஷ்ஷஜ் உக்ஷா ஸளத்ஜஷஹஷ்ஸஂ||௨௱௮௧||

நிஷாஜஂ ஜ்யஂஹதெ கூஂஶீ விகஃ கூஶஜதி வஞஊஂ|

---

230 T ◌ஂ ந

231 T ந்) மா

232 T ஜ்ஜு

233 T ◌ஂ ஜ்

234 T ◌ஂ உ

235 H தாஃ

236 T ◌ஂ ஜா

ஹயஹெஷாதா௱யூௗவஂ ஸஂவிஜ௱யாஷெவதஸ்லா௱ஂ||உா௮உ||

உஜாத்தாஉிஸ்லொொத்வதிஸ்லாந௸

கூந௱ஜாதொ ஹ௱உி ஜெ௲யொ ஊ௱ஜ௱ூ௱ஜாத்த உஜாஹ௱தஃ|
ஸ்லரிதஃ கூணுஊ௱ஙீயஸ்லவூாஂமெ ஷ௱உய ஷூ௱தஃ||உா௮ங||

வெஜா௱யநவாயு௸

கூஂஜஊாசூாஉயொ யஜூாஃ ஷூவூஜெவொஉிதாஷு யெ|
தாநு ஸவூாஙணூஸாரெஷிநு தசு தசு ஷ௱யொஜயெக||உா௮ச||
ணவஂ ஸயுக்ஷணஂ வெஜஂ யொயீதெஜ௱ாவயத௱வி|
ந தக கூஉஸஹஹெூ௱ஷு ஜஉிதா௱ஂ ௱க௱தெ ஷயூஂ||உா௮ரு||

வெஜஉஹிஊா

வெஜ ணவ வரொ யஜெூா வெஜ ணவ வாரஜவஃ|
வெஜ ணவ வா௱ஂ ஞுஹு ஸவூஂ வெஜஉயஜூஜக||உா௮கூ||
தஷ்லா௱யஃ வா௱ஂ ஷ௱ா௱ா௱ஂ வியிநெவ ஜ௱ரொஜூ௱வாக|
கூயு௱தவொவிஷெவிூவெ௱ரெஷ யஜூஸ்லநாதநஃ||உா௮ள||
யஜெூண ய ஜஊாஂ ஞுாஹீஂ விஜ௱ாஂ ஶிஷ௱ாய வொயயெக|
நநுஞி ஜெவதாஸ்லவூாஷுஂ விஷ௱ணா[237]விஜெக ஜயஂ||உா௮௮||

கூஜ௱யநாஹிதஜொஷஃ

யொ ஹிகூா ஞுாஹுணொ வெஜாந[238]நூ௱ஜெ ஷ௱வத்தூதெ|
ஞுஹுத௱ாஶீ ஸ விஜ௲யஃ கூஜூ௱ஊஜ௱ ஜதி ஷூ௱தஃ||உா௮கூ||
வெஜஹீநஸ௱ விஷ௱ஸ௱ ஸவூஶாஷூஷ௱ஜஹூதா|
வஷூஹீநஸ௱ ஜெஹஸ௱ ஸவூஹ௱ஷணதா யயா||உாகூ௦||
யொ நிராகூ௱திநா விஷ௱ஸ்ல ஜஜிஂ கூ௱ரதெ யஜா|
ஸ விஷ௱ஷூ தஜாவொதி ஸ௱ராவாநவயு௱ூ௱வஂ||உாகூக||
தஜாநிராகூ௱திஸ்லாயஂ ஷஹதெ வாவநஂ வா௱ஂ|
தஷ்லாஷிராகூ௱தெஃ வாவஞ கூ௱யூ௱ாக வஜீக்திஹொஜநஂ||உாகூஉ||
(நிராகூ௱திர௱யநாஹித ஜத௱கூூஃ|)
வெஜாஂஷு ஜொசியஂ ஞுஹு யெ கெ ஜ௱ஷ௱ஞி ஊாநவாஃ|

---

237 T ○ஂ நா

238 T நு கூ

தெ வொரஜரகஂ ஹ்ராஹ்ய ஜாயதெ ஹுவி ஶுகராஃ||உாகூரு||

ஸாஂஶவெஊாஃயநவமய

வெஊரஶெவிஸகஃ வராகஃ வ[239]ரஂ

யெ வஂஜி வியிநா ஷிஜொத்ரஊஃ|

தெ ஶ்ரிவமரூஹ உாநுஹய த-

ஶ்ஶா[240]ஷ்ஷதஂ வஊஓவாந்ஹுயுஃ வரஂ||உாகூச||

||ஐதூாஶ்ரெயஶீக்ஷாஊஶஂ ஸஂவஶணூ||

---

[239] T த்

[240] H ஶ்ஶா

Appendix 5

Ātreyaśīkṣāmūla and Taittirīya Prātiśākhya

Comparative References

Verse No.	*Ātreyaśīkṣāmūla*	*Sūtra No.*	*Taittirīya Prātiśākhya*
46.	*ye 'tra sāṁhitā varṇās samāmnātāś ca śāstrataḥ* ‖	1.1	*atha varṇasamāmnāyaḥ*
3.	*… ṣoḍaśehāditas svarāḥ* ।	1.5	*ṣoḍaśāditas svarāḥ*
4.	*… sparśāḫ pañcaviṁśatiḥ* ।	1.7	*adyāḫ pañcaviṁśatis sparśāḥ*
4.	*… catastro 'ntassthāḥ …*	1.8	*parāś catasro 'ntassthā*
5.	*ṣaḍ ūṣmāṇaḥ …*	1.9	*pare ṣaḍ ūṣmāṇaḥ*
6.	*krameṇa pañca pañca syus sparśānāṽ vargasaṁjñakāḥ* ।	1.10	*sparśānām ānupūrvyeṇa pañca pañca vargāḥ*
6-7.	*… caturṇām prathamādayaḥ* ‖ *pañcamasyottamaḥ …*	1.11	*prathamadvitīyatṛtīyacaturthottamāḥ*
7-8.	*hānyoṣmā prathamāś caiva visargaś ca dvitīyakāḥ* ‖ *aghoṣās syuḥ …*	1.12-13	*ūṣmavisarjanīyaprathamadvitīyā aghoṣāḥ; na hakāraḥ*
8.	*… tebhyo'nye ghoṣavanto halas smṛtāḥ* ।	1.14	*vyañjanaśeṣo ghoṣavān*
8.	*parivinyābhyupaprāvapratyadhīty upasargakāḥ* ‖	1.15	*āprāvopābhyadhipratiparivinīty upasargāḥ*
9.	*kāraśabdottaro varṇo varṇākhyā …*	1.16	*varṇaḫ kārottaro varṇākhyā*
47.	*akāreṇa vyavetas syāt kāraśabdo halām iha* ।	1.17	*akāravyaveto vyañjanānām*
48.	*anusvāre ca nāsikye jihvāmūlyavisargayoḥ* । *upadhmānīyavarṇe ca kāraśabdas tu neṣyate* ‖	1.18	*na visarjanīyajihvāmūlīyopadhmānīyānusvāra nāsikyānām*
49.	*rasya tv ephaḥ …*	1.19	*ephas tu rasya*

Cont.

(Cont.)

Verse No.	Ātreyaśīkṣāmūla	Sūtra No.	Taittirīya Prātiśākhya
49.	*… trayāṇāñ ca hrasvo varṇottaro …*	1.20	*hrasvo varṇottaras trayāṇām*
9.	*vyañjanānām akāraḥ …*	1.21	*akāro vyañjanānām*
10.	*vargottaras tu vargākhyā prathamaḥ …*	1.27	*prathamo vargottaro vargākhyā*
10.	*… ṛkāraś ca tathalkāras svareṣu vai* ı	1.31	*ṛkāralkārau hrasvau*
127.	*uccair udāttaḥ …*	1.38	*uccair udāttaḥ*
127.	*… nīcais tu nihataś cānudāttakaḥ* ı	1.39	*nīcair anudāttaḥ*
128.	*svaritas syāt samāhāraḥ …*	1.40	*samāhāras svaritaḥ*
28.	*… tasya pūrvan tv avagrahaḥ* ı	1.49	*tasya pūrvapadam avagrahaḥ*
198.	*athātra sarvavarṇānāỹ yājuṣāṇāṽ viśeṣataḥ* ı *uccāraṇaprasiddhyartham śabdasyotpattir ucyate* ıı	2.1	*atha śabdotpattiḥ*
224.	*kaṇṭhe tu saṽvṛte nādaḥ …*	2.4	*saṽvṛte kaṇṭhe nādaḫ kriyate*
224.	*… śvāsas syād vivṛte sati* ı	2.5	*vivṛte śvāsaḥ*
224.	*madhyasthe tu hakāraḥ …*	2.6	*madhye hakāraḥ*
224.	*… varṇaprakṛtayaś ca tāḥ* ı	2.7	*tā varṇaprakṛtayaḥ*
225.	*nādajās svaraghoṣās syuḥ …*	2.8	*nādo 'nupradānaṁ svaraghoṣavatsu*
225.	*… hacaturthā hakārajāḥ* ı	2.9	*hakāro hacaturtheṣu*
225.	*aghoṣāś śvāsajāḥ …*	2.10	*aghoṣeṣu śvāsaḥ*
229.	*akāroccāraṇe cauṣṭhau hanū nātyupasaṁhṛtau* ı *kāryau tu dīrghaplutayor na cātivivṛtā ime* ıı	2.12	*avarṇe nātyupasaṁhṛtam oṣṭhahanu nātivyastam*
235-236.	*hanū anativiśleṣe … okāroccāraṇe sati* ı	2.13	*okāre ca*
235.	*… oṣṭhau cātyupasaṁhṛtau* ı	2.14	*oṣṭhau tūpasaṁhṛtatarau*
233.	*ekāre … īṣadyutoṣṭhakau* ıı	2.15	*īṣatprakṛṣṭāv ekāre*

Cont.

(Cont.)

Verse No.	*Ātreyaśīkṣāmūla*	*Sūtra No.*	*Taittirīya Prātiśākhya*
233-34.	*ekāre … atiśliṣṭahanūrdhvayuk* ।	2.16	*upasaṁhṛtatare hanū*
233.	*… jihvāprāntau … sthānam īṣatśliṣṭahanūrdhvayuk* ।	2.17	*jihvāmadhyāntābhyāñ cottarāñ jambhyān sparśayati*
232-233.	*ṛvarṇe ḷti ca … hanū atyupasaṁhārye jihvāgram barsvake bhavet* ।	2.18	*upasaṁhṛtatare ca jihvāgram ṛkārarkāralkāreṣu barsveṣūpasaṁharati*
230.	*upaśleṣyam ivarṇoktau jihvāmadhyan tu tāluni* ।।	2.22	*tālau jihvāmadhyam ivarṇe*
233, 235.	*ekāre … jihvāmadhyaṁ sthānam atiśleṣavad dhanutālukam* ।	2.23	*ekāre ca*
231.	*oṣṭhāv uvarṇe … upaśleṣayutau tathā* ।	2.24	*oṣṭhopasaṁhāra uvarṇe*
232.	*ekamātrāntaratvasya syāt tu sarvatra sambhave*	2.25	*ekāntaras tu sarvatra prakṛtāt*
237.	*aikāraukārayor ādāv akāraḥ …*	2.26	*akārārdham aikāraukārayor ādiḥ*
240.	*aidautor ādyakārasya karaṇībhavadoṣṭhakaḥ* । *sa̐vṛtākhya iti prāhur varṇakramavicakṣaṇāḥ* ।।	2.27	*sa̐vṛtakaraṇataram ekeṣām*
237.	*ivarṇovarṇayoś śeṣau syātām adhyardhamātrikau* ।।	2.28 -29	*ikāro 'dhyardhaḥ pūrvasya śeṣaḥ; ūkārastūttarasya*
226.	*acāṁ sthānam upaśleṣo yatra …*	2.31	*svarāṇāṁ yatropasaṁhāras tat sthānam*
227.	*yad aṅgaṁ spṛśyate 'ṅgena halāṁ sthānan tad iṣyate* ।।	2.33	*anyeṣān tu yatra sparśanan tat sthānam*
228.	*aṅgena spṛśyate sthānaṁ yena tat karaṇaṁ halām* ।	2.34	*yena sparśayati tat karaṇam*
241.	*uccāraṇe kavargasya hanūmūlaṁ spṛśed budhaḥ* । *jihvāmūlena …*	2.35	*hanūmūle jihvāgreṇa kavarge sparśayati*
241.	*… cor uktau jihvāmadhyena tālu . . .*	2.36	*tālau jihvāmadhyena cavarge*

Cont.

(Cont.)

Verse No.	*Ātreyaśīkṣāmūla*	*Sūtra No.*	*Taittirīya Prātiśākhya*
242.	*jihvāgreṇa ṭavarge tu prativeṣṭya śiras spr̥śet* ı	2.37	*jihvāgreṇa prativeṣṭya mūrdhani ṭavarge*
242.	*jihvāgratas tavarge ca dantamūleṣv adhas tathā* ı	2.38	*jihvāgreṇa tavarge dantamūleṣu*
243.	*adhareṇottaroṣṭhan tu pavargoccāraṇe spr̥śet* ı	2.39	*oṣṭhābhyām pavarge*
243.	*jihvāmadhyasya pārśvābhyān tālu yoccāraṇe spr̥śet* ıı	2.40	*tālau jihvāmadhyāntābhyāy̐ yakāre*
244.	*jihvāñcalasya madhyena dantamūlopari kramāt* ı *āsannam atyāsannañ ca pradeśaṁ ralayos spr̥śet* ıı	2.41 -42	*rephe jihvāgramadhyena pratyag dantamūlebhyaḥ; dantamūleṣu lakāre*
245.	*adharoṣṭhāgrabhāgena bāhyenordhvadatas spr̥śet* ı … *ve* …	2.43	*oṣṭhāntābhyān dantair vakāre*
246.	*jihvāmūlīyapūrvāṇāṁ habhinnānān tathoṣmaṇām* ı *kavargādiṣu yat sthānan tad eva syur yathākramam* ıı	2.44	*sparśasthāneṣūṣmāṇa ānupūrvyeṇa*
247.	*karaṇānān tu yat teṣām madhyan tu vivr̥tam* …	2.45	*karaṇamadhyan tu vivr̥tam*
247.	*visargasya ca hasya syāt sthānañ ca karaṇaṅ galaḥ* …	2.46	*kaṇṭhasthānau hakāravisarjanīyau*
248.	*vargāntyā nāsikāmātrasthānakā hāt pare 'pare* ı	2.49	*nāsikyā nāsikāsthānā*
249.	*mukhāvayavanāsikyāḥ* …	2.50	*mukhanāsikyā vā*
249.	… *nāsikā nasvikāsataḥ* ı	2.52	*nāsikāvivaraṇād ānunāsikyam*
63.	*nīcāpūrvas tathoccordhvo dakāraḥ kevalāgamaḥ* ı	5.8	*nīcāpūrvo dakāra uccāparaḥ*
118.	*kakāraṣ ṣaparo yatra bhavet tasmin pare sati* ı *pūrvasthito visargas syāt sthitisandhir iti smr̥taḥ* ıı	9.3	*na kṣaparaḥ*
54.	*hrasvapūrvau padāntasthau ṅanau dvitvam pare 'py aci* ı	9.18 -19	*hrasvapūrvo ṅakāro dvivarṇam; nakāraś ca*

Cont.

(Cont.)

Verse No.	*Ātreyaśīkṣāmūla*	*Sūtra No.*	*Taittirīya Prātiśākhya*
53.	*acpūrvaṽ vyañjanordhvaỹ yad vyañjanan dvitvam āpnuyāt* ।	14.1	*svarapūrvaṽ vyañjanan dvivarṇaṽ vyañjanaparam*
54.	*sparśaś ca lavapūrvo yaḥ …*	14.2	*lavakārapūrvas sparśaś ca pauṣkarasādeḥ*
70.	*vakāraś ca pare sparśe … lakāraḥ … sparśe*	14.3	*sparśa evaikeṣām ācāryāṇām*
54.	*… yat tu rephāt parañ ca tat* ।	14.4	*rephāt parañ ca*
55.	*pūrvāgamaẖ kramāt tatra syād dvitīyacaturthayoḥ* ।	14.5	*dvitīyacaturthayos tu vyañjanottarayoẖ pūrvaḥ*
59.	*pāthaeṣo'tidhāmātibhūteparamapūrvikāḥ* । *tathopasargapūrvāś cāgamañ chakhibhujā iyuḥ* ॥	14.8	*upasargapāthaeṣo'tyātidhāmaparamabhūtepūrveṣu chakhibhujeṣu ca*
61-62.	*aghoṣād ūṣmaṇas sparśaparād yatra parasthitaḥ* ॥ *prathamo 'bhinidhānas syāt tasya sasthāna eva ca* ।	14.9	*aghoṣād ūṣmaṇaẖ paraẖ prathamo 'bhinidhānas sparśaparāt tasya sasthānaḥ*
60.	*prathamasyoṣmaṇi pare dvitīyādeśakaẖ pade* ।	14.12	*prathama ūṣmaparo dvitīyam*
70.	*dvirūpan nāpnuyād ūṣmā prathamordhve 'cpare 'pi vā* ।	14.16 -17	*ūṣmā svaraparaḥ; prathamaparaś ca plākṣiplākṣāyaṇayoḥ*
70.	*… visargo repha eva ca* ।	14.15	*avasāne ravisarjanīyajihvāmūlīyopadhmānīyāḥ*
71.	*savargīyānuttamordhve savarṇordhve ca hal tathā* ।	14.23 -24	*savarṇasavargīyaparaḥ; nānuttama uttamaparaḥ*
121.	*ādau prārambhakoṅkāre tv akāraẖ pādamātrikaḥ* । *sa tripādadvimātras syād ukāro mas tu mātrikaḥ* ॥	18.1	*oṅkāran tu praṇava eke 'rdhatṛtīyamātram bruvate*
112-113	*antyabhāge tu nihataẖ pādamātraẖ prakīrtitaḥ* ॥ *… tasyānte cānudāttas syād aṇumātro bhavet tadā* ।	19.3	*dviyama eke dviyamapare ṭā aṇumātrāḥ; tasyām eva prakṛtau*

Cont.

(Cont.)

Verse No.	*Ātreyaśīkṣāmūla*	*Sūtra No.*	*Taittirīya Prātiśākhya*
133.	*ivarṇotor yavatve saty uccayos svaryate ca yaḥ* । *sa ca kṣaiprābhidhas svāraḥ* ...	20.1	*ivarṇokārayor yavakārabhāve kṣaipra udāttayoḥ*
134.	*pade sthite 'py apūrve vā nīcapūrve yavākṣaram* । *svaryate yatra nityas syāt* ...	20.2	*sayakāravakāran tv akṣaraỹ yatra svaryate sthite pade 'nudāttapūrve 'pūrve vā nitya ity eva jānīyāt*
135.	*ucce nānāpadasthe 'pi śliṣṭena svaryate ca yaḥ* । *sa prātihata eva syāt* ...	20.3	*api cen nānāpadastham udāttam atha cet sāṁhitena svaryate sa prātihataḥ*
137.	*tasminn akāralopaś cet pṛthagbhūtapade tadā* । *svāro 'bhinihato jñeyaḥ* ...	20.4	*tasmād akāralope 'bhinihataḥ*
138.	*udāttapūrve tasmin syād ūbhāvas svaryate yadi* । *praśliṣṭākhyaḥ* ...	20.5	*ūbhāve praśliṣṭaḥ*
139.	*yā tv akhaṇḍapade vyaktis sā bhaved ardhamātrikā* । *yas tasyāḥ paratas svāraḥ pādavṛttas sa kathyate* ॥	20.6	*padavivṛttyām pādavṛttaḥ*
142.	*vyañjanena vyavahitaḥ pade tūdāttapūrvakaḥ* । ... *tairovyañjana ucyate* ॥	20.7	*udāttapūrvas tairovyañjanaḥ*
144.	*kṣaipre nitye prayatnas syāt svāre dṛḍhataro bhavet* ।	20.9	*kṣaipranityayor dṛḍhataraḥ*
144.	... *abhinihate*...	20.10	*abhinihate ca*
145.	*praśliṣṭaprātihatayos sa vai mṛdutaras smṛtaḥ* ॥	20.11	*praśliṣṭaprātihatayor mṛdutaraḥ*
146.	*sa tairovyañjane pādavṛtte cālpataras smṛtaḥ* ।	20.12	*tairovyañjanapādavṛttayor alpataraḥ*
166.	*bhavet parasvarāṅgaṽ vyañjanam prāyaśo 'pi hi* ।	21.1-2	*vyañjanaṁ svarāṅgam; tatparasvaram*
167.	*tatra pūrvasvarāṅgaṁ syād avasāne sthitañ ca yat* ।	21.3	*avasitam pūrvasya*

Cont.

(Cont.)

Verse No.	Ātreyaśīkṣāmūla	Sūtra No.	Taittirīya Prātiśākhya
168.	*yogādi …*	21.4	*saÿyogādi*
167.	*parāyuktam …*	21.5	*pareṇa cāsaṁhitam*
167.	*… anusvāro … bhaktir eva ca* ǁ	21.6	*anusvāras svarabhaktiś ca*
170.	*parāṅgam asavarṇaṁ syād antassthāparam eva yat* ǀ	21.7	*nāntassthāparam asavarṇam*
170.	*… yamāḥ* ǁ	21.8	*nāsikyāḥ*
170.	*parāṅge coṣmaṇi pare parāṅgaṁ sparśakaḥ …*	21.9	*sparśaś coṣmapara ūṣmā cet parasya*
128-129.	*pareṣām anudāttānāṁ svaritāt padavartinām* ǁ *saṁhitāyān tu pracaya udāttaśrutir iṣyate* ǀ	21.10	*svaritāt saṁhitāyām anudāttānām pracaya udāttaśrutiḥ*
64-65.	*syād yatrānuttamāt sparśād uttamaḥ parato yadi* ǁ *krameṇa syur yamās tatra nāntassthā parato yadi* ǀ	21.12-13	*sparśād anuttamād uttamaparād ānupūrvyān nāsikyāḥ; tān yamān eke*
115.	*hakārān naṇamā yatra dr̥śyante paratas tadā* ǀ *nāsikyatvam urasyatvaṁ has tu tatra dvir ucyate* ǁ	21.14	*hakārān naṇamaparān nāsikyam*
73-74.	*āpnuto ralayor yasmād ūrdhve saty acparoṣmaṇi* ǁ *r̥l̥svarārdhāv ādeśau tasmāt syāt svarabhaktitā* ǀ	21.5	*rephoṣmasaÿyoge rephas svarabhaktiḥ*
202.	*bhavanti nādapramukhāvarṇoccāraṇahetavaḥ*	22.1	*śabdaḥ prakr̥tis sarvavarṇānām*
46, 49.	*ye atra sāṁhitā varṇās samāmnātāś ca śāstrataḥ* ǁ *tān sarvān kāraśabdāntān …* *… varṇottaro bhavet* ǀ	22.4	*varṇakārau nirdeśakau*
275.	*gātradairghyan dhvaner dārḍhyaṅ kāṇṭhākāśāṇutā tathā* ǀ *tisro 'vasthā imāś śabdam uccaiḫ kurvanti tatra tu* ǁ	22.9	*āyāmo dāruṇyam aṇutā khasyety uccaiḫkarāṇi śabdasya*

Cont.

(Cont.)

Verse No.	*Ātreyaśīkṣāmūla*	*Sūtra No.*	*Taittirīya Prātiśākhya*
276.	*hrasvatā yā ca dehasya mṛdutā ca dhvaneś ca yā* । *mahattā kaṇṭhakhasyaitā nīcaiḥ kurvanti śabdakam* ॥	22.10	*anvavasargo mārdavam urutā khasyeti nīcaiḥkarāṇi*
116, 139.	*vivṛttimadhye virāmaś caikamātras syāt … yā tv akhaṇḍapade vyaktis sā bhaved ardhamātrikā*	22.13	*vivṛttivirāmas samānapada-vivṛttivirāmaḥ … ekamātro 'rdhamātra ity ānupūrvyeṇa*

Bibliography

Abhyankar, Kashinath Vasudev and G.V. Devasthali. 1978. *Vedavikṛtilakṣaṇasaṁgraha: A Collection of Twelve Tracts on Vedavikṛtis and Allied Topics.* Pune: Bhandarkar Oriental Research Institute.

Aithal, Parameswara. 1991. *Veda-lakṣaṇa Vedic Ancillary Literature: A Descriptive Bibliography* (Indian edn. 1993). Delhi: Motilal Banarsidass.

Allen, W. Sidney. 1953. *Phonetics in Ancient India,* repr. 1965. London: Oxford University Press.

Bandyopadhyay, Dhirendranath. 2000. *Samskrita Sāhityer Itihās [History of Sanskrit Literature]*, 2nd edn., repr. 2005. Kolkata: West Bengal State Book Board.

Banerji (Bhattacharya), Chhaya. 2009. *A Critical and Comparative Study of the Prātiśākhyas*. Kolkata: Sanskrit Pustak Bhandar.

Bhagavaddatta (ed.). 1921. *Atharvavedīyā Māṇḍukī Śikṣā,* rev. edn. 2009. New Delhi: Meharchand Lachhmandas Publications.

Bhaṭṭācārya, Gurunātha Vidyānidhi (ed. & tr.). 2004. *Vaidyamahāmahopādhyāya-śrīmad-gaṅgādāsa-viracitā Chandomañjarī,* 12th rev. edn. Kolkata: Sanskrit Pustak Bhandar.

Burnell, A.C. 1875. *On the Aindra School of Sanskrit Grammarians*, repr. 1986. Madras: Pioneer Book Services.

Chakrabarti, Sukla. 1996. *A Critical Linguistic Study of the Prātiśākhyas*. Calcutta: Punthi Pustak.

Chandra, Lokesh (ed.). 1981. *Sanskrit Texts on Phonetics: A Collection of Śikṣā Texts*, reproduced by Lokesh Chandra from the papers of the late Prof. Raghu Vira. New Delhi: Śata Piṭaka Series, Indo-Asian Literatures, vol. 282.

Chariar, P.B. Ananta (ed.). 1905. *The Taittirīyopaniṣadbhāṣyam by Śrī Kūranārāyaṇa Muni*. Conjeeveram: Sri Sudarsana Press.

Chatterjee, K.C. 1948. *Technical Terms and Technique of Sanskrit Grammar*, repr. Kolkata: Sanskrit Book Depot.

Chaturvedi, Rammurti. 2003. *Vaidikaśikṣāsvarūpavimarśaḥ*. Varanasi: Sampurnanand Sanskrit University.

Chaubey, Braj Bihari. 1972. *Vaidika-svarita-mīmāṁsā*. Hoshiarpur: Vaidik Sahitya Sadan.

Chitrao, M.M. Siddheshwar Shastri. 1964. *Bharatavarshiya Prachina Charitrakosha*. Poona: Bharatiya Charitrakosha Mandal.

Chowdhury, Tarapada (ed.). 1981. "Śaiśirīya-śikṣā". In Sharada Rani (ed.) *Vedic Studies: A Collection of the Research Papers of Prof. Raghu Vira*, pp. 403-22. New Delhi: Śata-Piṭaka Series, Indo-Asian Literature, vol. 272.

Coward, Harold G. and K. Kunjunni Raja (eds.). 1990. *Encyclopedia of Indian Philosophies*, vol. 5: *The Philosophy of the Grammarians*, repr. 2001. Delhi: Motilal Banarsidass.

Datta, Pradyot Kumar. 1994. *Pāṇini and Prātiśākhya: A Comparative Study in Etymological and Grammatical Approach*. Kolkata: Sanskrit Pustak Bhandar.

Deshpande, Madhav M. (ed. & tr.). 1998. *Śaunakīyā Caturādhyāyikā: A Prātiśākhya of the Śaunakīya Atharvaveda*. Harvard: Harvard University Press.

Devasthali, G.V. 1977-78. "Krama-Pāṭha". In *Annals of the Bhandarkar Oriental Research Institute*, **58/59**: 573-82.

Dikshitar, V. R. Ramachandra (ed.). 1938. *Bhāradvājaśikṣā with Nāgeśvara's Commentary*. Pune: Bhandarkar Oriental Research Institute.

Dīkṣita, Rāmanātha (ed.). 1961. *Sāmatantra: A Prātiśākhya of the Sāmaveda*. Varanasi: Vedic Research Committee, Banaras Hindu University.

Edgerton, Franklin. 1946. *Sanskrit Historical Phonology: A Simplified Outline for the Use of Beginners in Sanskrit*. New Haven: American Oriental Society.

Emeneau, M.B. 1946. "The Nasal Phonemes of Sanskrit". In *Linguistic Society of America* **22**(2): 86-93.

Franke, A. Otto (ed. & tr.). 1886. *Die Sarvasaṁmata-Śikṣā mit commentar.* Göttingen: Dieterichschen Univ.-Buchdruckerei.

Firth, John Rupert, 1946, "The English School of Phonetics". In *Transactions of the Philological Society,* pp. 92-132.

Ghosh, Manmohan (ed. and tr.). 1938. *Pāṇinīya Śikṣā,* repr. 1991. Delhi: V.K. Publishing House.

Ghosh, Pradip Kumar (ed. and tr.). 1994. *Niśśaṅka-śārṅgadeva-praṇīta-saṅgīta-ratnākara.* Kolkata: West Bengal State Music Academy.

Indra. 1973. *Prātiśākhyoṁ meṁ prayukta pāribhāṣika śabdoṁ kā ālocanātmāka adhyayana,* repr. 1991. Varanasi: Chaukhamba Vidyabhavan.

Jha, Udayanath (ed. and tr.). 2005. *Yājñavalkyaśikṣā,* 3rd edn. Varanasi: Chukhambha Publishers.

Kane, Pandurang Vaman. 1930. *History of Dharmaśāstra,* vol. 1. Pune: Bhandarkar Oriental Research Institute.

Kashikar, C.G. 2001. "On the Taittirīya Brāhmaṇa". In *Annals of the Bhandarkar Oriental Research Institute*, **82**(1/4): 43-56. Pune: Bhandarkar Oriental Research Institute.

Katre, S.M. 1941. *Introduction to Indian Textual Criticism.* Mumbai: Karnatak Publishing House.

Kauṇḍinnyāyana, Śivarāja Ācārya. 1992. *Kauṇḍinnyāyanaśikkṣā,* repr. 2009. Varanasi: Chowkhamba Vidya Bhawan.

Kielhorn, H. 1876. "Remarks on the Śikṣās". In *The Indian Antiquary,* pp. 141-44, repr. 1984. Delhi: Swati Publications.

Kirste, J. (ed.). 1889. *The Gṛihyasūtra of Hiraṇyakeśin.* Vienna: Alfted Hölder.

Krishnamacharya, V. (ed.). 1959. *Ṛgvarṇakramalakṣaṇa of Narasiṁhasūrī.* Adyar: Adyar Library and Research Centre.

Kulkarni, Nirmala R. 2006a. "Problems of Editing the Śikṣā Texts". In Nirmala Ravindra Kulkarni (ed.) *Vedic Studies*, pp. 213-25. Delhi: Bharatiya Kala Prakashan.

———, 2006b. "Ātreyaśikṣā: A Problem for Reconstruction". In Nirmala

Ravindra Kulkarni (ed.) *Vedic Studies*, pp. 260-64. Delhi: Bharatiya Kala Prakashan.

———, 2006c. "On the GOML MS of the Ātreya-śikṣā". In Nirmala Ravindra Kulkarni (ed.) *Vedic Studies*, pp. 265-75. Delhi: Bharatiya Kala Prakashan.

——— (ed.). 2004. *Lakṣaṇacandrika (A Commentary on the Taittirīya Prātiśākhya) by Mahādeva Rāmacandra Gadre.* Delhi: Bharatiya Kala Prakashan.

———, 1995. *A Grammatical Analysis of the Taittirīya-Padapāṭha.* Delhi: Sri Satguru Publications.

Lüders, Heinrich (ed. and tr.). 1894. *Die Vyasa-Çiksha besonders in ihrem Verhältnis zum Taittiriya-Pratiçakhya.* Göttingen: Dieterichsche Univ.-Buchdruckerei.

Mahulkar, D.D. 1981. *The Prātiśākhya Tradition and Modern Linguistics.* Vadodara: Dept. of Linguistics, Faculty of Arts, M.S. University of Baroda.

Mīmāṁsaka, Yudhiṣṭhira (ed.). 2009. *Śikṣā-sūtrāṇi: Āpiśali-pāṇini-candragomi-viracitāni.* Rewali: Ram Lal Kapoor Trust.

Mīmāṁsaka, Yudhiṣṭhira. 1984. *Saṁskṛta vyākaraṇa śāstra kā itihāsa,* vol. 2, 4th edn. Bahalgarh: Ram Lal Kapoor Trust.

Mishra, Vidhata. 1972. *A Critical Study of Sanskrit Phonetics.* Varanasi: The Chowkhamba Sanskrit Series Office.

Monier-Williams, M. 1899. *A Sanskrit–English Dictionary,* repr. 2005. Delhi: Motilal Banarsidass.

Oka, Krishnaji Govind (ed.). 1913. *The Nāmaliṅgānuśāsana (Amarakośa) of Amarasiṁha with the Commentary Amarakośodghāṭana of Kṣīrasvāmin.* Pune: Law Printing Press.

Oppert, Gustav. 1880. *Lists of Sanskrit Manuscripts in Private Libraries of Southern India,* vol. 1. Madras: Government Press.

———, 1885. *Lists of Sanskrit Manuscripts in Private Libraries of Southern India,* vol. 2. Madras: Government Press.

Parameshwaranand, Swami. 2001. *Encyclopaedic Dictionary of Purāṇas,* vol. 4. New Delhi: Sarup & Sons.

Pataskar, Bhagyalata (ed.). 2010. *Studies on the Śikṣās and the Prātiśākhyas.*

Pune: Adarsha Sanskrit Shodha Samstha.

Pathak, Madhukar. 1972. *Pāṇinīyaśikṣāyāḥ śikṣāntaraiḥ saha samīkṣā* (*A Comprehensive Study of the Pāṇinīya-śikṣā with Reference to Other Ancient Phonetical Works*). Varanasi: Vāṇīvilāsa Saṃskṛta Pustaka Samsthāna (distibutor).

Phaḍake, Bābā Śāstrī. 1898. *Kṛṣṇayajurvedīyaṁ Taittirīyāraṇyakam,* vol. 1. Pune: Ānandāśrama Mudraṇālaya.

———. 1927. *Kṛṣṇayajurvedīyaṁ Taittirīyāraṇyakam,* vol. 2. Pune: Ānandāśrama Mudraṇālaya.

Raghavan, V. 1966. *New Catalogus Catalogorum,* vol. 2. Chennai: University of Madras.

Ram, Sadhu (ed.). 1981. "Kauhali-śikṣā". In Sharada Rani (ed.) *Vedic Studies: A Collection of the Research Papers of Prof. Raghu Vira*, pp. 390-402. New Delhi: Śata-Piṭaka Series, Indo-Asian Literature vol. 272.

Ramanujan, P. 2000. "Śikṣā Śāstra and Accental Semantics". In Bidyut Lata Ray (ed.), *Facets of Vedic Studies*, pp. 43-58. New Delhi: Kaveri Books.

Saith, Shanti Saroop. 1941. *Catalogue of Sanskrit Manuscripts in the Punjab University Library,* vol. 2. Lahore: University of Punjab.

Sarasvatī, Madhusūdana. 1912. *Prasthānabheda.* Srirangam: Sri Vani Vilas Press.

Sarup, Lạkshman (ed. & tr.). 1920-27. *The Nighaṇṭu and the Nirukta of Śrī Yāskācārya,* repr. 2009. Delhi: Motilal Banarsidass.

Sastri, A. Mahadeva and K. Rangacarya (eds.). 1900. *The Taittirīyāraṇyaka with the Commentary of Bhaṭṭabhāskara Miśra,* vol. 1. Mysore: Government Branch Press.

———, 1902. *The Taittirīyāraṇyaka with the Commentary of Bhaṭṭabhāskara Miśra,* vol. 2 (Prapāṭhakas 5 to 6). Mysore: Government Branch Press.

Sastri, N. Subramania. 1956. *An Alphabetical Index of Sanskrit, Telugu & Tamil Manuscripts [Palm-leaf and Paper] in the Sri Venkateswara Oriental Research Institute Library, Tirupati [Śrīveṅkaṭeśvaraprāc yapariśodhanālayabhāṇḍāgārīya-likhitagranthasūcī].* Tirupati: Sri Venkateswara Oriental Research Institute.

Sastri, P.N. Pattabhirama. 1976. *Vyāsaśikṣā along with Vedataijasa Commentary of Sūrya-nārāyaṇa-sūrāvadhānin and the Sarvalakṣaṇamañjarīsaṅgraha of Rājā Ghanapāṭhin.* Varanasi: Veda Mimamsa Research Centre.

Sastri, R. Shama and K. Rangacarya (eds.). 1906. *Taittirīya Prātiśākhya with the Commentaries: Tribhāṣyaratna of Somayārya and Vaidikābharaṇa of Gārgya Gopāla Yajvan,* repr. 1985. Delhi: Motilal Banarsidass.

Sastri, R. Shama (ed.). 1920. *The Bodhāyana Gṛihyasūtra.* Mysore. Government Branch Press.

Sastri, S. Subrahmanya (ed.). 1943. *Saṅgītaratnākara of Śārṅgadeva with Kalānidhi of Kallinātha and Sudhākara of Siṁhabhūpāla,* vol. 1. Chennai: The Adyar Library.

Satwalekar, Sripad Damodar (ed.). 1957. *Kṛṣṇayajurvedīya-taittirīya-saṁhitā,* 2nd edn. Pardi: Svādhyāya-Maṇḍala.

Scharf, Peter M. 2013. "Linguistics in India". In Keith Allen (ed.) *The Oxford Handbook of the History of Linguistics*, pp. 230-32. Corby: Oxford University Press.

Sharma, Giridhar and Parameswarananda Sarma (eds.). 1961. *Vaiyākaraṇasiddhāntakaumudī (kārakaprakaraṇāntā), prathamo bhāgaḥ,* repr. 2004. Delhi: Motilal Banarsidass.

Sharma, Venkatarama (ed.). 1930. *Taittirīya-Prātiśākhya with the Bhāṣya Padakramasadana of Māhiṣeya,* repr. 2005. New Delhi: Meharchand Lachhmandas Publications.

Sharma, V. Venkatarama (ed.). 1934. *Vājasaneyi Prātiśākhya of Kātyāyana with the Commentaries of Uvaṭa and Anantabhaṭṭa.* Chennai: University of Madras.

Shastri, Mangal Deva (ed. and tr.). 1931. *The Ṛgvedaprātiśākhya with the Commentary of Uvaṭa,* vol. 2. Allahabad: The Indian Press.

——— (ed. and tr.). 1937. *The Ṛgvedaprātiśākhya with the Commentary of Uvaṭa,* vol. 3. Lahore: Moti Lal Banarsi Das.

——— (ed. and tr.). 1956. *The Ṛgvedaprātiśākhya with the Commentary of Uvaṭa,* vol. 1. Varanasi: Vaidika Svādhyāya Mandira.

Shringy, R.K. and Prem Lata Sharma (ed. and tr.). 1978. *Saṅgīta-ratnākara of Śārṅgadeva,* vol. 1. Varanasi: Motilal Banarsidass.

Śrīrāmacandra, Pullela (ed.). 1980. *Kauṇḍinyaśikṣā*. Hyderabad: Osmania University.

Staal, J.F. and Samuel Jay Keyser (eds.). 2003. *A Reader on the Sanskrit Grammarians*. Massachusetts: MIT Press.

Stautzebach, Ralf (ed.). 1994. *Pāriśikṣā und Sarvasammataśikṣā: Rechtlautlehren der Taittirīya-śākhā*. Stuttgart: Franz Steiner Verlag.

Suryakanta (ed. and tr.). 1933. *R̥ktantram: A Prātiśākhya of the Sāmaveda*, repr. 1970. Delhi: Meharchand Lachhmandas.

——— (ed. and tr.). 1939. *Atharva-Prātiśākhya*, repr. 2012. Delhi: Meharchand Lachhmandas Publications.

——— (ed.). 1940. *Laghur̥ktantrasaṅgraha and Sāmasaptalakṣaṇa*, repr. 1982. New Delhi: Meharchand Lachhmandas.

Tarlekar, Ganesh Hari (ed. and tr.). 2001. *The Puṣpasūtra: A Prātiśākhya of Sāmaveda*. Delhi: Indira Gandhi National Centre for Arts & Motilal Banarsidass.

Tripāṭhī, Rāma Prasāda (ed.). 1989. *Śikṣāsaṁgrahaḥ of Yājñavalkya and Others*. Varanasi: Sampurnanand Sanskrit University.

Varma, Siddheshwar. 1929. *Critical Studies in the Phonetic Observations of Indian Grammarians*, repr. 1961. Delhi: Munishiram Manoharlal.

Vira, Raghu. 1981. "Śākhās of the Yajurveda: The Discovery of a Unique Chart of Yajuṣa Recensions". In Sharada Rani (ed.) *Vedic Studies: A Collection of the Research Papers of Prof. Raghu Vira*, pp. 329-45. New Delhi: Śata-Piṭaka Series, Indo-Asian Literature, vol. 272.

Vira, Raghu (ed.). 1981. "*Āpiśali-śikṣā*". In Sharada Rani (ed.), *Vedic Studies: A Collection of the Research Papers of Prof. Raghu Vira*, pp. 346-69. New Delhi: Śata-Piṭaka Series, Indo-Asian Literature, vol. 272.

VishvaBandhu. 1959. *Catalogue of VVRI Manuscript Collection in Two Parts*, vols. 1-2. Hoshiarpur: Vishveshvaranand Vedic Research Institute.

Weber, Albrecht. 1855. "Der kāṇḍānukrama der Ātreyī-Schule des Taittirīyaveda". In Albrecht Weber (ed.) *Indische Studien* 3, pp. 373-401. Berlin: Ferd Dümmler's Verlagsbuchhandlung.

Whitney, William Dwight. 1879. *Sanskrit Grammar.* Leipzig: Breitkopf & Härtel.

——— (ed. and tr.). 1862. *Atharvaveda prātiśākhya or Śaunakīyā caturadhyāyikā,* repr. 2006. Delhi: Rashtriya Sanskrit Sansthan.

——— (ed. & tr.). 1868. *Taittirīya Prātiśākhya with Its Commentary the Tribhāṣyaratna,* repr. 1973. Delhi: Motilal Banarsidass.